Jean Tsushima

December 1997
NHG — Bedygn

Chartered accountants in England and Wales

STUDIES IN BRITISH BUSINESS ARCHIVES

series editors

LESLEY RICHMOND AND ALISON TURTON

already published in this series

LESLEY RICHMOND AND ALISON TURTON (eds.)

The brewing industry

L. A. RITCHIE (ed.)

The shipbuilding industry

Chartered accountants in England and Wales

A guide to historical records

edited by
WENDY HABGOOD

Manchester University Press
MANCHESTER and NEW YORK

distributed exclusively in the USA and Canada by St. Martin's Press

Published by Manchester University Press
Oxford Road, Manchester M13 9PL, UK
and Room 400, 175 Fifth Avenue, New York, NY 10010, USA

Distributed exclusively in the USA and Canada
by St. Martin's Press, Inc.
175 Fifth Avenue, New York, NY 10010, USA

British Library Cataloguing-in-Publication Data
A catalogue record is available from the British Library

Library of Congress Cataloging-in-Publication Data
Chartered accountants in England and Wales : a guide to historical records / edited by Wendy Habgood.
p. cm. – (Studies in British business archives)
Includes bibliographical references and indexes.
ISBN 0-7190-4229-1
1. Accounting–England–History–Sources. 2. Accounting–Wales–History–Sources 3. Institute of Chartered Acountants in England and Wales–Archives. I. Habgood, Wendy. II. Series.
HF5616.G72E543 1994
657'.0942–dc20 93-27913
CIP

ISBN 0-7190-4229-1 *hardback*

Printed in Great Britain
by Bookcraft (Bath) Ltd.

Contents

Foreword

I am very pleased to contribute a foreword to this book which summarises the results of a survey of accounting archives carried out in 1991 and 1992.

The Institute of Chartered Accountants in England and Wales was first made aware of the need for such a survey in 1988. In July of that year, John Hillyer, who was then Senior Partner of Hill Vellacott, now Chantrey Vellacott, in the course of gathering material for his firm's bicentenary exhibition at Chartered Accountants' Hall, discovered that many of the firm's archives had been destroyed. Concerned about the possible fate of other firms' records, he wrote to the then President, Jock Worsley, proposing that the Institute should launch an appeal to finance a survey of accounting archives. The survey would aim to locate the archives of member firms and also ensure their preservation for future historical research. The Institute strongly supported this initiative and, in October 1989, with the assistance of the Business Archives Council and Guildhall Library, launched the Archive Rescue Appeal. Many firms contributed to the appeal and, in January 1991, the Institute appointed a professional archivist to carry out the survey.

During the project, many historically valuable records were brought to light and listed for the first time, including the records of several long-established provincial firms whose once-familiar names have disappeared as a result of mergers. The Institute's own records, and those of its founding bodies, dating from the 1870s, have also been examined and listed. However, the survey has revealed the extent to which the archive material relating to the profession has already been lost, owing to rising costs of record storage; increased use of computers; and mergers (of which there have been many in recent years) and the associated reorganisation of office premises.

Those who have been involved in the project have, however, been encouraged by the number of firms who, as a result of the survey, have safeguarded their archives by depositing them in their local record offices where they may be permanently preserved and made accessible to researchers. I hope that other firms, whether or not they participated in the survey, will want to make similar or other suitable arrangements after reading this guide. In 1992 the Institute deposited its own archives in Guildhall Library, the record office of the City of London.

The guide includes entries for 182 firms, the Institute of Chartered Accountants in England and Wales, and the Institute's predecessor bodies. It will be welcomed by anyone whose research includes accounting, business, economic or financial history and by those interested in the development of the accountancy profession and the histories of particular firms.

The Institute can be justly proud that its member firms, through their generous contributions to the Archive Rescue Appeal and their co-operation in allowing access to their records, have made the survey and this guide possible. It is indebted to the members of the Archive Panel for their supervision of the project; to Peter Boys, for the scholarly essay he has written; to Wendy Habgood, the Survey Archivist, for the enthusiastic way in which she has conducted the survey and the hard work she has put into the task of compiling the guide; and to the Business Archives Council for making the publication of the survey possible.

W I D Plaistowe
President
The Institute of Chartered Accountants in England and Wales
February 1993

Acknowledgements

First and foremost the author would like to thank the chartered accountants, archivists and librarians who have provided information about the records in their care or have allowed access to their records for listing purposes. Without their considerable help the survey on which this book is based would not have been possible. Particular thanks are due to John Barrett, archivist of Price Waterhouse; Andrea Betteridge, Freda Miller and Eunice Willoughby, the administrators of the Institute's district societies in Liverpool, Manchester and Sheffield, who made the records of the founding bodies available; and Peter Gibb, Information Services Department, who kindly supplied a list of the Institute's own archives. In addition, The Royal Commission on Historical Manuscripts provided a computer listing of accountants' records which was invaluable for locating old and new deposits. Information about firms, past and present, was generously provided by the Institute's staff, in particular by Avril Dennis, John Lamming and Neil Williams of the Institute library, Anne Grayson and Wendy Town of the Members' Registration Department and the staff of the Information Services Department.

The author is especially grateful to the Archive Panel for their enthusiasm in overseeing the project and for steering it towards a successful conclusion. Under the chairmanship of Antony Barnes, Chairman of Chartered Accountants' Trustees Ltd, the Panel (Peter Boys, lecturer in accounting, University of Kent at Canterbury; Stephen Freeth, Guildhall Library; Edwin Green, Business Archives Council; John Hillyer, former senior partner of Hill Vellacott; and Professor Richard Macve, University College of Wales, Aberystwyth) made many helpful suggestions which improved the content of the book. Thanks are due, in particular, to Peter Boys who was very generous with his time and help in reading and commenting on all of the text. A debt of gratitude is also owed to Paul Glicker, the Institute's Director, Administration, and Caroline Baynes, of the Institute's Policy Coordination Department. Their constant guidance, support and enthusiasm throughout the project has been greatly appreciated.

The achievements of the survey owe a great deal to the labours of the survey staff. Gill Johnson, with unstinting persistence and enthusiasm, encouraged a large number of firms to participate in the survey; Judy Woolley word-processed the entire text with speed and accuracy and, in spite of working from an indecipherable manuscript, with unfailing good humour.

The author is grateful, also, to the series editors, Lesley Richmond and Alison Turton, who made numerous suggestions which have substantially improved the content and appearance of this guide.

Finally, thanks are due, in no small measure, to my husband, John, who has endured unending talk of accounting records throughout the eighteenth months of our marriage without complaint. He will, though, be as relieved as the author is that the book is now complete.

Wendy Habgood
February 1993

The origins and evolution of the accountancy profession

PETER BOYS
Lecturer in accounting
University of Kent at Canterbury

This introductory essay aims to provide some background information about the development of the accountancy profession and of firms of chartered accountants, so as to set the archival material identified in the survey in its historical context. The first section reviews the initial appearance of public accountants in England and Wales, the subsequent growth in their number, and possible reasons for this increase, mostly, but not exclusively, before the formation in 1870 of the first professional society of accountants in England. The second section contains a brief account of the origins and evolution of professional accountancy organisations in the British Isles and, as this project is especially concerned with member firms of the Institute of Chartered Accountants in England and Wales, a slightly more detailed history of that body. The third section outlines the development of professional firms from their beginnings, when accountants were in practice on their own account, to the large multi-national partnerships of today. The fourth section examines the changes in the type of work accountants have performed over the years, including some of the technical developments in accounting and auditing. Finally, in a concluding section, the material is brought together in summarised form.

This essay is primarily concerned with the development of firms of practising accountants, that is, individuals who hold themselves out to be in practice on their own account, or in partnership with others, as public accountants. However, many accountants have been influential in spheres outside the profession.

One particular area where accountants have played a significant role from an early date is in the development of company law. David Chadwick, MP, a partner in Chadwick, Adamson, Collier & Co, submitted evidence to the 1867 and 1877 Company Law Amendment Committees and was a member of the latter (Parker, 1986, p. 62). Subsequently, membership of each such Committee has included at least one person with an accountancy qualification. In addition, individual accountants have made submissions to these Committees and, starting with the Society of Incorporated Accountants and Auditors in 1905, professional accountancy bodies have submitted evidence (Edwards, 1980, p. iv). During the First World War many accountants were called upon to fulfil important posts in public service, another area of influence; for example:

> the Controllership of enemy banks, Financial Secretaryships of Ministries (Treasury, Munitions and Food), Controllerships of various kinds, and appointments as advisers to Government Departments (including those responsible for all three military services) on accounting control, audit and costing. (Howitt, 1966, p. 216)

Likewise, accountants were required for similar positions during the Second World War, and thereafter public appointments became customary. In their role as advisers, practising accountants, and particularly the more eminent ones, have influenced significantly the course of business history and industrial structure, far beyond their own profession. However, given the subject of this essay, none of these matters is dealt with here; the essay concentrates on firms rather than personalities.

Another caveat is that although the accountancy profession was established by accountants in practice, today more than half of the active members of the Institute of Chartered Accountants in England and Wales are employed in industry, commerce or the public sector. This essay does not deal with these accountants' contributions to the development of the accountancy profession or to business in general. The term 'professional accountant' is used in this essay, because of its historical association, to signify someone who offers services to the public and who is not, therefore, an employee of any type of organisation other than a firm of practising accountants.

Details of the most prominent accountants, in all walks of life, can be found in Jeremy (1984–86) and in Parker (1980b).

ORIGINS AND EARLY GROWTH OF PROFESSIONAL ACCOUNTANCY

Material on the pioneers of the profession is difficult to obtain. Some episodic evidence of the first practising accountants in England has been published; more work has been undertaken on the origins of Scottish accountants and in particular the founder members of the Institute of Chartered Accountants of Scotland (see, for example, Stewart, 1977).

It is claimed that the first professional accountant in Scotland was George Watson (1645–1723) who among other things was accountant to the Bank of Scotland (Brown, 1905, pp. 183–5). In England many of the early authors on accounting were writing masters and teachers of book-keeping who also described themselves as accountants. The earliest text in English on the subject, by Hugh Oldcastle, a London schoolmaster who taught arithmetic and bookkeeping, was published in 1543.

Murray (1930) commences his book with some quotations from *The Records of a Scottish Cloth Manufactory at New Mills, Haddingtonshire, 1681–*

1703 which show that one Alexander Heriot, a teacher of bookkeeping,

> does not seem to have had the actual charge of the books and accounts, but to have been called in specially to adjust entries, examine accounts, check balances and cash, and supervise stocktaking ... , or, in other words, to perform the duties which nowadays fall within the province of a professional accountant. (pp. 2–3)

Later, Murray states: 'The profession of a public accountant ... , as now understood, had not emerged, at least in Scotland, in the seventeenth century, but the employment of Alexander Heriot by the New Mills Company suggests something very similar' (p. 52). However, there is sufficient evidence for him to consider that there were professional accountants in Scotland by the beginning of the eighteenth century (p. 95). By contrast, he believes that in England public accountants had been practising since 'at least the commencement of the seventeenth century' (p. 59), and provides a number of examples to demonstrate this. Robert Hartwell advertised in 1623, and possibly earlier, that he taught amongst other things (pp. 59–60):

> Accompts for { Merchants, by order of Debitor and Creditor,
Retaylers of all sorts,
>
> Perfecting of Accompts in controuersie.

According to Murray this meant that 'he taught book-keeping, and also that he made up difficult or intricate accounts, or accounts that were [a] matter of difference' (p. 61). Further evidence from the seventeenth century that authors engaged in practical accounting is given (pp. 61–4):

> Richard Dafforne who 'Rectifieth Books of Accompts abroad or at home, whether in Proper factorage, or Company' (1670).
>
> John Collins writes 'his Lordship [the Lord Chancellor] was pleased to nominate me in divers References concerning suits depending in Chancery about intricate Accompts, to assist in stating thereof' and 'I spend part of my time in stating Merchants-Accompts, Ship-Accompts, or any controversial intricate Accompts, and in computing of Interest, the valuation or forbearance of Leases, Mortgages and Annuities' (1675).
>
> Thomas Browne gives notice that 'If any Person desires ... to make use of the Author, for the Auditing, Stating or Drawing up any Reports of Accompts, he is ... ready to serve ... ' (1670).

Murray concludes his comments (p. 64):

> Others must have been similarly employed, and although their number may not have been large, the profession of accountant, as now understood, was in existence and its utility recognised.
>
> The accomptant, however, still continued to be a teacher or a schoolmaster, and it was only in his spare time that he was able to assist merchants or litigants in practical affairs.

Murray then cites three writers from the eighteenth century. The first is Charles Snell, who provides the earliest known example of an accountant's report on a set of books of account following an investigation arising out of the famous South Sea Bubble (for further details, together with a copy of the report, see Worthington, 1895, pp. 14–24 and his Appendix I, pp. 108–17).

Information about practising accountants and the growth in their number at the end of the eighteenth and during the nineteenth century can be gleaned from trade directories. Although historians of the profession do make *ad hoc* references to such directories, there seems, unfortunately, to have been no systematic study of them. This is understandable; in the early years of publication, directories were not classified by occupation and thus it is a laborious task to extract the names of the few accountants who may be listed.

Ernest Cooper remarks in a paper read at the first autumn meeting of the Institute of Chartered Accountants in England and Wales (1886, p. 648):

> The earliest mention of a professional accountant I have found in the London Directory is the firm of Shortney and Millne, Merchants and Commercial Accomptants, who first appeared in 1776. In 1778 the firm appeared as Shortney and Co., Commercial Accomptants and Agents; in 1779 as F. Shortney. In 1785 as Shortney and Son. In 1789 the business of Agents took precedence of the business of accountants. Neither the name of Shortney nor that of Millne, so spelt, now appears in the London Directory.

However, Parker (1980a, annotation 12) states: '*Kent's London Directory*, 1775, mentions Terence Shortney, Merchant & Commercial Accomptant of 5 Church Row, Fenchurch St., the earliest known reference to a practising accountant in London.'

Worthington (1895, p. 31) cites James Davidson as the only accountant in one London directory of 1790, while from *The British Universal Directory* for the same year he extracted five names (pp. 31–2):

> Butler, William, Writing Master and Accomptant, 4 Oxford Court, Cannon Street.
> Davidson, James, Accomptant and Agent, 7 Fenn Court, Fenchurch Street.
> Gosnell, Thomas Knolles, Accomptant, New Crutched Friars.
> Rose and Clarkson, Accomptants and Agents, 78 Cannon Street.
> Shortney and Son, Commercial Accomptants, 38 St. Mary Axe.

As can be seen, the term 'writing master' is still in use; while the meaning of the word 'agent' is unclear, Worthington suggests it is a comprehensive term and could refer to 'commission, rent, house, land, insurance, or partnership and business transfer agents', or could possibly denote 'the practice of effecting arrangements between debtors and creditors' (p. 32). Many accountants carried on other occupations during these years; for example, one from Liverpool in 1790 was described as 'mercantile accomptant and dealer in tin plates' (Chalmers, 1883, p. 13).

Worthington's stated purpose in reviewing London trade directories was to gain some idea of the increase in the number of accountants (1895, p. 31). To this end he identified eleven in *Holden's Triennial Directory* of 1799, twenty-four in the 1809–11 issue and seventy-three in the 1822–24 edition (pp. 32–4; the full names, occupations and addresses are provided in his Appendix II, pp. 120–5). His observation on comparing the details from these sources is that 'the majority of these Accountants did not come to stay for a permanency' (p. 34). In the 1822–24 directory most of the occupations are shown simply as accountant, although many show a combination with other activities, mainly as agent or auctioneer, but also as appraiser, arbitrator, referee, and a dealer in British and foreign lace; there is no longer any reference to writing masters. Brown (1905, p. 234) and Cooper (1886, p. 648) provide three further figures from early directories: forty-seven (1817), forty-four (1820) and ninety-nine (1826–27).

In 1840 and thereafter the *Post Office Directory* was classified, and from this source it is known that there were 107 accountants practising in London at that time. In succeeding years the figures were: 140 (1841), 151 (1842), 160 (1843), 182 (1844), 210 (1845), 203 (1846) and 186 (1847) (Worthington, 1895, p. 42). Eldridge (1911, p. 203) continues the series to a later date: 264 (1850), 310 (1860), 467 (1870) and 590 (1875). In passing, Cooper (1886, p. 648) comments: 'In 1843 there were several firms which are still in existence [in 1886] under altered names.' Comparing this comment with Worthington's earlier, it suggests that practices in the mid- to late nineteenth century were of greater longevity than those in the early part of that century. However, this may also be contrasted with another statement made by Cooper (1921, pp. 42–3) thirty-five years later in his reminiscences of fifty-seven years in an accountant's office:

> I will first glance at the position in 1864, and at a few personalities. In the London Directory that year there were over 300 names of practising accountants. I am able to recognise only a few names, and none is still carrying on under the same name with the exception of my firm, whose name has not been changed since 1860. Only two firms, which in 1864 were, I believe, in a large way of business, now remain. The firm of Quilter, Ball, Jay & Co., then perhaps the leading firm, has in recent years been absorbed by another firm, and two others, now leading firms, had not come into existence.

This may reflect a change in the names of firms rather than their demise.

So far all the statistics have been for accountants in London, but Cooper (1886, p. 648) does give some overall figures for England and Wales:

> The Census of 1841 shows in England and Wales 4,260 accountants, and that of 1881, 11,517. Showing a growth in the 40 years of 170 per cent. against an increase of population of 62 per cent.
> Probably the Census figures include a large proportion of Bookkeepers and other persons not professional accountants.

Further random details of the position in the provinces are provided by other authors. Eldridge (1911, p. 202), incorrectly believing it to be the first reference in a directory, gives the names of three accountants who appeared in Bailey's *Western and Midland Directory, or Merchant's and Tradesman's Useful Companion* for 1783:

John Menzies, Accomptant, Basnet Street, Liverpool.
Henry Gandy, Accomptant, Castle Street, Bristol.
William Dyer, Agent and General Accomptant, Senall Street, Bristol.

According to Brown (1905, p. 233), 'In a Directory of Bristol and Bath for 1787 there appears the name of "Thomas Jones, Accomptant, Thomas Street, Bristol," who was probably the immediate predecessor of Edward Thomas Jones of that city, the author of the "English System of Book-keeping," published in 1796.'

Worthington (1895, pp. 93–5) and Brown (1905, pp. 233–5) supply, from directories of various years, additional figures indicating the growth in the number of accountants in the provinces:

Liverpool	5 (1790), 10 (1796), 3 (1808), 37 (1832), 69 (1849), 91 (1860), 100 (1864) and 139 (1870)
Manchester	2 (1794), 0 (1808), 14 (1815), 24 (1829), 32 (1832), 52 (1840), 66 (1850), 84 (1861), 88 (1864) and 159 (1871)
Birmingham	2 (1808) and 45 (1861)
Bristol	25 (1793–94), 2 (1808), 20 (1824), 24 (1827), 28 (1830) and 74 (1861).

It is of interest to compare the early statistics for England with those for Scotland at about the same time. For example, the first *Directory* of Edinburgh in 1773, which was known to be incomplete, included the names of seven accountants, whereas by the following year there were fourteen; a classified directory of 1805 contained seventeen names. In Glasgow, the first *Directory* of 1783 has the names of six accountants, and by 1807 this number had risen to ten (Brown, 1905, pp. 182–3).

All these figures have to be treated with a great deal of caution since they are taken from different directories, some of which are more comprehensive than others. Etor (1980, p. 3) nicely makes this point with respect to the number of accountants in Bristol at the end of the eighteenth century: a 1775 directory includes '31 accountants, and 45 bookkeepers' and 'one 1793 directory names 60 Bristol accountants. Another adds a *further* 90 names to the total! And both fail to mention that some of the other businessmen listed were practising public accountants as well.' This latter evidence shows how misleading the information given earlier may be, and indicates the need for further detailed and comprehensive study of trade directories, which have the potential to reveal valuable material about early accountants and the gradual rise of the profession in different towns and cities.

Having given some idea of the growth in numbers of accountants, especially during the nineteenth century, possible explanations for this increase will be examined. Naturally, the evolution of the accountancy profession reflects to a large degree changes in the economic, political, social and technological environment, and in particular the development from a commercial to an industrialised society, which in turn led to new or revised legislation in a number of areas. Parker (1986, p. 5) has identified four factors of special significance to the development of the profession: 'the growth of large-scale organizations and, in particular, of the railways; the development of the limited liability company; the high rate of insolvencies; and the introduction of income taxation'.

The great railway age in Britain spanned the period from 1830 to 1870, by which time most of the network was complete. Railway companies, originally formed by private Acts of Parliament, were large organisations. This necessitated the raising of substantial sums of money and the separation of ownership from control with the consequent need for an audit. The size of railways in terms of long-lived capital assets raised important issues of accounting principle and of disclosure in financial statements. Initially regulated by private legislation, railways, together with other public utilities, became controlled by public Acts of Parliament such as the Companies Clauses Consolidation Act, 1845. This required the directors to produce accounts and a balance sheet which had to be audited by at least two shareholder auditors, although provision was made for them to employ accountants at the company's expense (ss. 101–8). From 1844 the Board of Trade had had the powers to require railway promoters to estimate the cost of construction, traffic and working expenses, which, according to Worthington (1895, pp. 42–3), called for the services of accountants 'to prepare independent, accurate, and reliable returns'. Further legislation specifically relating to railway companies was eventually passed after a number of financial crises. The Railway Companies Act, 1867 provided that no dividend should be declared until the auditors had certified that the half-yearly accounts contained a full and true statement of the financial condition of the company and that the dividend was a *bona fide* payment out of profits in the judgement of the auditors (s. 30). A year later, the Regulation of Railways Act, 1868 revised the Companies Clauses Consolidation Act, 1845 so that the auditors of a railway company no longer had to be shareholders (s. 11), and, more significantly, prescribed the preparation of uniform accounting statements, which included the 'double-account' system (s. 3).

More general company legislation also had an influence on the accountancy profession. The Joint Stock Companies Act, 1844 allowed companies, for the first time, to be incorporated by registration. As a means of control, these companies had to file certain particulars with the Registrar of

Companies and provide regular returns, including the filing of a balance sheet (s. 43), which had to be audited by one or more auditors appointed by the company (s. 38). A major milestone in company law was achieved with the Limited Liability Act, 1855. In order to gain the privileges of limited liability a company had to comply with certain obligations; for example, one already registered under the 1844 Act had to submit its affairs to an audit in order to gain a certificate of solvency (s. 2). However, in the following year the Joint Stock Companies Act, 1856 repealed both the 1844 and 1855 Acts, abandoning most of the previous safeguards, including the compulsory audit. The 1856 Act relegated the audit provisions, including one which allowed auditors to employ accountants at the company's expense, to the optional Table B, Regulations for Management of the Company (articles 74–84). Nevertheless, most companies adopted these provisions (Gower *et al*, 1979, p. 48, n. 59).

To begin with, the winding-up provisions of legislation regulating companies were of as much significance to the profession as those relating to auditing. The Companies Act, 1862 consolidated previous company law and created the position of official liquidator. In most cases a professional accountant was appointed to this post. Worthington (1895, pp. 50–1) illustrates just how important this Act was to accountants: during the period 1863 to 1893, '44,435 companies were registered, of which number 26,074 have died a natural death, or been wound up, or amalgamated with, or absorbed by, some other concern'. 1866 was a year of financial crisis, with the collapse of many large companies and banks, dominated by that of Overend, Gurney & Co Ltd. Two prominent accountants, William Turquand and Robert Harding, who would become the first two presidents of the Institute of Chartered Accountants in England and Wales, were appointed as liquidators of this company (Jones, 1981, p. 43). Their remuneration for this liquidation amounted to almost £72,000 over a number of years to 1893, together with nearly £15,000 for their clerks (Worthington, 1895, pp. 54–5).

Legislation specific to certain types of organisation also helped the profession, particularly in gaining audit work. For example, following the failure of the City of Glasgow Bank in 1878, the Companies Act, 1879 imposed a compulsory annual audit on all banking companies registered, or re-registered, thereafter with limited liability (s. 7). Most banks registered as limited liability companies between 1880 and 1882 (Balogh, 1947, p. 6). Unlike the general company legislation of 1856 and 1862, the audit sections of the 1879 Act did not contain the provision for the auditors to employ accountants at the company's expense, which led Edey and Panitpakdi (1956, p. 370) to suggest that 'the appointment of professional auditors was becoming more usual'.

At about the same time scope for the employment of accountants as auditors was increased with local government legislation and that relating to friendly societies, industrial and provident societies, and building societies. (The first text on auditing, *Auditors: Their Duties and Responsibilities under the Joint-Stock Companies Acts and the Friendly Societies and Industrial and Provident Societies Acts*, was written by Pixley and published in 1881.) Other legislation around this time also led to the potential employment of accountants by prescribing the form of accounting information for certain undertakings, such as gas and electricity, and life assurance companies.

It was not until the Companies Act, 1900 that all companies were once again subjected to a compulsory audit. Subsequent Companies Acts gradually introduced more stringent accounting requirements and strengthened the position of the auditor; the 1948 Act specified that auditors of public companies had to belong to one of a number of recognised professional associations or be authorised by the Board of Trade (s. 161).

The growth of the British economy during the nineteenth century was punctuated from time to time by financial crises which, in turn, were followed by an increase in the number of insolvent and bankrupt traders. To deal with these the laws of bankruptcy were amended at regular intervals, starting with the Bankruptcy Act, 1824, which was consolidated in the following year. Some of the amendments benefited accountants and it was the influence of this legislation which eventually led to the formation of professional accountancy societies. For example, the Act of 1831 created not only the Bankruptcy Court but also the position of official assignees appointed by the Lord Chancellor to administer bankrupts' estates. Official assignees had to be 'Merchants, Brokers, or Accountants, or Persons who are or have been engaged in Trade' (s. 22), the first statutory recognition of accountants.

By the very nature of bankruptcy, accounts have to be prepared which reflect the financial position of the debtor's affairs. Thus, for example, the Relief of Insolvent Debtors Act, 1842 allowed a trader owing less than £300 to present to the Bankruptcy Court a petition containing a 'full and true Schedule of his Debts' so as to be granted protection (s. 1). This provision, according to Woolf (1912, p. 174), 'obviously would result in increased employment and remuneration for the profession'. Similarly, the Bankrupt Law Consolidation Act, 1849 required a bankrupt to prepare and file with the court a balance sheet and accounts (s. 160). Worthington (1895, p. 70) suggests that it was this provision which 'very largely assisted in bringing many Accountants into prominent notice before the commercial world, and some members of the profession established their reputation solely in connection therewith'.

The Bankruptcy Act, 1869 abolished the official assignee, and instead the administration of a debtor's property was placed in the hands of a trustee in bankruptcy who was to be appointed by the creditors (s. 14), thereby giving the latter greater control. The consequence of this was that many unscrupulous and unskilled persons solicited for such appointments and the resulting dissatisfaction reflected badly on competent accountants, who, in order to protect their reputations and to distinguish themselves from the unqualified, started to form professional societies. In 1883, the Bankruptcy Act of that year introduced the position of the official receiver to superintend the conduct of a debtor and the administration of his estate (s. 68). This restored control once more to the courts and, consequently, reduced the flow of work to the accountancy profession. Fortunately for accountants, however, they were by this time engaged in other tasks.

Reflecting on the increase in numbers of accountants in London, Cooper (1886, p. 648) confirms the close relationship between this growth and the changes in bankruptcy legislation: the almost fourfold increase from 1820 to 1843 was tentatively attributed by him to the Bankruptcy Law Consolidation Act of 1825; the increase of nearly 150 per cent between 1860 and 1883 was due to the stimulating effect of the Bankruptcy Act of 1869; and the slight decrease from 1883 to 1886 resulted from the depressing effect of the Bankruptcy Act of 1883.

Income tax, too, has played its part in the development of the profession. Dating from 1799, it was reintroduced in 1842, although the rates at which the tax was levied were relatively low until the First World War when it became of greater significance to accountants. The first text on the subject, written by Murray and Carter, was published in 1895. The two World Wars imposed excess profits duty and excess profits tax. More recently, corporation tax, which changed the system for taxing companies' profits, and capital gains tax were introduced in 1965, followed by value added tax in 1973. All these forms of taxation, together with death duties under various names, have provided a specialised source of work for accountants. This is in contrast to the United States, where such work is performed by lawyers. Parker (1986, pp. 40–1) suggests that the reason for the position in the United Kingdom is that the skills required for taxation work were similar to those for bankruptcy.

DEVELOPMENT OF PROFESSIONAL ACCOUNTANCY BODIES

There are currently six major accountancy bodies in the British Isles: the Institute of Chartered Accountants in England and Wales; the Institute of Chartered Accountants of Scotland; the Institute of Chartered Accountants in Ireland; the Chartered Institute of Public Finance and Accountancy; the Chartered Association of Certified Accountants; and the Chartered Institute of Management Accountants. These six bodies have evolved from some seventeen former associations. All six bodies have published, at some time or another, at least one account of their history, as has one of the former societies; a classified bibliography of these histories is provided in Appendix I, p. 44.

Professional bodies serve a number of purposes, including: uniting individuals with similar problems and interests; enhancing the status of the members; protecting the interests of the public who utilise their members' services; protecting the interests and livelihood of members; imposing a code of ethics on members; setting examinations to demonstrate that a certain level of skill and ability has been reached by members; representing members' interests on committees of government and other official bodies; issuing guidance on technical and professional standards; and providing disciplinary measures to enforce these standards.

There are a number of reasons for the early proliferation and subsequent combination of accountancy institutes in the British Isles. The first is that societies of accountants were formed originally on a local basis centred around important towns and cities. For example, the oldest bodies, founded in Scotland, were: the Institute of Accountants in Edinburgh, 1853 (granted a royal charter in 1854 when it became the Society of Accountants in Edinburgh); the Institute of Accountants in Glasgow, 1853 (granted a royal charter in 1855 when it became the Institute of Accountants and Actuaries in Glasgow); and the Society of Accountants in Aberdeen (granted a royal charter at the time of its formation in 1867). That these first societies were founded in Scotland was perhaps due to the high standard and practical nature of Scottish education, but was more likely due to the links which accountants had with the legal profession. In particular, accountants wished to influence potential changes in Scottish bankruptcy law in the 1850s, since insolvency work formed an important part of their business (Parker, 1986, pp. 14–17).

In England five accountancy societies were founded in the 1870s. These, and their dates of formation, were: the Incorporated Society of Liverpool Accountants (1870); the Institute of Accountants in London (1870); the Manchester Institute of Accountants (1871); the Society of Accountants in England (1872); and the Sheffield Institute of Accountants (1877). Originally, all but the Society of Accountants in England were local societies based in commercial and industrial centres in England. However, after representations from provincial practitioners who did not wish to join the Society of Accountants in England (which had lower entry requirements than the local societies), the Institute of Accountants in London became a national body in 1872 and changed its name to the Institute of Accountants (Howitt, 1966, p. 9). Although there was rivalry between these two national bodies, the desirability of a united profession was soon seen. The Institute of Chartered Accountants in England and Wales (ICAEW), incorporated by royal charter on 11 May 1880, was formed by the amalgamation of these five accountancy societies.

New bodies at first allowed entry to those with suitable practical experience, but shortly after formation a body usually admitted members only by examination, together, in some cases, with a formal period of practical training or a requirement to serve articles of clerkship. Such a procedure precluded some persons with practical experience and there was then the tendency for those excluded to form their own professional organisation. This process has been repeated a number of times in the course of the development of the accountancy profession in the British Isles, and provides a second reason for the multiplicity of accountancy bodies.

The ICAEW only held its monopoly in England and Wales for a short time before new rivals emerged. First and foremost was the Society of Accountants and Auditors, founded in 1885, which was open to those who, for one reason or another, were unable to qualify for membership of the ICAEW. A small body, the Scottish Institute of Accountants, founded in 1880, merged with the Society in 1899. The Society changed its name in 1908 to the Society of Incorporated Accountants and Auditors and in 1954 to the Society of Incorporated Accountants (SIA).

The Institute of Chartered Accountants in Ireland (ICAI) was incorporated by royal charter in 1888.

A further wave of new bodies began in Scotland in 1891 with the Corporation of Accountants and in England just after the turn of the century with three societies: the Institution of Certified Public Accountants (1903), the London Association of Accountants (1904) and the Central Association of Accountants (1905). The stimulus for the formation of these bodies at this particular time was the Revenue Act, 1903. This specifically recognised that, in addition to barristers and solicitors, members of an incorporated society of accountants could represent taxpayers before the Commissioners (s. 13). Interestingly, by 1941, through a series of combinations, all four bodies mentioned in this paragraph had amalgamated under the title of the Association of Certified and Corporate Accountants. The reasons for the various mergers included the relatively small number of members, a common history and aims, and confusion among the public caused by the multiplicity of associations with similar titles (Osbourn and Bell, 1954, pp. 53–4). The name of this body was shortened in 1971 to the Association of Certified Accountants, and, following the granting of a royal charter in 1974, it became the Chartered Association of Certified Accountants (ACCA) in 1984.

A third and final reason for the number of accountancy bodies is that some have specialised in one particular field of accounting. Specialising in public finance and dating from the beginnings of great reform within local government, the Corporate Treasurers' and Accountants' Institute was established in 1885 to further the objectives common to all municipal and other similar financial officers and as a forum for discussion on municipal finance (Sowerby, 1985, pp. 3, 5). In 1901 it became the Institute of Municipal Treasurers and Accountants and, following the granting of a royal charter in 1959, the Chartered Institute of Public Finance and Accountancy (CIPFA) in 1973. The other specialist body, the Institute of Cost and Works Accountants, was set up in 1919. To some extent this reflects the later development of cost and management, as compared with financial, accounting, but the timing was heavily influenced by the First World War which had established the need for scientific costing techniques. In 1972, this body changed its name to the Institute of Cost and Management Accountants and, after the granting of a royal charter in 1975, became the Chartered Institute of Management Accountants (CIMA) in 1986.

By the 1920s, as most of the newer societies insisted on the passing of examinations before entry was allowed, the doors of existing professional organisations were closed to certain practising accountants and so yet another wave of new bodies formed at or about this time (Stacey, 1954, pp. 124–31). None of these more minor bodies is dealt with here, although like their predecessors they have amalgamated to a certain extent.

The unification of the three Scottish societies in 1951 to form the Institute of Chartered Accountants of Scotland (ICAS) followed a long period of co-operation amongst them. For example, in 1892 a joint examining board was established and thenceforth admission to membership was by a common examination; and in 1915 a Joint Committee of Councils was set up. The reasons for the eventual amalgamation were: the increased part played by the profession within the national economy; to give more weight to expressions of corporate opinion; and because the prestige of a chartered accountant could be increased by being a member of a unified institute (*A History of the Chartered Accountants of Scotland*, 1954, p. 75).

The last successful scheme of integration took place in 1957 when members of the SIA were absorbed into the three national bodies of chartered accountants, the ICAEW, the ICAS and the ICAI. The stimuli for this arrangement were various and included: similar standards of training and examinations; confusion in the public's mind between the two qualifications; problems of partnerships existing among and between members of the ICAEW and the SIA; and difficulty in obtaining students (Howitt, 1966, pp. 159–60).

Thus by 1957 there were six major bodies of accountants, though at that time not all had received royal charters.

Further attempts have been made at unification. One scheme envisaged reducing all six major bodies to just three national bodies of chartered accountants; in 1970 all parties, apart from the ICAEW, voted in favour of this proposal. A positive consequence of this failure was the setting up, in 1974, of the Consultative Committee of Accountancy Bodies (CCAB) to act as a co-ordinating organisation for all six bodies. More recently, two attempts by the ICAEW to merge with just one of the other institutes have also failed: with the ICAS in 1989 and with CIPFA in 1990.

These, then, are the reasons for the current state and shape of the organisation of the accountancy profession in the British Isles. As the guide is concerned only with accountants who are members of the ICAEW, a more detailed look will be taken at this body.

At the time of its formation in 1880, the ICAEW had 599 members; by 1890 the figure had nearly trebled to about 1,700; by the golden jubilee in 1930 membership had reached 9,000, and by 1970 it was almost 50,000. In 1992 membership exceeded 100,000, approximately the same as that of the other five bodies combined. Initially, members were in, or employed in, public practice, but, slowly, they began to enter industry and commerce. Those in the former category now represent only about 45 per cent of the total.

For the first forty years the ICAEW was a male preserve and it took a change in legislation, the Sex Disqualification (Removal) Act of 1919, before women were admitted. Mary Harris Smith, the first female member, was admitted in 1920, and in 1924 Ethel Watts was the first woman to become a chartered accountant by examination. In 1992 female members formed only 13 per cent of total membership, although of those newly admitted some one-third were women.

There have always been two categories of member, Associate and Fellow, who are entitled to use the designatory letters ACA and FCA respectively. The qualifications necessary to become a fellow have varied over the years.

The ICAEW is governed by a council, subject to the requirements of the royal charter of 1880 (a supplemental charter was granted in 1948) and the bye-laws, first adopted in 1882 and subsequently revised substantially. The council was originally forty-five in number but is now made up of sixty elected and not more than twenty co-opted members, from whom are chosen annually a President, a Vice-President, and, since 1966, a Deputy-President. It was not until 1943 that the first non-practising member, F R M de Paula, was elected to Council, and not until 1979 that the first women were so elected.

The main purpose of the ICAEW has always been to elevate the profession's standing by enforcing strict rules of conduct and by requiring a high standard of education and training. As a self-regulatory body its supervisory status has increased since the mid-1980s with delegated statutory responsibility for members undertaking insolvency work, investment business and auditing.

From its inception members were governed by, and disciplined for any violations of, a code of ethics which has evolved over time, especially during the 1970s when emphasis was placed on the importance of professional independence. With effect from 1980 a Joint Disciplinary Scheme (JDS) was introduced, in conjunction with the ICAS and the ACCA, to deal with 'public interest' cases. Under the JDS, for the first time, firms as well as individuals could be disciplined.

To begin with, admission to the ICAEW was open to those with suitable practical experience, but thereafter entry was largely restricted to those who additionally had passed internally administered examinations, first held in 1882. A period of practical experience has always been required before admittance. This had to be gained in public practice until 1991, when training outside public practice was permitted. Potential members served articles of clerkship until 1973, since when they have entered into a training contract. The length of service required has depended on the general level of education of the trainee. For graduates, the period has always been three years. For non-graduates, articles were originally for five years; four-year articles were introduced for certain candidates in 1963 and by 1973 five-year articles had been abolished. Apart from a preliminary examination as a test of general education, last held in 1963, examinations have been on a two-stage basis, with the second stage divided into two parts, under various names, since 1965. Students with a recognised accounting degree, first established in 1945, have always been exempt from the first stage. To reflect changes in accountants' work, the number of papers and the subjects examined have been revised from time to time. Preparation for these examinations has been left to independent tutors.

From the outset the council was reluctant to issue guidance on technical matters, fearing resentment by, or embarrassment to, members. However, with the creation of the Taxation and Financial Relations Committee, the first Recommendation on Accounting Principles was issued in 1942. Following criticisms of financial reporting in the 1960s, the Accounting Standards Steering Committee was formed in 1970 (from 1976 the Accounting Standards Committee (ASC), constituted under the CCAB). The first in the series of Statements on Auditing was issued in 1961 and the Auditing Practices Committee (APC) was formed in 1973, but, following criticism of auditors, it too was constituted under the CCAB in 1976. The ASC and APC issued, for the first time, prescriptive standards, as well as other forms of guidance. Prior to the issue of a standard or guideline, a draft is published and comments are invited from interested parties. In 1990 the ASC was replaced by the Accounting Standards Board, overseen by the new, independent Financial Reporting Council. In 1991 the APC was restructured with greater authority and renamed the Auditing Practices Board.

Although slow, perhaps, in dealing with technical issues, the ICAEW has played an important role in influencing government legislation which impinges on members. This is especially true in the case of insolvency, company and taxation law, and when gaining recognition within legislation, for example, to audit certain types of organisation.

Reflecting the local origins of the ICAEW, district societies were established from the start and their number has steadily grown as membership of the ICAEW has increased. The first ones were: Liverpool (a continuation of the Incorporated Society of Liverpool Accountants, 1870), Manchester (1881), Sheffield (1882), Birmingham (1882) and the Northern (1883, although it would seem that this should read 1882) (Howitt, 1966, pp. 165–70). In 1992 there were twenty-two district societies, some with a number of branches. Professional firms similarly had strong regional origins, and in many cases their development has been on a local basis, while in others they have become national and indeed international practices.

DEVELOPMENT OF PROFESSIONAL FIRMS OF ACCOUNTANTS

Little has been written on the general development of accountancy firms in the British Isles. One reason for this may be that ready sources of information are few. The barest details of a firm's name, its partners and various practising locations can be obtained from trade and professional directories, as can information about amalgamations between firms. Another source is professional announcements in the Press; for example, a notice in the first issue of *The Accountant* (October 1874, p.16) shows that the firm of Edward Thomas Peirson was established in 1853. The reasons behind the various changes in size and names of professional practices are more difficult to ascertain. The lack of information arises partly because accountants, conducting their business either as sole practitioners or in partnership, are required to disclose little about their operations, unlike incorporated bodies. It is fortunate, then, that a number of firms of all sizes have published their histories. A bibliography of these histories, classified by firm, is provided in Appendix II. It should be borne in mind that histories have, quite naturally, only been written of the firms which have survived; other firms have not survived and it is impossible, although of interest, to establish why this is the case.

The form and content of these published histories differ quite considerably. They are written variously by retired partners, journalists, in-house committees, and in one case by a professional historian. The histories place different emphases on certain points, but they usually detail the origins of the firms and their gradual expansion. Little information is included about the technical aspects of the profession's work, for example, how accounting principles and auditing methods have changed over time.

Firms themselves are not always aware of their histories, especially that part which pre-dates the inception of the ICAEW. A letter in *Accountancy* (July 1990, p. 4) illustrates this point: although it had always been thought that Voisey & Co had been established in 1878, in fact, Lewis Voisey, the firm's founder, was in practice from at least 1872, when he attended the inaugural meeting of the Society of Accountants in England (*Rules and Regulations of the Society of Accountants in England*, 1875, p. 4).

The history of the ICAEW (Howitt, 1966, p. 227) defines what it terms a 'founder firm' as 'one which can claim continuous partnership descent from a signatory to the Charter or a member of the first Council', or which had been in existence for at least 100 years in 1965. It then provides, in Part II, section 11, brief details of some forty such firms in 1965; a number of these can trace their origins to more than one founder firm. The listing is by no means comprehensive and in some cases the detail in the entries is inaccurate.

Available evidence suggests that there are seven English firms of accountants which can trace their histories continuously to before 1820; of these, three go back as far as the eighteenth century, the oldest having its origins in 1780. Of the seven firms, four were founded in Bristol, while three emanated from Liverpool. The names of these firms, either at the time they were absorbed into other practices or at inception, the date of formation, the name of the practice into which they were absorbed or their current name, and the date of the amalgamation when appropriate, are:

Tribe, Clark & Co (1780), Bristol; merged with Deloitte, Plender, Griffiths & Co (1969), now Coopers & Lybrand.

Edward Thomas Jones (1788), Bristol; now Chantrey Vellacott.

Joseph Redish (1796), Liverpool; now Kidsons Impey, but the Liverpool office of Hodgson Impey merged with Pannell Kerr Forster (1990).

Harmood Banner & Co (1805), Liverpool; merged with Deloitte & Co (1974), now Coopers & Lybrand.

Stead, Taylor & Stead (1816), Liverpool; merged with Harmood-Banner, Cash, Stone & Mounsey (1963), now Coopers & Lybrand.

Curtis, Jenkins, Cornwell & Co (1816), Bristol; merged with Cooper Brothers & Co (1966), now Coopers & Lybrand.

Grace, Ryland & Co (1818), Bristol; merged with Thomson McLintock & Co (1969), now KPMG Peat Marwick.

Edward Thomas Jones moved to London and commenced business there in 1821 (*Hill Vellacott*, 1988, p. 13). This is probably the oldest London firm which has continuous descent to the present day. Other practices, known to have been formed in England before 1837 and which can trace continuous existence, are:

Powell, Jerome & Co (1821), Birmingham; merged with C Herbert Smith & Russell (1927), now Ernst & Young.

Ashworth, Mosley & Co (1825), Manchester; merged with Robson Rhodes (1980).

Lewis & Mounsey (1825), Liverpool; merged with Harmood Banner & Son (1948), now Coopers & Lybrand.

John Watson (pre-1827), Sheffield; now Watson Wheatcroft.

Carter & Co (1827), Birmingham; merged with Cooper Brothers & Co (1960), now Coopers & Lybrand.

Viney Merretts (1828), London; merged with Binder Hamlyn (1980), now BDO Binder Hamlyn.

Josolyne Layton-Bennett & Co (*c.* 1830), London; merged with Arthur Young, McClelland, Moores & Co (1981), now Ernst & Young.

Welton & Bond (1833), London; merged with Deloitte, Plender, Griffiths & Co (1918), now Coopers & Lybrand.

Smithson, Blackburn & Co (1834), Leeds; merged with Pannell Kerr Forster (1984).

Carlill, Burkinshaw & Ferguson (1835), Hull; merged with Hodgson, Harris & Co (1970), now Kidsons Impey, but the Hull and Beverley offices merged with Price Waterhouse (1990).

In contrast to most of the above, the firm of Begbies, founded in London by George Coryndon Begbie in 1837 shortly after Queen Victoria ascended the throne, was, 150 years later, still practising under the identifiable name of its founder as a five-partner firm in Grays Inn (Boys, 1988).

Most founder firms have their origins in the earlier part of the Victorian era. A review of the brief histories of founder firms in Howitt (1966, pp. 227–47), together with a search of firms' histories and an analysis of the firms in which the forty-five members of the first council of the ICAEW were partners (Parker, 1980c, carried out a similar exercise), shows that there are at least seventy-five practices which meet the criteria of founder firms (see Appendix III for full details). There is likely to be a bias towards large firms in the analysis which follows because of the sources from which the information has been gathered.

Details of the eighteen earliest founder firms have so far been given; the remainder were founded as follows (in a number of cases the precise date at which a firm was established is not known with any certainty, but, if anything, its origins are likely to be earlier than that assumed): 1840s sixteen; 1850s sixteen; 1860s eighteen; and 1870s seven. Of these fifty-seven practices, no fewer than thirty-one can trace their development forward to just five current-day firms, as follows: Ernst & Young eight; Touche Ross & Co eight; Coopers & Lybrand five; KPMG Peat Marwick five; and Price Waterhouse five.

An indication of the relative size and importance of certain firms before the formation of a professional accountancy body in London, and the significance of the work they undertook, is found in the *Report from the Select Committee on Limited Liability Acts* (1867) which contains the following evidence presented by W K Henderson, an accountant, on the concentration of liquidation work into the hands of six firms as at the end of 1866 (q. 926):

Liquidators	*Number of Companies*	*Amount £*
Harding, Whinney, and Gibbons	61	20,259,600
Coleman, Turquand, Young[s], & Co.	29	18,416,000
Kemp, Cannan, Ford, & Co.	12	13,660,000
Price, Holyland, and Waterhouse	8	5,200,000
Chatteris and Nicholls	5	4,915,000
Quilter, Ball, & Co.	5	1,100,000
Sundries, consisting of 91 persons	139	28,558,600
	259	92,109,200
Deduct Companies represented by two Houses	2	6,000,000
	257	86,109,200

The firm of Harding & Co. represent one-fourth of all the capital in liquidation.

The firm consists of three partners … .

Coleman & Co. represent upwards of one-fifth of the capital, and have four partners engaged in liquidations.

The six firms mentioned in the table can all trace their histories through to the present day, although the only name which is recognisable easily is Price, Holyland, and Waterhouse, which became Price Waterhouse. The first two named are both now part of Ernst & Young (although the two names of Young refer to different individuals); the third and fifth firms merged in 1921 and are now part of Touche Ross & Co; and the last firm, under the style Welton & Bond, was absorbed by Deloitte, Plender, Griffiths & Co in 1918, as already shown.

Another indicator of the leading accountants, and consequently of their firms, at particular moments in history is the influence which they have had on the professional accountancy bodies. For example, the first council of the Institute of Accountants in London, in 1870, consisted of the following twelve members (Howitt, 1966, p. 7):

Name	*Name of firm in 1870*	*Current Name*
John Ball	Quilter, Ball & Co	Coopers & Lybrand
G A Cape	Cape & Harris	MacIntyre Hudson MacIntyre & Co Saffery Champness
H Croysdill	Croysdill, Saffery & Co	Saffery Champness
W W Deloitte	Deloitte, Dever, Hollebone & Griffiths	Coopers & Lybrand
R Fletcher	Robert Fletcher & Co	KPMG Peat Marwick
J B Gibbons	Harding, Whinney, Gibbons & Co	Ernst & Young
R P Harding	Harding, Whinney, Gibbons & Co	Ernst & Young

C F Kemp	Kemp, Cannan, Ford & Co	Touche Ross & Co
S L Price	Price, Holyland, Waterhouse & Co	Price Waterhouse
William Quilter	Quilter, Ball & Co	Coopers & Lybrand
William Turquand	Turquand, Youngs & Co	Ernst & Young
John Young	Turquand, Youngs & Co	Ernst & Young

The foregoing paragraphs illustrate both the continuity and the change which have occurred in the accountancy profession over a period of 200 years or so, with the names of a few firms still recognisable while the majority have disappeared. This shows the great transformation which has occurred in the organisation of accountancy practices.

At the time of the formation of the ICAEW in 1880 most firms of accountants were small in size. Accountants either practised on their own or in partnership with one or two others. The largest practice at about that time was probably Turquand, Youngs, Weise, Bishop & Clarke, which had six partners; there was both a John and an Alexander Young. When firms were small it was possible for all partners' names to feature in the title of their firm, as in the example just quoted. As and when partners retired and new ones were admitted, so the name of the firm could change in line with those of the partners. Over the years, as accountancy partnerships gradually grew in size, so it became impracticable to call the practice by the name of all the partners. Furthermore, once a firm's name had been established and become well known there was a reluctance to change it and lose the goodwill which had been built up. Similarly, when firms amalgamated it was not always possible to include all the names of the merged practices. Even when joint names were adopted, they were frequently shortened a few years later. In recent years there has been a tendency for firms to shorten their names still further, perhaps to make them easier to remember and to create a better corporate identity. One such phenomenon has been the disappearance of the '& Co' at the end of the name. These alterations in name make it difficult to write about the histories of the firms in a way which is easily comprehensible. In what follows, wherever possible, the style of the firm is that in use at the time of the events described.

A small number of names of current-day firms have featured frequently in the paragraphs above; in fact, today the accountancy profession is dominated by the 'big six'. In alphabetical order, these are: Arthur Andersen; Coopers & Lybrand; Ernst & Young; KPMG Peat Marwick; Price Waterhouse; and Touche Ross & Co. The significance of these six firms can be seen from the number of quoted companies which they audit and the fees derived from these and other audits: 'Research shows that 97% of the FT-SE 100 companies are audited by the big six, who together also audit nearly 84% of the UK's largest 500 companies by market capitalisation' (Bagnall and Lea, 1992). This concentration of power into the hands of a few has occurred largely over the last twenty-five years. For example,

Briston and Kedslie (1985) have shown that, between 1928 and 1968, the concentration of audits of all listed companies carried out by the top twenty firms went from 29.60 per cent to 38.89 per cent, while for the top eight the figures were 21.12 per cent to 28.65 per cent. However, the comparable figures for 1984, the date at which the survey was carried out, were 75.78 per cent and 57.20 per cent. The reasons for this change are that listed companies have merged, with the audit generally transferred to the auditor of the acquiring company, and also firms of auditors have themselves amalgamated.

The size of the big six firms can be seen from the following figures extracted from a survey of the top fifty firms (*Accountancy*, July 1992, p. 16):

Firm	*Fee income £ million*	*Partners*	*Professional staff*	*UK offices*
Coopers & Lybrand	577.0	715	6,972	38
KPMG Peat Marwick	494.7	600	6,992	47
Price Waterhouse	400.5	482	4,602	26
Ernst & Young	398.9	411	5,081	30
Touche Ross & Co	349.7	396	4,401	25
Arthur Andersen	330.8	234	3,578	10

To give some indication of just how large these firms are, the tenth-ranked firm has a fee income which is only about 20 per cent of that of the sixth largest firm, while the thirtieth-placed firm is just one tenth the size of the tenth largest firm.

Firms have grown to their current size mostly by mergers, particularly in recent years among large and medium-sized firms, leading to a decline in the number of the latter. However, to put this into perspective, even today the vast majority of practising members of the ICAEW are in practice on their own or in partnership with fewer than four others. Hence there would seem to be a polarisation of the accountancy profession into a small number of very large international practices and a large number of very small ones, with only a few medium-sized firms in between.

Despite the enormous size of some accountancy firms, they are not incorporated businesses, although the Companies Act 1989 does now permit auditors of companies to adopt the corporate form. It would seem, however, that only about ten had taken advantage of this provision by June 1992 (Singleton-Green, 1992).

In 1989 there were eight large international firms, known colloquially as the 'big eight'. However, in September 1989 two of them, Ernst & Whinney and Arthur Young, merged to form Ernst & Young, and in April 1990 another two, Coopers & Lybrand and Deloitte Haskins & Sells, merged their United Kingdom firms to form Coopers & Lybrand Deloitte, shortened in June 1992 to Coopers & Lybrand. Thus the 'big eight' were reduced to the 'big six'. Earlier, in 1987, Peat Marwick Mitchell had merged with the tenth-placed firm, KMG Thomson McLintock, to form Peat Marwick McLintock, changed to KPMG Peat Marwick from October 1991. In the material which follows reference will be made to these constituent firms, not only because they have played a significant part in the evolution of the profession, but also because there is relatively more information about their development. However, because of their diverse origins and developments, and the differing availability of complete and up-to-date material, all nine firms do not receive equal treatment. For example, some of the histories are written from an American perspective, with little detail given about the British partnerships, and, as most of the histories were published some years ago without having been updated, less is known about developments in recent years when the pace of change has been greatest. Nevertheless, as the histories are the main source of explanation, they are reviewed to identify similarities and differences in the evolution of these nine firms.

One factor which hampered and may have delayed the expansion of firms, particularly in later years, was the Joint Stock Companies Act, 1856, which limited partnerships to twenty partners. This restriction was repealed for partnerships of accountants, solicitors and members of the Stock Exchange by the Companies Act 1967, leading to an upsurge in mergers between accountancy firms. In order to circumvent the earlier limitation, separate partnerships had to act in association with one another with cross-partnership agreements or other working relationships.

The analysis which follows will concentrate first on the firms' growth at a national level and will be divided into two historical periods, one before and one after the Second World War. Consideration will then be given to the expansion of the partnerships on an international basis. In each case, the nine firms covered will be dealt with in alphabetical order.

National growth of firms before the Second World War

Arthur Andersen, as will be seen, is unlike the other large firms, having its origins almost exclusively in America. Although it had a correspondent relationship with a British firm from the 1930s, it did not open an office in England until 1957.

Arthur Young also had American beginnings, but merged later with the British firms of Broads, Paterson & Co and McClelland, Moores & Co. Little has been written on the development of the British partnerships, apart from some brief notes on the history of the London office. Broads, Paterson & Co was established in London in 1869 as Broad & Broad, while McClelland, Moores & Co was formed, in 1958, by the merger of two Glasgow-based practices which had been established in 1824 and 1856. These partnerships had both opened offices in London, one in 1922, the other in 1924/25. With the lack of available evidence, it is not possible to comment further on the growth or otherwise of these firms before the Second World War.

Coopers & Lybrand was founded in 1854, by William Cooper, who was subsequently joined by his brothers, Arthur, Francis and Ernest; the name Cooper Brothers & Co was adopted on 1 January 1861 (*A History of Cooper Brothers & Co*, 1954, pp. 1–2). The firm's policy was originally that business should be conducted from the London office only, in order that it could maintain its standards and the personal supervision which the partners believed to be so important. The first branch office was opened in Liverpool in 1920, more than sixty years after the founding of the firm, with a second in Birmingham in 1946 (p. 37).

Deloitte Haskins & Sells was founded in 1845 by William Deloitte. At an early stage in the firm's history, there had been a branch office in Manchester, under the style Deloitte & Halliday, but this partnership was terminated in 1877 (Kettle, 1958, pp. 7, 20). Deloitte played a significant role in the development of railway accounting, and it is suggested that 'Deloitte's early association with the Great Western Railway [dating from 1849] was a major factor in laying the foundation of the firm's practice' (pp. 17, 22). Further, he was called upon by the auditors of the Great Northern Railway to investigate the famous Redpath frauds uncovered in 1856 and it was through this that his name became known to the general public (pp. 22–4). The firm only opened provincial offices 'when the volume of existing business in the district justified doing so as a matter of business convenience' (p. 139). The growth of the firm's business in South Wales, particularly the audit of the Powell Duffryn Company (the firm was first appointed auditors in 1864), led to the need for resident staff in Cardiff. However, a branch office was not opened there until 1912, again more than sixty years after the foundation of the firm, and a further office was opened in Swansea in 1923 (pp. 14, 147). A small office had been opened in Truro in 1920, but this was discontinued in 1945 (p. 139). In 1918, the firm gained valuable clients by absorbing the London practice of Welton & Bond (formerly Quilter, Ball & Co, established in 1833), which had failed to secure a succession of younger partners (p. 108).

The origins of Ernst & Whinney in the United Kingdom can be traced to a number of firms, but the main ones are: Harding & Pullein, London (1848), which by 1894 had become Whinney, Smith & Whinney; Brown & Fleming, Glasgow (1880); and J E Coleman & Co, London (*c.* 1840), Turquand & Edwards, London (*c.* 1850) and Youngs & Co, London (*c.* 1840), all three of which combined in 1857 to form Coleman, Turquand, Youngs & Co (Jones, 1981, pp. 20–1, 256–9). In 1926, Whinney, Smith & Whinney opened its first regional office in Leeds when the firm became sole auditors of the Yorkshire Penny Bank, which insisted that they be resident in Leeds (p. 163). In 1928, by merging with an established practice, Thomas Smethurst & Co, the firm acquired an office in Manchester to serve a large and growing client, Dunlop Rubber (pp. 163–4). Brown, Fleming & Murray opened a London office in 1919 to service its client, the Anglo-Persian Oil Company, which had transferred its accounts department from Glasgow to London in 1915 (p. 168).

Peat, Marwick, Mitchell & Co was founded in 1867 as Robert Fletcher & Co, when Fletcher, due to various assignments in England such as the reorganisation of the London, Chatham & Dover Railway, left his Aberdeen partnership and opened an office in London (Morrison, 1980). In 1875 Fletcher was asked to investigate the affairs of Middlesbrough Corporation. This led to an office being opened in Middlesbrough. The growth in work around this town led to branch offices being opened in Barrow-in-Furness, York, Darlington, Leeds and, much later, Newcastle upon Tyne (Morrison, 1981). The name of W B Peat & Co was adopted by the firm in 1891. Until 1910 the firm was content to develop in London and Middlesbrough, but in the following ten years it grew to a dozen offices in the United Kingdom (Wise, 1982, p. 17).

The London firm of Price Waterhouse was founded in 1849 by Samuel Lowell Price. In 1900, the practice of Lovelock, Whiffin & Dickinson, London, was acquired so as to secure Arthur Lowes Dickinson's services as senior partner for Price, Waterhouse & Co's American firm, established in 1890 (Richards, 1950, pp. 9–10). To begin with the partners were reluctant to open offices outside London, 'partly because they wished to control entirely the use of the Firm's name but also in deference to clients' wishes that staff with homes in the district where the clients' offices were located should not be allowed to examine their private books' (pp. 8–9). This aversion must have been overcome, since regional offices were opened in Liverpool, in 1904, and in Newcastle upon Tyne, in 1912 (*The Reporter*, December 1987). In 1920, the firm acquired the practice of Monkhouse, Goddard & Co (founded in 1868) which originally carried on business in Newcastle upon Tyne, but had offices in other towns in the north of England and one in London (Richards, 1950, p. 6). Price, Waterhouse & Co opened further provincial offices in Leeds (1928), Cardiff and Manchester (1932), and Birmingham (1939) (*The Reporter*, December 1987).

KMG Thomson McLintock was founded in Glasgow in 1877 by Thomson McLintock (Winsbury, 1977, p. 11). Prior to the First World War business in London necessitated much travelling, but following the appointment of Thomson McLintock as liquidator of the Northern Equitable Insurance Co Ltd, which had moved its head office from Glasgow to London, the firm opened an office in London in 1914 (pp. 17, 21, 28). The relative size, growth and importance of these two offices can be seen from the following: 'In 1919 gross fees in Glasgow were £28,000 and in London

£13,000. By 1927 these figures were £45,000 and £102,000 respectively, and by 1933 £37,000 and £159,000' (p. 22). In 1934 the two practices split (p. 20), not to be reunited until 1959 (p. 4). Besides London and Glasgow, the only other offices established before the Second World War were in Manchester and Birmingham, which were opened in the 1920s, with the Manchester office opening an offshoot in Sheffield in 1934 (p. 77). The Manchester office resulted from the firm's involvement with the amalgamation of two companies which eventually formed a division of ICI (p. 82) and the Birmingham office from the acquisition of Charles Baker & Co (p. 77).

Touche Ross & Co was founded by George A Touche in 1899 when he opened an office in London; a branch office was opened in Birmingham at some time before 1935 (Richards, 1981, pp. 4–5, 21). Thus, at the outbreak of the Second World War, George A Touche & Co was not large; there were sixty-seven members of staff (p. 21).

Although many of the firms had opened offices in other parts of the country away from their original base and had gained important reputations before the Second World War, it can hardly be said that they were national firms. Since the Second World War, and especially in the last twenty-five years, firms have grown rapidly in size, particularly by merger, so as to provide greater regional and national coverage.

National growth of firms after the Second World War

As has already been noted, Arthur Andersen & Co opened its London office in 1957. The firm has had the policy of expanding by organic growth, rather than by merger, but in 1979, when placed twelfth in the *Accountancy Age* league table (27 July 1979, p. 12), it amalgamated with the fourteenth-placed firm, Tansley Witt & Co, the origins of which go back to 1866. Not all the offices of Tansley Witt & Co joined the Arthur Andersen & Co fold; those which did were London, Bristol, Gloucester, Liverpool, Manchester and Worcester; other offices merged with four other major firms. One reason for the merger would seem to have been to acquire some well-known audit clients such as Cadbury Schweppes. Arthur Andersen & Co was one of the big eight firms worldwide, but in Britain, where its audits were largely those of American subsidiaries, it only ranked tenth in the league table of firms even after its merger with Tansley Witt & Co (Hopkins, 1980, pp. 51–3).

Arthur Young, McClelland, Moores & Co, which had been formed by the merger between Arthur Young & Company and McClelland, Moores & Co in 1968, amalgamated, in 1970, with Haldane, Brown & Co, an Edinburgh firm founded in 1823 which had opened a London office in 1911. Of more significance was the amalgamation in 1981, when the firm was ninth in the league table (*Accountancy*, July 1980, p. 11), with fourteenth-placed

Josolyne Layton-Bennett & Co, which itself had been formed in 1971 by the merger between Josolyne, Miles & Cassleton Elliott (the result of the merger in 1967 of Josolyne, Miles & Co, established *c.* 1830, and Cassleton Elliott & Co, established in 1917) and Layton-Bennett, Billingham & Co, established in 1883 (Boys, 1989).

Cooper Brothers & Co, wishing to extend its practice in the provinces, amalgamated, in 1950, with an old-established firm, Alfred Tongue & Co, based in Manchester with branches in Glasgow and Sheffield, and, two years later, with Aspell, Dunn & Co, an established Leicester firm (*A History of Cooper Brothers & Co*, 1954, p. 18). The reasons why Aspell, Dunn & Co wished to merge were twofold (*C&L Journal*, June 1979, p. 29): 'Because of a number of amalgamations and takeovers of clients by larger companies, there was a danger of their practice being diminished. The other great attraction was the access to knowledge which the larger firm could provide.' A further merger followed, in 1957, with a Glasgow-based firm. In the 1960s there were six mergers, with firms in: Birmingham; Bristol; Newcastle upon Tyne; Coventry; Northampton, Wellingborough and Bedford; and Manchester. In addition, offices were opened in Leeds, Newcastle upon Tyne (prior to the relevant merger), Middlesbrough and Cardiff. The 1970s saw two further mergers with firms in Leeds and Bradford, and the opening of offices in Southampton, Reading, Nottingham and Edinburgh (p. 26). The reasons for this geographical expansion are clearly stated:

> First there was the need to serve the larger client companies at each of their business locations in the UK. Second there was the realisation that a wide network of offices was in itself a powerful argument in favour of being selected for major investigation tasks. Third, this was the era of nationalisation and of corporate merger into larger and larger groups – two powerful factors in their own right pushing firms like Cooper Brothers towards a national capability. (p. 26)

Furthermore, it is suggested that the requirement under the Companies Act, 1948 to produce an audit report on group accounts 'must have been another, perhaps unconscious, spur to expand in the provinces'. Although not stated explicitly, the well-known clients gained by the merger with the Birmingham-based firm of Carter & Co would suggest that this may have been an additional reason; however, the client list may only have influenced the choice of firm in a particular location with which it was best to merge. The reasons for opening offices in Edinburgh and Reading are also given (p. 29):

> with the growing number of clients in the area and the increasing tendency of US and UK companies to open a Scottish head office in Edinburgh, the decision was made, and an office opened in St Andrew Square.

and

> It was partly the desire to move from the high rent and rates of the City, and also to eliminate some of the travelling from the Birmingham office to Oxfordshire, that an office was opened in Reading in 1973. An added reason was the growth of industrial estates on the West side of London in Slough and Bracknell. Being close to Heathrow airport this area has attracted many American companies who have established UK and even European headquarters in the vicinity.

Some idea of the growth of Coopers & Lybrand since the Second World War can be seen from the following figures: in 1945 the United Kingdom firm had a staff of 173 and in 1979 this had risen to 2,445 (p. 3).

In 1956, the date at which Deloitte, Plender, Griffiths & Co's published history ends, the firm had only four United Kingdom offices, London, Cardiff, Swansea and Manchester. The last-named was opened, in 1949, to accommodate the growing workload in the north-west (Kettle, 1958, p. 138). Other, more recent information, although brief, can be found in a Special Merger Issue of the *Deloittes Newsletter* (1 May 1974), published at the time of Deloitte & Co's merger with Harmood Banner & Co, when the firms were, respectively, first and tenth in the *Accountancy Age* league table (3 August 1973, p. 8). The *Newsletter* shows that Deloitte & Co had engaged in a number of mergers in the 1960s and early 1970s with firms in Leeds, Glasgow, Edinburgh, Newport, Newcastle upon Tyne, Belfast, Norwich, Bristol, Liverpool, Southampton and Aberdeen. In addition a Nottingham office was opened in 1973. Harmood Banner & Co was founded in Liverpool in 1805 and had opened a London office in 1906; it too had engaged in a number of mergers, particularly in the 1960s and early 1970s, with firms throughout the United Kingdom, including two of Liverpool's oldest firms.

Whinney, Smith & Whinney established an office in Birmingham in 1956 when it amalgamated with a local firm, and expanded this office with a further merger there in 1962 (Jones, 1981, p. 119, ref. 21). British Petroleum had grown rapidly in the early 1960s and its auditors, Brown, Fleming & Murray, were concerned that they might lose this client if they too did not expand in a similar vein. This led to the merger in 1965 between Brown, Fleming & Murray and Whinney, Smith & Whinney to form Whinney, Murray & Co (pp. 208–9). There were further mergers, particularly in the 1970s, both by these and by the other predecessor firms of Ernst & Whinney, in addition to organic growth. Jones (p. 221) summarises the position:

> In the 1970s alone Whinney Murray amalgamated with the following practices: Smith & Garton based in Huddersfield and Leeds (1971), Fraser, Lawson & Laing, Glasgow (1973), Buckley, Hall, Devin, Hull and Leeds (1973-74), McWilliam, Smith & MacLean, Inverness (1976), Woolley & Waldron, Southampton (1977), and Mason & Sons in London (1977), while Turquands Barton Mayhew merged with Howell & Hanbidge, Sheffield

(1974), Reid & Mair, Glasgow (1978) and Davidson Smith, Wighton & Crawford, Edinburgh (1978), having opened their own offices at Luton and Norwich in 1974 and 1976 respectively.

Whinney, Murray & Co had opened offices in Liverpool (1968) and Aberdeen (1975). Turquand, Youngs & Co had merged with Barton, Mayhew & Co in 1972 to form Turquands Barton Mayhew & Co, which in turn amalgamated with Whinney, Murray & Co in 1979, giving the combined firms much greater national coverage (pp. 222–3). Later in 1979, the by now Ernst & Whinney merged with Baker, Sutton & Co, a London practice with 35–40 per cent of its fees generated from insurance work (p. 207), and in 1980 with FitzSimons & Cameron of Belfast (p. 221). Mergers between predecessor firms of Whinney, Murray & Co illustrate further reasons for, and routes to, mergers. A C Palmer & Co, a Leicester-based firm, audited the British United Shoe Machinery Co, which, seeking the services of a London-based firm, suggested the selection of a practice which could act as joint auditors. The joint audit, with Barton, Mayhew & Co, begun after 1944, led to correspondent arrangements from 1961 and a full merger in 1972 (pp. 170–1). In another case, Turquand, Youngs & Co formed a joint practice with Ware, Ward & Co in 1960 before a full merger in 1963 (p. 210).

It would seem that acquisitions of other practices played only a minor part in the growth of some firms; for example, writing of Peat, Marwick, Mitchell & Co, Wise (1982, p. 17) states: 'After World War II the partnership acquired a few firms, such as Edwin Guthrie & Co., Wykes & Co., and Sharp, Parsons & Co. (Birmingham only), but these moves did not add substantially to the partnership's volume or profitability.' This could not be said of the merger with KMG Thomson McLintock in 1987.

Only the early history of Price Waterhouse has so far been published, hence there is little material on the development of the firm since 1950. However, a chronology of significant events in the history of the firm (*The Reporter*, December 1987) shows when and where offices were opened and the mergers in which it has engaged; these, on the whole, have been with firms with significant regional practices. Offices were opened in: Glasgow (1950); Edinburgh (1976); Aberdeen (1981); and Middlesbrough and Windsor (1983); while amalgamations occurred with: Howard Smith, Thompson & Co, Birmingham, and Hudson Smith, Briggs & Co, Bristol (1963); Mellors, Basden & Mellors, Nottingham (1966); Bolton, Bullivant & Co, Leicester, and Daniel Mahony, Taylor & Co, London (1969); Ashworth, Rowan, Craig, Gardner & Co, Belfast, and Sturges, Fraser & Co, London (1971); and Whittaker, Bailey & Co, Southampton (1975). More recently, in 1990, Price Waterhouse acquired two of the three Humberside offices of Hodgson Impey, at the time when most of the offices of that firm merged with Kidsons (*Accountancy*, April 1990, p. 8). The general growth in the size of Price Waterhouse can be seen from the following: eighty-six partners and staff (1900); fifteen partners and 544 staff (1950); 176 partners and 2,911 staff (1983); and 298 partners and 4,438 staff (1987) (*The Reporter*, December 1987).

Thomson McLintock & Co's growth began in the 1960s. With the split between the Glasgow and London offices, the firm had a history of decentralisation and it adopted a federal structure of partnerships. This encouraged other practices to join the firm since they were able to retain some autonomy (Winsbury, 1977, pp. 72–3). The first sign of expansion came when Thomson McLintock & Co merged with Aston, Wilde & Co in Birmingham in 1963 (p. 77). Two further mergers occurred in 1966: the Newcastle upon Tyne office, opened some years earlier as a result of gaining a client based there, merged with the local firm of Squance & Co and the Manchester office merged with the Leeds-based firm of Sir Charles H Wilson & Co (p. 80). All these mergers gave the firm better national representation, except in the south-west of England. Apart from small offices in Bristol and Cardiff opened in 1946 (p. 162), this gap in coverage was filled by a merger with the Bristol-based firm of Grace, Ryland & Co in 1969 (p. 86). In 1970, Thomson McLintock & Co set up in Belfast with a small practice, May & Co, and in 1974 opened an Exeter office and extended its Leicester office, set up in the 1950s by the London office, with the merger with Baker Bros., Halford & Co (p. 89). Many of the firms just mentioned were themselves formed by mergers. Winsbury sums up the position in 1977 as follows: 'The process of completing the coverage in England and Wales was therefore a rather English blend of chance and planning, a mixture of *ad hoc* answers to specific local problems and situations, and deliberate thought-out policy' (pp. 91–2). The firm also expanded in Scotland but this was more of a conscious decision in response to competition from other firms. The late 1950s and early 1960s saw a number of Scottish companies taken over by large non-Scottish groups, and in their wake firms of accountants moved into Scotland to service them, merging with Scottish-based firms in the process. Thomson McLintock & Co was large enough to withstand this invasion, receiving no formal proposals for a merger, and from 1965 extended its coverage of Scotland by opening an Edinburgh office and amalgamating with other firms (pp. 92–102).

George A Touche & Co was re-styled Touche, Ross, Bailey & Smart in 1960. With twelve partners and a staff of nearly 200 in 1961, the firm made the decision to expand nationally by merger (Richards, 1981, p. 31). It merged, with effect from 1963, with Kemp, Chatteris & Co, a City of London practice of similar size. The merger was effected by a working agreement and this was followed by similar arrangements with A T Niven & Co of Edinburgh and Wilson, Stirling & Co of Glasgow from 1964, Foster & Stephens of Birmingham from 1965, and Radford, Edwards & Co of Manchester from 1966 (p. 32). With the passing of the Companies Act 1967 truly national partnerships could be formed, and Touche, Ross, Bailey & Smart operated in such a way from 1 May 1969, one of the first, if not the first, to do so; the shortened name of Touche Ross & Co was adopted later in that year (p. 37). The firm continued to grow by opening new offices in Bristol and Leeds in 1970 and 1971 respectively, and by amalgamating with the Leicester practice of F W Clarke & Co in 1970 (pp. 39–40) and, in 1975, with the Liverpool firm, Edmund D White & Sons, which also had an office in London (p. 43). A more significant event occurred in 1979 when Touche Ross & Co, seventh in the *Accountancy Age* league table (27 July 1979, p. 12), merged with ninth-placed Mann, Judd & Co; this improved national coverage, with new offices in Burnley, Cardiff, Chepstow, Dartford, Newcastle upon Tyne, Newport, Plymouth, Swansea and Wolverhampton and expanded existing ones in London, Birmingham, Bristol, and Manchester (Richards, 1981, p. 49). Mann, Judd & Co, founded in Glasgow in about 1815, opened a London office in 1919; in 1937 the offices became separate practices. The London firm expanded in the 1960s and 1970s through a number of mergers, and it was this practice which amalgamated with Touche Ross & Co (pp. 90–3). The growth of Touche Ross & Co since the Second World War can be seen from the following: 'at the end of the Second World War the firm consisted of three partners and a staff of about 35, as compared with the present [1981] 157 partners and a staff of around 2,300' (p. 136).

The merger movement continued into the 1980s and 1990s. To begin with, medium-sized firms merged with one another; for example: Clark Pixley with Fryer, Whitehill & Co to form Clark Whitehill in 1982; Hodgson Harris with Chalmers, Impey & Co to form Hodgson Impey in 1985; and Dearden Farrow joined Binder Hamlyn in 1987. Then came the amalgamations of the largest firms. First, those placed second and tenth respectively (*Accountancy*, August 1986, p. 7), Peat, Marwick, Mitchell & Co and KMG Thomson McLintock, combined in 1987 to form the largest of all firms at that time, Peat Marwick McLintock. Next, Ernst & Whinney merged with Arthur Young, respectively fifth and eighth in the league table (*Accountancy*, July 1989, p. 10), to form Ernst & Young in September 1989 (*Accountancy*, August 1989, p. 12), the combined firm moving temporarily to second position. Then Coopers & Lybrand merged with the United Kingdom practice of Deloitte Haskins & Sells, by then the third- and fifth-placed firms (*Accountancy*, July 1989, p. 10), to form the largest United Kingdom firm, Coopers & Lybrand Deloitte from April 1990 (*Accountancy*, February 1990, p. 10); in most of the rest of the world Deloitte Haskins & Sells merged with Touche Ross & Co. These mega-mergers were followed by others among the medium-sized firms. Kidsons and Hodgson Impey, respectively sixteenth and eighteenth in the league table, merged in May

1990 to form Kidsons Impey (*Accountancy*, April 1990, p. 8). Spicer & Oppenheim amalgamated with Touche Ross & Co from August 1990, when these firms were respectively placed ninth and sixth (*Accountancy*, August 1990, p. 7). More recently, in July 1992, Stoy Hayward, tenth, merged with Finnie & Co, twentieth (*Accountancy*, July 1992, p. 11), and Baker Tilly, seventeenth largest firm, took over Milne Ross, ranked somewhere in the middle twenties, from September 1992 (*Accountancy Age*, 2 July 1992, p. 1).

A further comment on the amalgamation in the United Kingdom of Spicer & Oppenheim with Touche Ross & Co in 1990 is worthwhile. The former, strong in the financial services sector, lost a number of clients in the wake of 'Big Bang' in 1986 and suffered further from the Stock Market crash of 1987, while the latter was in need of extra staff, having gained a number of clients when Deloitte Haskins & Sells merged with Touche Ross & Co in America and elsewhere but not in the United Kingdom (Waller, 1990).

International growth

The phenomenon of geographical expansion has not been purely a national one; just as significant has been the opening of overseas offices, the growth of international links and mergers, or at least agreements, between firms of accountants in more than one country. Interestingly, much of the earliest expansion by United Kingdom firms was in America, often occurring before regional offices had been opened at home.

According to Wise (1982, p. 1), Barrow, Wade, Guthrie & Co (1883) is acknowledged as the first accountancy firm organised in America; the firm merged with Peat, Marwick, Mitchell & Co in 1950. Edwin Guthrie, a partner in the Manchester firm of Thomas, Wade, Guthrie & Co, went as a receiver in a bankruptcy case to New York in 1883 and, discovering that there were few auditors or accountants there, established a practice (p. 2). Other United Kingdom firms opened offices in America shortly afterwards, for example Price, Waterhouse & Co (1890), Deloitte, Dever, Griffiths & Co (1890) and George A Touche & Co (1900).

Although the formation of the major American practices began later than their British counterparts, there is evidence that there were public accountants in the United States as early as the end of the eighteenth century (Sinclair, 1946, p. 130). Haskins & Sells commenced practice together in New York in 1895, although the partnership was a continuation of Haskins's practice begun in 1886 (Foye, 1970, p. 13); Arthur Young can trace its origins back to 1893; two Scots joined forces in 1897 under the style Marwick, Mitchell & Co, although this was a continuation of a practice started by Marwick in 1895 in New York (Wise, 1982, pp. 5, 7); Lybrand, Ross Bros & Montgomery was founded in 1898; Ernst & Ernst was formed in 1903; and Arthur Andersen commenced business in 1913 in Chicago as Andersen, Delany & Co, adopting the name Arthur Andersen & Co in 1918 (Littler, 1974, pp. 2, 5).

In the following paragraphs the development of the international aspects of accountancy will be considered by reviewing, once again in alphabetical order, the big eight firms, together with KMG Thomson McLintock.

The American firms began to open offices in Europe after the First World War with the flow of American capital abroad. At first representative arrangements were made with native practices to serve American clients overseas; for example, in 1930 Arthur Andersen & Co made arrangements to be represented in Europe, South America and the Far East by McAuliffe, Davis & Hope and had affiliations with other firms to be represented elsewhere in the world (Littler, 1974, pp. 46–7). In 1949, the joint arrangement was formalised with Turquand, Youngs, McAuliffe & Co (Turquand, Youngs & Co had merged with McAuliffe, Davis & Hope in 1938) to form Arthur Andersen, Turquand, Youngs & Co (Robertson, 1949, pp. 145, 149). However, in order to obtain greater supervision of its American clients, and with the increase in work generally, Arthur Andersen & Co opened its own offices in Europe, the London one opening in 1957 when the arrangement with Turquand, Youngs & Co in Europe ceased (Littler, 1974, pp. 48–9).

The American practice of Arthur Young & Company was founded in 1893, in Chicago, and went under the style Stuart & Young until 1906 (Burton, 1948, pp. 15, 21). In 1923, the firm opened its first overseas office in London, in partnership with Broads, Paterson & Co, under the name Arthur Young, Broads, Paterson & Co. The connection between the two firms came about because one of Broads, Paterson & Co's American clients had become a joint audit with Stuart & Young in 1904, and subsequently further work had been exchanged. In 1966 the firms amalgamated under the common name of Arthur Young & Company.

Cooper Brothers & Co decided in 1946 to establish an international accounting organisation represented by indigenous firms; before that time it had established itself in a number of overseas countries (*C&L Journal*, June 1979, p. 33). In Europe, offices which had been opened in Brussels (1921) and Paris (1930) were closed during the Second World War but reopened in 1945 and 1949 respectively; further offices were opened in Antwerp (1948) and Rotterdam (1949) (*A History of Cooper Brothers & Co*, 1954, pp. 37–8). In America, an office was opened in 1926 in New York, and in 1948 Cooper Brothers & Co became associated with Scovell, Wellington & Company, which had offices throughout the country (p. 40). An office was opened in Montreal in 1936 and in 1948 a close association was formed with McDonald, Currie & Co, so that Cooper Brothers & Co's business was carried on under its own name wherever McDonald, Currie & Co had offices (pp. 39–40). In 1957 the international firm of Coopers & Lybrand was formed, initially with the following participants: Cooper Brothers & Co; McDonald, Currie & Co; and Lybrand, Ross Bros & Montgomery; each firm continued to practise under its own name (*L. R. B. & M. Journal*, January–March 1958, p. 1). Lybrand, Ross Bros. & Montgomery, formed in Philadelphia in 1898, had expanded on a national basis. With an increase in American investment in Great Britain and on the Continent, the firm was represented in Europe by Jackson, Pixley & Co prior to 1924. As work expanded after the First World War, direct contact was established with clients abroad by opening offices in Berlin (1924), Paris (1926) and London (1929). Seen from an American perspective, it was the tremendous increase in American investment abroad after the Second World War and the need to service clients which inevitably led to the formation of the international grouping (*L. R. B. & M. Journal*, January–March 1958, pp. 1, 10–11; *Fiftieth Anniversary*, 1949, p. 12). The change to a single international name, Coopers & Lybrand, did not take place until 1973 (*C&L Journal*, June 1979, p. 38). Cooper Brothers & Co also had, early on, strong representation in Africa, sometimes amalgamating with local firms: between 1931 and 1954 offices were established in nineteen locations in nine countries, of which all but three were opened after the Second World War (*A History of Cooper Brothers & Co*, 1954, pp. 38–9). In 1948, through three mergers, offices were opened in the main cities of Australia, as were offices in New Zealand (p. 39).

In the late 1880s Deloitte, Dever, Griffiths & Co carried out a number of investigations in America, and in 1890 the firm opened an office in New York. Other offices were opened in America and agency arrangements were made to represent the firm elsewhere, including Canada (Kettle, 1958, pp. 47–8). In conjunction with another practice, Deloitte, Plender, Griffiths & Co, as the firm was by then known, opened offices in South Africa from 1906, and from after the Second World War was represented in East Africa (pp. 88–90). From 1908 offices were opened in South America (pp. 93–4), in the Far East in 1910 (p. 97) and in the 1920s a number of offices were opened in Europe (p. 115). Some of these were established in conjunction with other British firms, practising under joint names. As early as 1901 Haskins & Sells established an office in London by acquiring the City firm of Conant & Grant. This occurred following an engagement for an American client, the Barnum & Bailey Circus, and in the knowledge that other American organisations were expanding into Europe (Foye, 1970, p. 18). Again, it was the flow of American capital abroad after the First World War which led Haskins & Sells to open other offices overseas (p. 70). In 1905 Haskins & Sells collaborated with Deloitte, Plender, Griffiths & Co in the investigation of two insurance companies (p. 31) and subsequently considered having a closer relationship with the firm. Talks took place in the early

1930s but it was not until 1952 that the two firms merged (p. 101), each practising under its own name (in its home country) and as a composite partnership styled Deloitte, Plender, Haskins & Sells (Kettle, 1958, p. 141). The common name of Deloitte Haskins & Sells was adopted in 1978.

The expansion of Whinney, Smith & Whinney abroad shows the importance of a client's initial lead. As a result of the Midland Bank increasing its business with American banks, it was suggested in 1912 that its auditors, Whinney, Smith & Whinney, might enter into an agency agreement with the New York and Philadelphia firm of MacPherson & Co. This was not thought appropriate and Whinney, Smith & Whinney opened its own office in New York in 1914. This had to close in 1917 because of the war and was not reopened; instead, in 1918, Whinney, Smith & Whinney asked the Cleveland-based firm of Ernst & Ernst, which had an office in New York, to act on its behalf (Jones, 1981, pp. 106–7). Similarly, Ernst & Ernst required overseas facilities as its clients took up opportunities abroad, particularly in Europe, so in 1924 a working agreement was drawn up with Whinney, Smith & Whinney to represent the firm there (*Ernst & Ernst*, 1960, pp. 73–4). Over the years this collaboration developed with cross-partnership agreements until finally, in 1979, the international partnership of Ernst & Whinney was formed (Jones, 1981, p. 107). Much of Whinney, Smith & Whinney's growth in the United Kingdom during the inter-war years came from American-based companies which had been introduced by Ernst & Ernst (p. 144). Whinney, Smith & Whinney had also entered into a number of correspondent arrangements before the First World War with firms in Australia, New Zealand, South Africa and Canada, and in the inter-war years offices were set up on the Continent, in many cases in conjunction with other practices. This expansion mirrored that of clients (pp. 174–6). Another constituent firm of Ernst & Whinney, McAuliffe, Davis & Hope, founded in 1895, built up a strong base in the Far East during the early twentieth century in the hope of gaining the audits of various rubber and tea companies whose London agents were already clients (pp. 94, 102–3).

Marwick, Mitchell & Co, formed in 1897, opened an office in London in 1904 and one in Glasgow in 1908. In 1911 Sir William Peat met James Marwick and they reached agreement for their firms to work together. However, in 1919 this arrangement was terminated, only to be resurrected in 1925 when the firms started to practise under the common style Peat, Marwick, Mitchell & Co (Wise, 1982, pp. 13–15).

From an early date Price, Waterhouse & Co performed work abroad for clients, including visits to India and, shortly after 1870, to the West Indies and North America (Richards, 1950, p. 5). In 1889, the firm was engaged to investigate 'a group of [American] breweries prior to amalgamation and subsequent flotation of the company on the London market' (p. 8). As a result of increasing work in America, the firm opened a branch office in

New York in 1890 under the control of a manager, L D Jones, and a year or so later W J Caesar took charge of an office in Chicago. Price, Waterhouse & Co decided to close these offices and in 1895 Jones and Caesar began to practise together under the style Jones, Caesar & Co, while continuing to act on agency terms for the London firm. However, before the turn of the century, the two practices were combined and the joint practice was carried on under both styles (p. 9). In 1896, Price, Waterhouse & Co entered into an agency agreement with Davey Flack & Co of Melbourne, Australia, which, in 1946, became part of the international firm of Price Waterhouse & Co, practising under that name, and representing the firm throughout Australia and New Zealand (p. 9). Other offices were opened overseas in the early part of the twentieth century as follows: Montreal and Cairo (1907); Buenos Aires (1913); Petrograd (1916); Paris (1917); and Rotterdam (1919) (*The Reporter*, December 1987). A number of these offices, in their early years, were run in conjunction with other British firms (DeMond, 1951, pp. 148–51).

As acknowledged in its own history, Thomson McLintock & Co was slow to enter the international arena (Winsbury, 1977, pp. 128–9). This may have been because the founder's son, Sir William McLintock, who led the firm from 1920 to 1947, was uninterested in overseas business, as epitomised by his reputed statement: 'It is bad enough men signing my name in Birmingham and Paris, but never in Buenos Aires' (p. 129). The firm had opened and closed an office in Paris in the early 1930s and established one in Lisbon in 1965. By the mid-1960s it would have been too costly to set up its own overseas offices and the firm had outgrown the possibility of operating on a correspondent basis. The only option was to set up a federation of national firms consistent with the firm's philosophy in the United Kingdom. The American firm, Main Lafrentz, was in a similar position, needing stronger international connections really as a defensive strategy so as not to lose clients, and made the initial move to link up with Thomson McLintock & Co. Once more, it was the expansion overseas by a client, Grand Metropolitan Hotels, which led to a ready response from Thomson McLintock & Co (pp. 128–31). The international organisation, a co-ordinating body and not a practising firm, was begun in 1964 and was known as McLintock Main Lafrentz – International (p. 133). Later, in 1979, this association expanded and became a group of independent national firms, with strong European representation, known as KMG (Klynveld Main Goerdeler). Thomson McLintock & Co changed its name to KMG Thomson McLintock in 1985.

George A Touche formed a separate firm in New York in 1900 when he entered into partnership with J B Niven, a fellow Scot, under the style Touche, Niven & Co (Richards, 1981, p. 94). This practice grew steadily if unspectacularly. In 1947, at the time of post-war economic expansion, the firm merged with two other American practices, George Bailey & Co and Allen R Smart & Co, to form Touche, Niven, Bailey & Smart (p. 96). The Canadian firm, George A Touche & Co, founded in 1909 in Toronto, expanded rapidly and the merger in 1919 with Webb Read & Co (or Webb, Reid & Co, see Swanson, 1972, p. 55) made it the first nation-wide firm in Canada. In 1958 this firm merged with another Canadian firm, P S Ross & Sons, to form Ross, Touche & Co. All three of the Touche national practices recognised the need for greater international expansion after the Second World War to meet the needs of their clients throughout the world. During the 1950s various meetings took place and a common name, Touche, Ross, Bailey & Smart was adopted in 1960 (Richards, 1981, pp. 6, 100–3). Offices had been opened elsewhere in the world, often in conjunction with other firms; for example, there was one in Java between 1910 and 1914 under the style Deloitte, Plender, Touche & Co (p. 6).

A number of reasons have so far been given for mergers between two firms, for example to give greater regional, national and international coverage. Mergers between large or growing firms and those which are smaller can be explained in this way. With national and international mergers between two large practices, the extent to which their activities and locations fit together can be a major consideration. For example, when Coopers & Lybrand merged with the United Kingdom firm of Deloitte Haskins & Sells, it was stated that:

> We have found in many aspects of our activities that our strengths are complementary, rather than overlapping. A very visible example is in our audit client base, where the financial services and retailing strengths of Deloitte clients complement the manufacturing position of Coopers. There are other examples of complementary activity in Tax, Corporate Finance, Business Services, Insolvency and Management Consulting. (*Our Merger*, 1989)

Similarly, the international merger between KMG and Peat Marwick International was a good fit both geographically and in terms of industry specialisation. The former was strong in manufacturing, particularly in Europe, while the latter's strength lay in banking and finance (Cypert, 1991, p. 27).

Although this essay has so far dealt mostly with the development, both nationally and internationally, of the largest firms, some mention should be made of medium and small firms. The development of these firms would seem to be fairly similar to that of their larger counterparts, albeit on a smaller scale (see, for example: *Hill Vellacott* (1988), now Chantrey Vellacott; Letts (1980) on MacIntyre Hudson, now also MacIntyre & Co; Medlam (1980) on Pannell Fitzpatrick & Co, now Pannell Kerr Forster; and *Russell Limebeer* (1978), now Fraser & Russell). Some firms lower down the league table have taken the decision not to amalgamate with other partnerships; for example, Dixon Wilson has remained a City of London practice for over 100 years, although since 1978 there has been a partner resident in Paris (Hardie, 1988, pp. 5, 19). Another City-based practice, Comins & Co, established in 1890 as Schultz & Comins, opened an office in New York in 1895, 'Only the sixth British firm to do so', although it was closed in 1909; however, the practice is now part of an international association, ICC (Inter Continental Consultants), instigated by the firm in 1972 (*Comins & Co*, 1990). Many medium-sized firms are concentrated in particular cities or regions rather than being national firms, while smaller practices will have just the one office. Where medium-sized firms have expanded on a regional basis, it has been, in most cases, by merger or by taking over small practices. Naturally, development of these firms internationally, when it has occurred, has been on a small scale too, some having a few overseas offices while others rely on correspondent arrangements.

CHANGING NATURE OF THE WORK OF ACCOUNTANTS

One of the earliest and most detailed accounts of the work performed by a professional practice in the early nineteenth century is to be found in the history of Bristol-based Curtis, Jenkins, Cornwell & Co. In 1821 two-thirds of the total time charged was for bankruptcy work, followed by accountancy and then executorship. However, just seven years later, in 1828, the position had changed substantially, with accountancy work, which included auditing, arbitration, estate management, advising on bookkeeping systems, and partnership dissolutions, representing over 50 per cent of the workload, followed by executorship and then bankruptcy (Cornwell, 1991, p. 60). This lack of reliance on bankruptcy work at such an early date is contrary to received wisdom; whether this firm was an exception it is difficult to tell.

Jones (1981) provides the most detailed breakdown of a firm's activities over any length of time. Harding & Pullein, founded in 1848, performed virtually no audit work in its first ten years; insolvency work generated most of the fee income. In 1860 auditing contributed 2.4 per cent of fees and this percentage did not rise above 20 per cent until the 1880s. In 1890 auditing and insolvency were level pegging at 40 per cent each and by 1895 auditing had become the major source of income, contributing just over 50 per cent (p. 50). The audit fees as a percentage of total fees of Whinney, Smith & Whinney (as Harding & Pullein were styled from 1894) fluctuated quite considerably in the first half of the twentieth century as follows: 58.6 per cent in 1905, 35.4 per cent in 1910, 44.6 per cent in 1915, 38.3 per cent in 1920, 48.5 per cent in 1925 and 67.4 per cent in 1930. During the war, audit fees rose as high as 73.9 per cent but had fallen to 59.7 per cent by 1960. Until 1925 the other substantial fee generator was insolvency work, in the 1930s and early 1940s accountancy work played a more important role, and then after the Second World War taxation formed the second most significant item of work (p. 99).

Richards (1950, p. 4) comments on the work which Price, Holyland & Waterhouse carried out in the 1860s:

> The principal work undertaken by the Firm in these early years consisted of liquidations, bankruptcies and arbitrations but another important contribution to the practice was the introduction of prospective borrowers of money to those who had funds available and were prepared to lend them; the auditing practice in those years was comparatively negligible and mainly consisted of the audit of estate accounts.

However, by 1887 'Audit work had begun to take a more important place in the practice, as distinct from the liquidations and bankruptcies which held a predominant position in earlier days' (p. 7).

Similarly with Cooper Brothers & Co, the early years of the firm were dominated by bankruptcies, liquidations and receiverships, but by the end of the first fifty years of business in 1904 'Auditing had become the backbone of the practice' (*L. R. B. & M. Journal*, January–March 1958, p. 2).

However, in contrast to the above, the history of a Birmingham firm, established in 1867 as Howard Smith & Co, includes the recollection from a one-time articled clerk who qualified in 1898 that: 'the firm was not keen to undertake bankruptcy and liquidation work, and ... its practice consisted mainly of auditing the accounts of collieries, manufacturing, engineering and steel companies, and ... those of the Corporation of Birmingham' (*Howard Smith Thompson & Co*, 1967, p. 5).

George A Touche & Co, having begun to practise later than other large United Kingdom firms, gained most of its early fees from directorships, receiverships and reconstructions, rather than from audits, although by 1915 audit fees formed the largest part of the firm's income (Richards, 1981, p. 16).

Thomson McLintock & Co's London office at first relied on 'special work', particularly advising on, and arranging, mergers, but in the 1920s, realising that this work was too unpredictable, a special audit manager was appointed 'to develop the "bread and butter" of audit work' (Winsbury, 1977, p. 32).

It is of special interest that within the records of Hill Vellacott, now Chantrey Vellacott, there is a copy of a letter from the firm showing that it was engaged in agreeing taxation liabilities for clients as early as 1880/81 (*Hill Vellacott*, 1988, p. 44).

The steady increase in the size of firms and the type, variety and complexity of some of the work necessitated the setting up of specialist departments. As taxation became more significant after the First World War, so firms set up specialist tax departments; for example, Thomson McLintock & Co employed a tax specialist in 1920, which greatly aided in the expansion of the firm (Winsbury, 1977, p. 34); Cooper Brothers & Co set up a separate tax department between the two World Wars (*A History of Cooper Brothers & Co*, 1954, p. 16); and 'Whinney, Smith & Whinney, Barton, Mayhew and Brown, Fleming & Murray (in London) all set up separate specialist departments to deal with these matters in the inter-war years, Turquand, Youngs following suit in the 1950s' (Jones, 1981, p. 163). After the Second World War, Cooper Brothers & Co extended its system of departmentalisation, establishing departments for 'executorship work, liquidations and receiverships, registration and share transfer work, costing and organisation, secretarial work and investigations' (*A History of Cooper Brothers & Co*, 1954, pp. 16–17). In fact, it is claimed that Cooper Brothers & Co was probably the first firm to enter the management consultancy field when it set up its organisation department in 1946 (*C&L Journal*, June 1979, p. 30). Other firms set up management consultancy practices as follows: George A Touche & Co, in 1952 (Richards, 1981, p. 30); Peat, Marwick, Mitchell & Co, in 1957 (Wise, 1982, p. 84); and Thomson McLintock & Co, in 1959 in London jointly with both Brown, Fleming & Murray and Mann, Judd & Co (Winsbury, 1977, p. 90).

Smaller regional firms were aware of their inability to offer specialist services to their audit clients, as is evidenced by this extract concerning the Bristol firm, Curtis, Jenkins, Cornwell & Co: 'Prior to 1963, the firm had become conscious of its inability to provide adequate services in the expanding "consultancy" field – a feeling shared by a number of other local firms. This led to an informal arrangement with a major London firm' (Cornwell, 1991, p. 157). Curtis, Jenkins, Cornwell & Co established a taxation department as a direct result of the 1965 Budget, but

> more widely, (and in a combination with other parallel developments such as the growth in consultancy work), it foreshadowed an inevitable and increasing requirement for specialisation and a consequent (if tardily recognised) decline in the independent viability and fortunes of the average medium-sized provincial firm. (p. 159)

The relative importance currently of each type of work can be seen from league tables of the firms. Fee income for the big six firms is split on average as follows: audit and accountancy 42 per cent; tax 23 per cent; consultancy 26 per cent; and insolvency 9 per cent (*Accountancy*, July 1992, p. 17). These averages may be misleading since they can hide significant variations among firms; for example, KPMG Peat Marwick generates 52 per cent of its fee income from audit and accountancy, Ernst & Young 29 per cent from tax, Arthur Andersen 53 per cent from consultancy, and Touche Ross & Co 12 per cent from insolvency. Lower down the league table more reliance is placed on audit and accountancy, followed by tax work, with only a small percentage of fees coming from consultancy and insolvency, apart from a few firms which specialise in these areas.

The evolution of professional firms is of interest to the accounting historian not only because of their influence and effect on the social and economic development of the country, but also because they have been responsible for the way in which accounting principles and auditing methods and procedures, to take just two examples, have developed. In more recent years these have been influenced by international considerations. These important, more technical, changes are not well documented in firms' histories, although they are mentioned on odd occasions.

Hill Vellacott, now Chantrey Vellacott, descended from the practice of Edward Thomas Jones, who is best remembered for *Jones's English System of Book-keeping* (1796), an exposition of a form of modified single-entry. The journal and ledger had additional columns so that sub-totals of transactions could be obtained periodically from each book and compared; as long as these totals agreed there was no need to 'call over' each and every entry. By 1820 Jones had revised and refined his ideas, such that the extra columns for control totals appeared in a special 'balance book'. This system was used within the firm for over 100 years and well into the twentieth century. It is akin to what is known today as batch control and it is suggested that Jones's system was the forerunner of ledger abstracts, worksheets and, more recently, computer spreadsheets (*Hill Vellacott*, 1988, pp. 15–17).

One of the few examples of the origins and development of accounting principles is the following: 'The double-account system had been specifically designed to cope with railway accounting problems. William Deloitte, as the auditor of the Great Western Railway, laid claim to having devised the method, though Quilter, Ball & Co also demanded credit' (Jones, 1981, p. 31).

In terms of audit techniques, the historian is interested in the type of work or tests which the auditor performed, the way in which audit evidence was gathered, and the depth of auditing in terms of either an arithmetical check on the accuracy of the books and records or a more rigorous verification of the assets and liabilities of a business.

One accessible piece of information is the way in which auditors word their reports; the following example, which also gives some idea of the work performed, is quoted in *Howard Smith Thompson & Co* (1967, p. 9):

> We have examined the books, accounts and vouchers of the Company, tested by actual enumeration its assets and securities, and certify that in our opinion this Balance Sheet truly sets forth the position of the company on the 30th day of June 1879. Howard S. Smith & Slocombe, Auditors.

According to Richards (1950, p. 7), Edwin Waterhouse was believed to have been 'responsible for the introduction at an early date, of the system of audit schedules which is now in force in all offices of the associated firms throughout the world, and also in the offices of many other accountants'. Audit schedules record and support the audit work undertaken. Edwin

Waterhouse was a partner in Price, Waterhouse & Co from 1865 to 1905, which narrows, to some extent, the time at which these audit schedules were introduced.

Audit programmes, setting out the detailed work to be performed, seem to have been introduced fairly early on too. An illustration in *Hill Vellacott* (1988, p. 28) shows that audit programmes were used by this firm in the late nineteenth century, although, unfortunately, no reference is made to them in the text. Some time in the late 1920s or early 1930s George Touche drew up comprehensive audit programmes to improve standards (Richards, 1981, p. 21). After the war and with the introduction of the Companies Act, 1948 changes to these programmes were required. Richards continues: 'In its approach to auditing by the use of a standard programme designed to test internal controls, and also the use of standard balance sheet audit programmes, the firm was among the pioneers' (pp. 27–8).

Histories of professional firms contain some material on detailed audit work such as asset verification. For example, Kilpatrick (1942, pp. 12–13) cites the following example from W W Deloitte's letter book dated 18 June 1856:

> The stock of rails at Newport must be taken by me and you had better have an account taken by the various parties in charge of the rails along the line. The account will be taken as on the 30th June to correspond with your accounts but I need not see the rails until after that date.

Richards (1981, p. 25) asserts that by 1949 George A Touche & Co was regarded as a firm with high professional standards: 'This view was justified; audit procedures such as the circularisation of debtors and attendance at stocktaking, for example, were applied in appropriate cases by the firm long before they were widely used in the United Kingdom.'

After the Second World War returning members of professional firms found themselves out of touch with current practice. This led Cooper Brothers & Co to review and update its audit procedures and set them down in writing, both to act as a training medium and to standardise practices in all offices no matter where they were situated. The Audit Manual was produced in 1946 and was published in 1966 as *Manual of Auditing* by Vivian Cooper. In 1948 an internal check questionnaire was developed, influenced to some extent by associated firms in Australia and the United States, and in 1952 model audit files were introduced (*A History of Cooper Brothers & Co*, 1954, p. 16; *C&L Journal*, June 1979, pp. 15–16).

Thomson McLintock & Co, coming somewhat later to the national scene than other large firms, recognised the need to protect its good name by such things as 'inter-office inspection, conformity to the firm's view of technical issues, [and] prescription of audit standards' (Winsbury, 1977, p. 115).

Similarly, when firms entered the international arena, they wished the overseas audits to meet their own standards. Arthur Andersen & Co (Littler, 1974, pp. 47–8) sent staff over to Europe in 1945 to supervise work; one report comments: 'The first order of business was to supervise the carrying out of the 1945 audits on a basis consistent with our own standards.' Arthur Andersen & Co's philosophy was that its overseas offices should be staffed by nationals of the country; non-nationals would 'be used only to the extent necessary to train the nationals in our policies, auditing procedures and accounting concept[s]' (p. 51).

Likewise, the formation of international firms required greater harmonisation of practice. Referring to the international practice of Touche Ross & Co, Richards (1981, p. 117) comments: 'In some countries auditing standards were by no means comparable with those in the U.S., Canada and the United Kingdom', so the firm set about the task of ensuring that there were adequate standards in all member firms. The Touche Ross Audit Process (TRAP) was developed jointly by the American, British and Canadian firms. According to Richards, TRAP was developed by 'drawing on the Canadian firm's experience of analytical audit techniques' and 'is a new approach to planning and designing an audit, the basic idea being to perform each procedure with specific objectives in mind and to use the carefully-recorded and evaluated results of all procedures as input for continued planning' (p. 34).

When Peat Marwick International was formed in 1978 'One of the organization's most important initial tasks was the production of a new international audit manual that would enable partners and staff in every country to know the auditing standards required by Peat Marwick throughout the world' (Wise, 1982, p. 78).

There have also been technological changes which to some extent have affected the development of auditing. For example, the introduction of comptometers in the 1930s relieved the audit clerk of the tedious task of adding up columns of figures, while the introduction of computers in the 1960s required the development of new auditing techniques (Jones, 1981, p. 213).

SUMMARY AND CONCLUSION

Accountants had begun to set up in public practice by the end of the eighteenth century, often engaged in other activities, many of which today would be thought of as highly inappropriate. More legitimate work arose in the nineteenth century from legislation in the areas of insolvency and company law, especially that relating to railway companies. A compulsory audit for all companies was introduced in 1900, and successive Acts increased the requirements for both auditing and financial reporting. The First World War increased the level of taxation, making this an important part of an accountant's work; later, after the Second World War, management consultancy began to form a significant proportion of some firms' fee income.

By the 1870s there were sufficient accountants in practice for them to come together, initially on a local basis, to establish professional bodies and thereby raise the standards required of accountants in practice to protect their own interests and those of the public. The ICAEW was incorporated in 1880 with under 600 members. Membership grew steadily over the first ninety years to nearly 50,000, but increased more spectacularly from 1970, reaching 100,000 by 1992. The ICAEW is responsible for the standard of education and training of its students and members, for their ethical conduct and for disciplinary measures which may be necessary to enforce professional standards. After the Second World War, and especially since the 1970s, it played a much more active role in establishing recommendations and standards on accounting and auditing.

Many of today's largest firms were formed during the first half of the Victorian era at a time when legislation encouraged the employment of accountants and before the inauguration of professional bodies. Most of these firms have grown by amalgamation, often with others whose origins pre-date their own. Few of the oldest firms have retained their independence; these were mostly founded in the provinces and it is the London practices which have come to dominate the market by their national expansion.

There have been a number of reasons for the growth in the size of accountancy partnerships. First and foremost, accountancy is a service industry; as clients grow so the firm must follow. A comment in *A History of Cooper Brothers & Co* (1954, p. 5) neatly sums up the position: 'A firm grows not only by reason of the industry of its partners and staff, but also because its clients grow and set new standards to which it must adapt itself.'

Companies are rarely concentrated in one location, particularly when they have grown by merger and takeover. Thus, to provide an effective service no matter where clients are based, accountants opened local offices. When industrial corporations engage in mergers and takeovers, the audit of the company taken over usually goes to the acquiring company's auditors, as they are likely to be large and to be able to provide the necessary services or specialisms. The concentration of industry into a small number of large corporations has had the corollary that the audits of these companies are also in the hands of a few. A similar phenomenon occurred with the programme of nationalisation after the Second World War. Additionally, as some companies grew, so they shed their local auditors in favour of the prestige of a major international firm. All this has led to mergers between accountancy firms as a defensive measure to avoid losing clients when the latter expanded.

National and international expansion has occurred simultaneously in many cases. With the flow of British capital abroad around the turn of the century, British firms opened offices in America; after both the First and the Second World Wars, with the flow of American capital to Europe, American firms followed. Today big business is operated by international giants which require the services on a global basis of multi-national firms of accountants.

Firms have grown in different ways and at different speeds: some by natural growth, opening new offices at home and abroad; some by an active takeover and merger policy; while others have adopted some middle course. Before a full merger has taken place, firms have often entered into a joint partnership or a correspondent relationship to be represented by the other firm wherever it practised.

As a result of the complexities of the legal, technological, political and economic environment, firms offer a range of specialised services. These can be provided more easily by large accountancy practices, thus giving a further stimulus to growth via merger, for both large and small firms. Also, firms need to have a number of technical support services such as research and training. Winsbury (1977, p. 124) suggests that the high cost of training was one reason for smaller practices wishing to merge with Thomson McLintock & Co.

Other reasons for mergers have been to expand the client base, especially by acquiring smaller practices with a number of high-profile clients, and to obtain additional skilled staff.

The consequence, particularly with the rapid growth from the 1960s onwards, of all these amalgamations would seem to be the polarisation of the accountancy profession into a small number of very large international practices, known as the 'big six', and a large number of very small ones, with only a few medium-sized firms in between.

Appendix I
BIBLIOGRAPHY OF HISTORIES OF PROFESSIONAL ACCOUNTANCY BODIES IN THE BRITISH ISLES

The histories in this bibliography are classified alphabetically under the current name, or the last name before amalgamation, of the major national professional bodies. These are followed by a section listing histories of local societies and founder bodies and then by an 'other' section containing histories which cannot easily be classified into the previous sections.

CHARTERED ASSOCIATION OF CERTIFIED ACCOUNTANTS

'The Association', *Certified Accountant* (December 1974) pp. 585–91.

[Osbourn, F C and R T Bell (comps.)], *Fifty Years: The Story of the Association of Certified and Corporate Accountants, 1904–54* (London, The Association of Certified & Corporate Accountants, 1954) ix + 70 pp.

CHARTERED INSTITUTE OF MANAGEMENT ACCOUNTANTS

Banyard, C W, *The Institute of Cost and Management Accountants: A History* (London, The Institute of Cost and Management Accountants, 1985) 105 pp.

Loft, Anne, *Coming into the Light: A Study of the Development of a Professional Association for Cost Accountants in Britain in the Wake of the First World War* (London, The Chartered Institute of Management Accountants, 1990) 158 pp.

'1919–1969: Portrait of a Profession', *Management Accounting*, Vol. 47 (March 1969) pp. 91–5.

CHARTERED INSTITUTE OF PUBLIC FINANCE AND ACCOUNTANCY

[Poynton, T L], *The Institute of Municipal Treasurers & Accountants: A Short History, 1885–1960* (London, The Institute of Municipal Treasurers & Accountants, [1960]) vii + 166 pp.

Sowerby, Tom, *The History of the Chartered Institute of Public Finance and Accountancy, 1885–1985* (London, The Chartered Institute of Public Finance and Accountancy, 1985) vi + 123 pp.

INSTITUTE OF CHARTERED ACCOUNTANTS IN ENGLAND AND WALES

H[arper], A C, *The Institute of Chartered Accountants in England and Wales: A Short Sketch of its Inception, 11th May, 1880* (London, for private circulation only, 1930) 11 pp.

Hopkins, Leon, *The Hundredth Year* (Plymouth, Macdonald & Evans, 1980) vii + 168 pp.

[Howitt, Sir Harold *et al* (comps.)], *The History of the Institute of Chartered Accountants in England and Wales, 1880–1965, and of its Founder Accountancy Bodies, 1870–1880: The Growth of a Profession and its Influence on Legislation and Public Affairs* (London, Heinemann, 1966) xiv + 269 pp. (Reprinted New York and London, Garland Publishing, 1984.)

Magnus, Philip, *The History of the Institute of Chartered Accountants in England and Wales, 1880–1958* (Unpublished, incomplete typescript, [1958]) 109 pp.

Margerison, Tom, *The Making of a Profession* (London, The Institute of Chartered Accountants in England and Wales, 1980) 43 pp.

INSTITUTE OF CHARTERED ACCOUNTANTS IN IRELAND

Robinson, H W, *A History of Accountants in Ireland* ([Dublin], The Institute of Chartered Accountants in Ireland, 1964) xii + 485 pp. (Reprinted New York and London, Garland Publishing, 1984.) 2nd edition (1983) xiv + 443 pp.

INSTITUTE OF CHARTERED ACCOUNTANTS OF SCOTLAND

A History of the Chartered Accountants of Scotland from the Earliest Times to 1954 (Edinburgh, The Institute of Chartered Accountants of Scotland, 1954) xi + 183 pp. (Reprinted New York and London, Garland Publishing, 1984.)

Kedslie, Moyra J M, *Firm Foundations: The Development of Professional Accounting in Scotland* (Hull, Hull University Press, 1990) xix + 335 pp.

McDougall, E H V, *Fifth Quarter–Century: Some Chapters in the History of the Chartered Accountants of Scotland* (Edinburgh, The Accountants' Publishing

Co for the Institute of Chartered Accountants of Scotland, 1980) xv + 101 pp.

SOCIETY OF INCORPORATED ACCOUNTANTS

Garrett, A A, *History of the Society of Incorporated Accountants, 1885–1957* (Oxford, Oxford University Press, 1961) xviii + 360 pp. (Reprinted New York and London, Garland Publishing, 1984.)

LOCAL SOCIETIES AND FOUNDER BODIES

Centenary 1882–1982, ([Birmingham], The Birmingham and West Midlands Society of Chartered Accountants, [1982]) 23 pp.

Hargraves, Ian, *Centenary 1870–1970* ([Liverpool], The Liverpool Society of Chartered Accountants, [1970]) 21 pp.

The History of the First Fifty Years of the Society ([Cardiff], The South Wales and Monmouthshire Society of Chartered Accountants, 1963) 22 pp.

Hoe, Alan M, *The First Hundred Years: Centenary 1877–1977* ([Sheffield], The Sheffield & District Society of Chartered Accountants, [1977]) 39 pp.

Middleton, S A, *A History of the Northern Society of Chartered Accountants* ([Newcastle upon Tyne], The Northern Society of Chartered Accountants, [1982]) 88 pp.

Walker, Stephen P, *The Society of Accountants in Edinburgh, 1854–1914: A Study of Recruitment to a New Profession* (New York and London, Garland Publishing, 1988) x + 373 pp.

OTHER

APC: The First Ten Years ([London], Auditing Practices Committee of CCAB, 1986) 84 pp.

[Brown, Anthony (ed.)], *The First One Hundred Years, 1883–1983* ([Liverpool], The Liverpool Chartered Accountant Students' Association, [1983]) 14 pp.

Davies, R U (ed.), *Watchdogs' Tales: The District Audit Service – the First 138 Years* (London, HMSO, 1987) viii + 250 pp.

Appendix II
BIBLIOGRAPHY OF HISTORIES OF ACCOUNTANCY FIRMS IN THE BRITISH ISLES

The existence of firms' histories is not always easy to establish because they are usually published privately and do not always include full bibliographic details. Therefore, there may be many more which have not come to light, particularly of the smaller and medium-sized firms. The histories in this bibliography are classified alphabetically under the name of the firm at the time its history was written, with the current name of the firm in parentheses. Where current firms have a published history under the name of a predecessor or constituent firm, this is cross-referenced under the current name.

Although the listing is essentially of histories of firms in the British Isles, others have been included selectively where international mergers have had an impact on the development of a British Isles firm. These overseas firms' histories are similarly cross-referenced and thus, for example, references to Haskins & Sells are identified with Coopers & Lybrand because of the merger in the

United Kingdom between Coopers & Lybrand and Deloitte Haskins & Sells, even though the latter firm amalgamated with Touche Ross & Co throughout most of the rest of the world.

The listing includes not only the histories of the actual firms, but also, in some cases, those of the firms' premises and biographies of partners.

Items which are not firm-specific have been included in a 'miscellaneous' section at the end of this bibliography.

ARTHUR ANDERSEN

Boys, Peter, 'What's in a Name – Firms' Simplified Family Trees: Arthur Andersen & Co', *Accountancy*, Vol. 103, No. 1145 (January 1989) p. 101.

[Higgins, John A *et al*], *The First Fifty Years, 1913–1963* (Chicago, Arthur Andersen & Co, 1963) xi + 201 pp. (Reprinted New York and London, Garland Publishing, 1986.)

[Littler, Mark *et al*], *The First Sixty Years, 1913–1973* (Chicago, Arthur Andersen & Co, 1974) xiii + 189 pp.

Spacek, Leonard, *The Growth of Arthur Andersen & Co., 1928–1973: An Oral History* (Arthur Andersen & Co, 1985) 349 pp. (Reprinted New York and London, Garland Publishing, 1989.)

A Vision of Grandeur (Arthur Andersen & Co, SC, 1988) 204 pp.

ARTHUR YOUNG [NOW ERNST & YOUNG]

Boys, Peter, 'What's in a Name – Firms' Simplified Family Trees: Arthur Young', *Accountancy*, Vol. 103, No. 1145 (January 1989) p. 102.

[Burton, J C (ed.)], *Arthur Young and the Business he Founded (Personal Reminiscences)* (New York, Arthur Young & Company, 1948) viii + 71 pp.

Keating, James, 'Arthur Young: The Man behind the Name', *The Arthur Young Quarterly*, Vol. 1, No. 2 (summer 1980) pp. 14–21.

ASHWORTH, MOSLEY & CO [NOW ROBSON RHODES]

Allured, Joseph (comp.), *A Short History of Ashworth, Mosley & Co., Chartered Accountants, Manchester, 1825–1980* (Bowdon, Cheshire, typescript, 1980) 6 pp.

BAKER, SUTTON & CO [NOW ERNST & YOUNG]

The Story of Baker Sutton & Co. ([London, Baker, Sutton & Co], 1 vol., loose leaf typescript, [1978]) [21] pp.

BAKER TILLY

Boys, Peter, 'What's in a Name – Firms' Simplified Family Trees: Baker Tilly', *Accountancy*, Vol. 103, No. 1146 (February 1989) p. 138.

BARROW, WADE & GUTHRIE [NOW KPMG PEAT MARWICK]

Anyon, James T, *Recollections of the Early Days of American Accountancy, 1883–1893* (Privately printed, 1925) 68 pp. (Reprinted Osaka, Nihon Shoseki, 1974.) Reprinted in Stephen A Zeff (ed.), *The U.S. Accounting Profession in the 1890s and Early 1900s* (New York and London, Garland Publishing, 1988) pp. 45–98.

BARSTOW & MILLAR [NOW PANNELL KERR FORSTER]

A Short History of Barstow & Millar C.A., 1878–1978 ([Edinburgh, Barstow & Millar, 1978]) [2] pp.

BARTON, MAYHEW & CO [NOW ERNST & YOUNG]

Coulson, H O H, *History of Barton, Mayhew & Co* (Draft typescript, incomplete) [44] pp.

BDO BINDER HAMLYN

Boys, Peter, 'What's in a Name – Firms' Simplified Family Trees: BDO Binder Hamlyn', *Accountancy*, Vol. 103, No. 1146 (February 1989) p. 139.

See also: VINEY MERRETTS

BEGBIE, ROBINSON, COX & KNIGHT [NOW BEGBIES]

A Hundred Years of Accountancy, 1837–1937 ([London], Begbie, Robinson, Cox & Knight, [1937]) 38 pp.

BEGBIES

Boys, Peter, 'When Small Means Successful', *Accountancy*, Vol. 101, No. 1134 (February 1988) pp. 112–13.

See also: BEGBIE, ROBINSON, COX & KNIGHT

CHANTREY VELLACOTT

See: HILL VELLACOTT

CLARK WHITEHILL

Boys, Peter, 'What's in a Name – Firms' Simplified Family Trees: Clark Whitehill', *Accountancy*, Vol. 103, No. 1147 (March 1989) p. 96.

COMINS & CO

Comins & Co Centenary, 1890–1990 (London, Comins & Co, [1990]) [4] pp.

COOPER BROTHERS & CO [NOW COOPERS & LYBRAND]

Cooper, Ernest, 'Fifty-seven Years in an Accountant's Office', in *Proceedings of the Autumnal Meeting of the Institute of Chartered Accountants in England and Wales* (London, Gee & Co, 1921) pp. 41–73. (Reprinted New York and London, Garland Publishing, 1982.)

A History of Cooper Brothers & Co., 1854 to 1954 (London, Batsford for Cooper Brothers & Co, 1954) xi + 116 pp. (Reprinted New York and London, Garland Publishing, 1986.)

COOPERS & LYBRAND

Benson, Henry, *Accounting for Life* (London, Kogan Page in association with the Institute of Chartered Accountants in England and Wales, 1989) xi + 241 pp.

Boys, Peter, 'What's in a Name – Firms' Simplified Family Trees: Coopers & Lybrand', *Accountancy*, Vol. 103, No. 1147 (March 1989) p. 97.

C&L Journal, 125th Anniversary Issue, No. 31 (June 1979) 41 pp.

The Early History of Coopers & Lybrand (New York and London, Garland Publishing, 1984) [Includes: *Fiftieth Anniversary, 1898–1948* (Lybrand, Ross Bros. & Montgomery, 1949) 168 pp. and *L. R. B. & M. Journal*, Vol. 39, No. 1 (January–March 1958) 20 pp.]

See also: COOPER BROTHERS & CO; COOPERS & LYBRAND DELOITTE; W H CORK, GULLY & CO; CURTIS, JENKINS, CORNWELL & CO; DELOITTE & CO; DELOITTE HASKINS & SELLS; DELOITTE, PLENDER, GRIFFITHS & CO; HASKINS & SELLS

COOPERS & LYBRAND DELOITTE [NOW COOPERS & LYBRAND]
Our Merger (Coopers & Lybrand and Deloitte Haskins & Sells, 1989) [8] pp.

W H CORK, GULLY & CO [NOW CORK GULLY, PART OF COOPERS & LYBRAND]
Cork, Sir Kenneth (with Hugh Barty-King), *Cork on Cork* (London, Macmillan, 1988) xi + 265 pp.
Tickler, Walter, 'W H Cork Gully & Co', *C&L Journal*, No. 35 (December 1980) pp. 18–20.

CRAIG GARDNER & CO
Farmar, Tony, *A History of Craig Gardner & Co.: The First 100 Years* (Dublin, Gill & Macmillan, 1988) 239 pp.

CURTIS, JENKINS, CORNWELL & CO [NOW COOPERS & LYBRAND]
Cornwell, S V P, *Curtis Jenkins Cornwell & Co.: A Study in Professional Origins, 1816–1966* (New York and London, Garland Publishing, 1991) 189 pp.

DELOITTE & CO [NOW COOPERS & LYBRAND]
Deloittes Newsletter, Special Merger Issue (1 May 1974) [8] pp.

DELOITTE HASKINS & SELLS [NOW COOPERS & LYBRAND]
Boys, Peter, 'What's in a Name – Firms' Simplified Family Trees: Deloitte Haskins & Sells', *Accountancy*, Vol. 103, No. 1148 (April 1989) pp. 118–19.

DELOITTE, PLENDER, GRIFFITHS & CO [NOW COOPERS & LYBRAND]
[Kettle, Sir Russell], *Deloitte & Co., 1845–1956* (Oxford, Oxford University Press for Deloitte, Plender, Griffiths & Co, 1958) xi + 171 pp. (Reprinted New York and London, Garland Publishing, 1982.)
Kilpatrick, James, *Deloitte, Plender, Griffiths & Co.: Russian Interlude* (London, Wyman & Sons, 1943) 31 pp.
— *Deloitte, Plender, Griffiths & Co.: Some Notes on the Early Days of the Firm* (London, Wyman & Sons, 1942) 32 pp.

DIXON WILSON
[Hardie, Sir Charles], *Dixon Wilson Centenary, 1888–1988: A Brief History* (London, Dixon Wilson, [1988]) 32 pp.

ERNST & ERNST [NOW ERNST & YOUNG]
Ernst & Ernst: A History of the Firm (Cleveland, Ohio, Ernst & Ernst, 1960) 85 pp.

ERNST & WHINNEY [NOW ERNST & YOUNG]
Boys, Peter, 'What's in a Name – Firms' Simplified Family Trees: Ernst & Whinney', *Accountancy*, Vol. 103, No. 1149 (May 1989) p. 88.
Jones, Edgar, *Accountancy and the British Economy, 1840–1980: The Evolution of Ernst & Whinney* (London, Batsford, 1981) 288 pp.

ERNST & YOUNG
See: ARTHUR YOUNG; BAKER, SUTTON & CO; BARTON, MAYHEW & CO; ERNST & ERNST; ERNST & WHINNEY; TURQUAND, YOUNGS, MCAULIFFE & CO; WARE, WARD & CO

A F FERGUSON & CO [NOW ALSO FERGUSON MAIDMENT & CO]

A F Ferguson & Co., Chartered Accountants, India: History of the Firm (Unpublished draft, *c.* 1965) 34 pp.

History of A F Ferguson & Co. – Pakistan Firm ([Karachi], typescript, 1965) 18 + 3 + 8 pp.

FERGUSON MAIDMENT & CO

See: A F FERGUSON & CO

FINNIE & CO [NOW STOY HAYWARD]

Boys, Peter, 'What's in a Name – Firms' Simplified Family Trees: Finnie & Co', *Accountancy*, Vol. 103, No. 1149 (May 1989) pp. 90–1.

FRASER & RUSSELL

See: PIKE, RUSSELL & CO; RUSSELL LIMEBEER

GRACE, DARBYSHIRE & TODD [NOW KPMG PEAT MARWICK]

The Pedigree of Tyndall over 150 years, 1818–1974 ([Bristol], The West of England Trust Limited, [1974]) 36 pp.

A Short History of Grace, Darbyshire and Todd, Chartered Accountants of Bristol, 1818–1957 ([Bristol], Grace, Darbyshire & Todd, [1957]) [15] pp.

GRANT THORNTON

Boys, Peter, 'What's in a Name – Firms' Simplified Family Trees: Grant Thornton', *Accountancy*, Vol. 103, No. 1150 (June 1989) p. 98.

Hubbard, Peter, *Grant Thornton: A Brief History* (typescript, 1991) 18 pp.

GRIFFITHS, MILES, SULLY & CO

See: J & A W SULLY & CO

HASKINS & SELLS [NOW COOPERS & LYBRAND]

[Foye, Arthur B *et al*], *Haskins & Sells: Our First Seventy-five Years* ([New York], Haskins & Sells, 1970) 192 pp. (Reprinted New York and London, Garland Publishing, 1984.)

Haskins & Sells: The First Fifty Years, 1895–1945 (Haskins & Sells, 1947) 101 pp.

HILL VELLACOTT [NOW CHANTREY VELLACOTT]

Boys, Peter, 'Two Toasts to Hill Vellacott', *Accountancy*, Vol. 102, No. 1139 (July 1988) p. 67.

Etor, John R, 'Edward Thomas Jones (1767–1833), Public Accountant' (Paper given at the Third International Congress of Accounting Historians, London, 1980) 25 pp.

Hill Vellacott: An Historical Account of their Development since 1788 ([London], Hill Vellacott, [1988]) 48 pp.

HODGSON IMPEY [NOW KIDSONS IMPEY]

Boys, Peter, 'What's in a Name – Firms' Simplified Family Trees: Hodgson Impey', *Accountancy*, Vol. 103, No. 1150 (June 1989) p. 99.

HOWARD SMITH, THOMPSON & CO [NOW PRICE WATERHOUSE]

Howard Smith Thompson & Co, 7th November 1867 to 7th November 1967: The First 100 Years ([Birmingham, Howard Smith, Thompson & Co, 1967]) 11 pp.

KEMP, CHATTERIS & CO [NOW TOUCHE ROSS & CO]
Kemp, Chatteris & Co, 1857–1957 ([London], Kemp, Chatteris & Co, [1957]) [2] pp.

KIDSONS [NOW KIDSONS IMPEY]
Boys, Peter, 'What's in a Name – Firms' Simplified Family Trees: Kidsons', *Accountancy*, Vol. 104, No. 1151 (July 1989) p. 102.

KIDSONS IMPEY
See: HODGSON IMPEY; KIDSONS

KINGSFORD, GARLANT & CO [NOW SPAIN BROTHERS & CO]
Kingsfords ([1956]) 12 pp.

KPMG PEAT MARWICK
Cypert, Samuel A, *Following the Money: The Inside Story of Accounting's First Mega-merger* (New York, American Management Association, 1991) xx + 279 pp.
See also: BARROW, WADE & GUTHRIE; GRACE, DARBYSHIRE & TODD; PEAT MARWICK MCLINTOCK; PEAT, MARWICK, MITCHELL & CO; THOMSON MCLINTOCK & CO

LARKING & LARKING [NOW LARKINGS]
Larking & Larking, Centenary, 1888–1988: One Hundred Years of Growth ([Maidstone], Larking & Larking, [1988]) [16] pp.

LARKINGS
See: LARKING & LARKING

LITTLEJOHN FRAZER
Boys, Peter, 'What's in a Name – Firms' Simplified Family Trees: Littlejohn Frazer', *Accountancy*, Vol. 104, No. 1151 (July 1989) p. 104.

LOVEWELL BLAKE
'Lovewell Blake – A Short History?', *EASCA News*, Vol. 3, No. 2 (April 1991) p. 7.

MACINTYRE & CO
See: MACINTYRE HUDSON

MACINTYRE HUDSON [NOW ALSO MACINTYRE & CO]
Letts, Stanford, 'Looking Back over a Century', *Accountants Weekly* (15 August 1980) pp. 26–7.
— *MacIntyre Hudson, May 1880–May 1980* (MacIntyre Hudson, [1980]) 42 pp.

MANN JUDD GORDON [NOW ALSO TOUCHE ROSS & CO]
Interim Account ... of a Going Concern: Some Essays on the History of the Firm of Mann Judd Gordon & Company, Chartered Accountants Glasgow, circa 1817 to 1967, on the Occasion of the 150th Anniversary of its Foundation (Glasgow, Mann Judd Gordon & Co, 1967) 57 pp.

MOORE & SMALLEY
100 Years of Moore & Smalley: A Brief History ([Preston], Moore & Smalley, 1992) 6 pp.

MOORE STEPHENS
Boys, Peter, 'What's in a Name – Firms' Simplified Family Trees: Moore Stephens', *Accountancy*, Vol. 104, No. 1152 (August 1989) p. 83.

MOORES ROWLAND

Boys, Peter, 'What's in a Name – Firms' Simplified Family Trees: Moores Rowland', *Accountancy*, Vol. 104, No. 1152 (August 1989) p. 82.

MORRIS GREGORY

A History of One Hundred Years of Accountancy Practice, 1852–1952 (Manchester, Morris, Gregory & Co, [1952]) 7 pp.

NEVILLE RUSSELL

Boys, Peter, 'What's in a Name – Firms' Simplified Family Trees: Neville Russell', *Accountancy*, Vol. 104, No. 1152 (August 1989) p. 83.

PANNELL FITZPATRICK & CO [NOW PANNELL KERR FORSTER]

[Medlam, Wilfred *et al*], *A History of Pannell Fitzpatrick & Co* ([London], Pannell Kerr Forster, [1980]) 45 pp.

PANNELL KERR FORSTER

Boys, Peter, 'What's in a Name – Firms' Simplified Family Trees: Pannell Kerr Forster', *Accountancy*, Vol. 104, No. 1153 (September 1989) pp. 80–1.

Wilding, Diana W, with C Everett Johnson, *A Tradition of Excellence. A Commitment to Progress – A 75-year Perspective* (Pannell Kerr Forster, 1986) 98 pp.

See also: BARSTOW & MILLAR; PANNELL FITZPATRICK & CO

PEAT MARWICK MCLINTOCK [NOW KPMG PEAT MARWICK]

Boys, Peter, 'What's in a Name – Firms' Simplified Family Trees: Peat Marwick McLintock', *Accountancy*, Vol. 104, No. 1153 (September 1989) p. 82.

PEAT, MARWICK, MITCHELL & CO
[NOW KPMG PEAT MARWICK]

Dawe, Donovan (with Adrian Oswald) *11 Ironmonger Lane: The Story of a Site in the City of London* (London, Hutchinson, 1952) 144 pp.

Morrison, Kenneth, 'PMM in the Past: The Founders', *PMM Platform* (summer 1980) pp. 24–5.

— 'PMM in the Past: James Marwick', *PMM Platform* (winter 1980) pp. 24–5.

— 'PMM in the Past: The First PMM Office', *PMM Platform* (spring 1981) pp. 24–5.

Wise, T A, *Peat, Marwick, Mitchell & Co.: 85 years* ([New York], Peat, Marwick, Mitchell & Co, 1982) 107 pp.

PIKE, RUSSELL & CO [NOW FRASER & RUSSELL]

Pike, Russell & Co.: An Account of a London Firm of Chartered Accountants, 1903–1973 (London, Pike Russell & Co, [1973]) 59 pp.

PRICE WATERHOUSE

Boys, Peter, 'What's in a Name – Firms' Simplified Family Trees: Price Waterhouse', *Accountancy*, Vol. 104, No. 1154 (October 1989) p. 160.

DeMond, C W, *Price, Waterhouse & Co. in America: A History of a Public Accounting Firm* (New York, Price Waterhouse & Co, 1951) ix + 356 pp. (Reprinted New York, Arno Press, 1980.)

Falkner, A C, 'The United Kingdom Firm – The Second Fifty Years', *PW Quarterly*, (winter 1969) pp. 8–11.

Jones, Edgar (ed.), *The Memoirs of Edwin Waterhouse: A Founder of Price Waterhouse* (London, Batsford, 1988) 248 pp.
Richards, G E (comp.), *History of the Firm: The First Fifty Years, 1850–1900* ([London], Price Waterhouse & Co, 1950) 13 pp.
'Some Significant Events in the History of the UK Firm', *The Reporter*, No. 50 (December 1987).
See also: HOWARD SMITH, THOMPSON & CO

RAWLINSON & HUNTER
Spooner, R, *Rawlinson & Hunter, Chartered Accountants: Its Formation, Development and Growth, 1933–1984* ([London], Rawlinson & Hunter, 1990) 38 pp.

ROBSON RHODES
Boys, Peter, 'What's in a Name – Firms' Simplified Family Trees: Robson Rhodes', *Accountancy*, Vol. 104, No. 1154 (October 1989) pp. 158–9.
Harvey, David, 'Robson Rhodes: From One Client to World Prominence', *Accountants Weekly* (11 October 1974) pp. 20–1.
See also: ASHWORTH, MOSLEY & CO

RUSSELL LIMEBEER [NOW FRASER & RUSSELL]
Russell Limebeer: A London Firm of Chartered Accountants (London, Russell Limebeer, [1978]) 27 pp.

SAFFERY CHAMPNESS
Boys, Peter, 'What's in a Name – Firms' Simplified Family Trees: Saffery Champness', *Accountancy*, Vol. 104, No. 1155 (November 1989) p. 122.

SPAIN BROTHERS & CO
See: KINGSFORD, GARLANT & CO

SPICER & OPPENHEIM [NOW TOUCHE ROSS & CO]
Boys, Peter, 'What's in a Name – Firms' Simplified Family Trees: Spicer & Oppenheim', *Accountancy*, Vol. 104, No. 1155 (November 1989) p. 123.

STOY HAYWARD
Boys, Peter, 'What's in a Name – Firms' Simplified Family Trees: Stoy Hayward', *Accountancy*, Vol. 104, No. 1154 (October 1989) p. 159.
Hale, Brian, 'Stoy Hayward Goes International in Major Merger', *Accountants Weekly* (24 January 1975) pp. 14–15.
See also: FINNIE & CO

J & A W SULLY & CO [NOW ALSO SULLY & CO AND GRIFFITHS, MILES, SULLY & CO]
[Sully, Alfred Victor], *Towards the Centenary, 1865–1951: Notes on the Origin and History of an Accountancy Practice* ([London], J & A W Sully & Co, 1951) 40 pp.

SULLY & CO
See: J & A W SULLY & CO

THOMSON MCLINTOCK & CO [NOW KPMG PEAT MARWICK]
House, Jack, *A Tale of Two Houses* ([Glasgow], Thomson McLintock & Co, 1980) xiv + 74 pp.

Winsbury, Rex, *Thomson McLintock & Co – The First Hundred Years* (London, Seeley, Service & Co for Thomson McLintock & Co, 1977) xi + 164 pp.

TOUCHE ROSS & CO

Boys, Peter, 'What's in a Name – Firms' Simplified Family Trees: Touche Ross & Co', *Accountancy*, Vol. 104, No. 1156 (December 1989) pp. 134–5.

'Origins of Today's Firm', *Touche Ross Review*, Merger Special (winter 1979/80) pp. 8–9.

Richards, Archibald B, *Touche Ross & Co., 1899–1981: The Origins and Growth of the United Kingdom Firm* (London, Touche Ross & Co, 1981) xiv + 145 pp.

Swanson, Theodor, *Touche Ross: A Biography – The Life and Services of a Multinational Partnership in the Expanding Profession of Accounting and Management Consulting* (Touche Ross & Co, 1972) 96 pp. (Reprinted New York and London, Garland Publishing, 1990.)

See also: KEMP, CHATTERIS & CO; MANN JUDD GORDON; SPICER & OPPENHEIM; WILSON, STIRLING & CO

TURQUAND, YOUNGS, MCAULIFFE & CO
[NOW ERNST & YOUNG]

Robertson, D W, 'Turquand, Youngs, McAuliffe & Co.', *The Arthur Andersen Chronicle* (July 1949) pp. 142–9.

VINEY MERRETTS [NOW BDO BINDER HAMLYN]

At Your Service – Viney Merretts (London, Viney Merretts, 1974) [20] pp.

Viney Merretts, Chartered Accountants for 150 Years in the City of London, 1828–1978 (London, Viney Merretts, [1978]) [8] pp.

WARE, WARD & CO [NOW ERNST & YOUNG]

Ware, Ward & Co.: A History of the Firm, 1867 to 1971 ([Bristol], Ware, Ward & Co, 1973) 13 pp.

WHITAKER & REDFEARN

Redfearn, G D (comp.), *The Whitaker and Redfearn Practice: A Short History of the Origins and of the First Sixty Years of the Partnership* ([Penzance], typescript, 1986) 6 pp.

WILSON, STIRLING & CO [NOW TOUCHE ROSS & CO]

[Stewart, James C], *Wilson, Stirling & Co., 1864–1964* ([Glasgow], Wilson, Stirling & Co, [1964]) 14 pp.

MISCELLANEOUS

Hopkins, Leon, *The Hundredth Year* (Plymouth, Macdonald & Evans, 1980) vii + 168 pp. [Especially chapter 5]

— 'The Victorians who Founded a Profession', *Accountants Weekly* (9 May 1980) pp. 22–5.

[Howitt, Sir Harold *et al* (comps.)], *The History of the Institute of Chartered Accountants in England and Wales, 1880–1965, and of its Founder Accountancy Bodies, 1870–1880: The Growth of a Profession and its Influence on Legislation and Public Affairs* (London, Heinemann, 1966) xiv + 269 pp. [Especially pp. 227–47] (Reprinted New York and London, Garland Publishing, 1984.)

Jeremy, David J (ed.), *Dictionary of Business Biography: A Biographical Dictionary of Business Leaders Active in Britain in the Period 1860–1980* (London,

Butterworth, 1984–86) 5 Vols. [Includes the following accountants: Barton, Sir Harold Montague; Benson, Henry Alexander; Chadwick, David; Cooper, Arthur; Cooper, Ernest; Cooper, Sir Francis D'Arcy; Deloitte, William Welch; De Paula, Frederic Rudolf Mackley; Dickinson, Sir Arthur Lowes; Edwards, Sir Ronald; Fells, John Manger; Garcke, Emile Oscar; Garnsey, Sir Gilbert Francis; Guthrie, Edwin; Harding, Sir Robert Palmer; Harmood-Banner, Sir John Sutherland; Jenkinson, Sir Mark Webster; Jones, Theodore Brooke; McLintock, Sir William; Mayhew, Sir Basil Edgar; Peat, Sir William Barclay; Plender, William; Quilter, William; Smallpeice, Sir Basil; Stamp, Josiah Charles; Touche, Sir George Alexander; Waterhouse, Edwin; and Whinney, Frederick]

Parker, R H (ed.), *British Accountants: A Biographical Sourcebook* (New York, Arno Press, 1980).

— 'Those First Councillors ... a Golden Heritage', *Accountancy*, Vol. 91, No. 1041 (May 1980) pp. 36–42.

Robinson, H W, *A History of Accountants in Ireland* ([Dublin], Institute of Chartered Accountants in Ireland, 2nd edition, 1983) xiv + 443 pp. [Especially chapter 22]

Stewart, Jas. C, *Pioneers of a Profession: Chartered Accountants to 1879 – Being Biographical Notes on the Members of the Scottish Chartered Societies, 1854 to 1879* (Edinburgh, Scottish Committee on Accounting History, The Institute of Chartered Accountants of Scotland, 1977) xii + 181 pp. (Reprinted New York and London, Garland Publishing, 1986.)

Vanstone, Harold B, *Accountancy in Manchester* (Privately printed, 1992) 27 pp.

— 'Accountancy in Manchester: Three Decades of Change', *Manchester Memoirs being the Memoirs and Proceedings of the Manchester Literary and Philosophical Society*, Vol. 127 (1987–88) pp. 98–108.

Appendix III
FOUNDER FIRMS

The term 'founder firm' is not a recognised title but one which was used in the ICAEW's history (Howitt, 1966, p. 227) where it is defined as a firm which 'can claim continuous partnership descent from a signatory to the Charter or a member of the first Council'. Although this definition refers to 'a signatory to the Charter', it is presumed that it actually means a signatory to the *petition* for the Charter. There were six petitioners named in the Charter, all of whom became members of the first council, hence this definition is somewhat tautological. Founder firms are also defined as those which could claim to have been in existence for at least 100 years in 1965.

The information in this appendix has been compiled from a number of sources, including: *Lists of Members* of the ICAEW, the London *Post Office Directory*, firms' histories and information provided by a number of firms. However, it should be noted that in some cases the dates are only approximate, and that further information may come to light which may refute, or add to, this appendix. Unfortunately, it was not possible to include in this appendix all the information which came to light during the survey.

The following listing is split into two sections corresponding to the two definitions above. In both sections it will be seen that a number of the founder firms have divided at some stage in their history, so that their descent can be traced through to more than one current firm.

Founder firms descended from the first council members

The first council consisted of forty-five members. However, five firms had two representatives each (see items 12, 14, 15, 16 and 29 below). Firms which have descended from a member of the first council are listed in alphabetical order by council member. The name of the firm, where this was different from that of the member, follows together with the location, both in 1880, then the date, in parentheses, when the firm was originally established (where firms had merged prior to 1880 this is the founding date of the oldest constituent firm), and finally the current name or names of the firm.

1. Jarvis William Barber, Barber Brothers & Wortley, Sheffield (1867), Barber, Harrison & Platt.
2. Josiah Beddow, Josiah Beddow & Son, London (*c.* 1845), Littlejohn Frazer.
3. John Blackburn, H W & J Blackburn, Bradford (1844) and Leeds, Robson Rhodes and Ernst & Young.
4. James Charles Bolton, J C Bolton & Son, London (pre–1864), Pannell Kerr Forster.
5. George Augustus Cape, Cape & Harris, London (1864), MacIntyre Hudson, MacIntyre & Co and Saffery Champness.
6. Edward Carter, Carter & Carter, Birmingham (1827), Coopers & Lybrand.
7. William Cash, Cash & Stone, London (1861), Coopers & Lybrand.
8. David Chadwick, Chadwicks, Collier & Co, London and Manchester (1860), Cooper Lancaster and Coopers & Lybrand.
9. Anthony Wigham Chalmers, Chalmers & Wade, Liverpool (1796), Kidsons Impey and Pannell Kerr Forster.
10. Arthur Cooper, Cooper Brothers & Co, London (1854), Coopers & Lybrand.
11. Joseph Davies, Davies, Voisey & Davies, Warrington (pre–1872), Voisey & Co.
12. William Welch Deloitte and John George Griffiths, Deloitte, Dever, Griffiths & Co, London (1845), Coopers & Lybrand.
13. Walter Newton Fisher, Birmingham (pre–1880), Coopers & Lybrand.
14. Edwin Guthrie and Charles Henry Wade, Thomas, Wade, Guthrie & Co, Manchester (1875), KPMG Peat Marwick and Touche Ross & Co.
15. Robert Palmer Harding and Frederick Whinney, Harding, Whinney & Co, London (1848), Ernst & Young.
16. Alfred Cotton Harper and Edward Norton Harper, E Norton Harper & Sons, London (*c.* 1873), Hays Allan.
17. Charles Fitch Kemp, C F Kemp, Ford & Co, London (1857), Touche, Ross & Co.
18. George Walter Knox, Knox & Burbidge, Sheffield (1869) and Knox, Craig & Co, London, Pannell Kerr Forster and Knox Cropper.

19. George Herbert Ladbury, Ladbury, Collison & Viney, London (1828), BDO Binder Hamlyn.
20. Roderick Mackay, R Mackay & Co, London (1867) and Middlesbrough, KPMG Peat Marwick.
21. Francis Nicholls, Nicholls & Leatherdale, London (*c.* 1858), Booth White.
22. Edward Thomas Peirson, Coventry (1853), Kidsons Impey and Edward Thomas Peirson & Sons.
23. Samuel Lowell Price, Price, Waterhouse & Co, London (1849), Price Waterhouse.
24. Thomas William Read, Liverpool (1860), Touche Ross & Co.
25. Joseph John Saffery, J J Saffery & Co, London (1855), Saffery Champness.
26. Thomas George Shuttleworth, Tasker & Shuttleworth, Sheffield (pre-1877), Grant Thornton.
27. George Edwin Swithinbank, G E Swithinbank & Co, London (pre–1876) and G E Swithinbank, Briggs & Co, Bristol, Price Waterhouse.
28. John Henry Tilly, Tilly & Co, London (pre–1868), Baker Tilly.
29. William Turquand and John Young, Turquand, Youngs & Co, London (*c.* 1840), Ernst & Young.
30. William Henry Watson, John Watson & Sons, Sheffield (pre–1827), Watson Wheatcroft.
31. Thomas Abercrombie Welton, Quilter, Ball & Co, London (1833), Coopers & Lybrand.
32. John Unwin Wing, Wing, Wing, Lilly & Co, Sheffield (pre–1877) and Wing, Wing, Lescher & Co, London, Hawsons and Buzzacott & Co.

It would appear, from the evidence available, that eight firms which were represented by partners on the first council have since disappeared. Again these firms are listed in alphabetical order by council member. The name of the firm, where this was different from that of the member, follows together with the location, both in 1880, and then the date when the firm seems to have disappeared.

Alfred Allott, London, 1883.
John Bath, John Bath & Sons, London, 1888.
Henry Bolland, Gibson, Bolland & Jackson, Liverpool, 1904.
Thomas Browning, Manchester, 1905.
Edward Hart, Hart Brothers, Tibbetts & Co, London, 1988. (This firm, given its date of disappearance, is correctly included by Howitt as a founder firm.)
Henry Grosvenor Nicholson, H G Nicholson & Co, Manchester, 1908.
Frederick Tendron, London, 1899.
James Waddell, J Waddell & Co, London, 1883.

Founder firms over 100 years old in 1965, and not listed above

Firms are listed in the order of their longevity, starting with the name of the founder or the earliest known name of the firm, followed by the original location and the date of formation in parentheses, and finally the current name or names of the firm.

33. Josiah Wade, Bristol (1780), Coopers & Lybrand.
34. Edward Thomas Jones, Bristol (1788), Chantrey Vellacott.
35. Harmood Banner & Son, Liverpool (1805), Coopers & Lybrand.
36. Thomas Crook & Son, Liverpool (1816), Coopers & Lybrand.
37. Robert Fletcher & Co, Bristol (1816), Coopers & Lybrand.
38. John Moxham, Bristol (1818), KPMG Peat Marwick.
39. J S James & Son, Birmingham (1821), Ernst & Young.
40. William Broome, Manchester (1825), Robson Rhodes.
41. Thomas Whinneray, Liverpool (1825), Coopers & Lybrand.
42. John Honey, London (*c.* 1830), Ernst & Young.
43. Edward Bolton, Leeds (1834), Pannell Kerr Forster.
44. J G Carlill, Hull (1835), Kidsons Impey and Price Waterhouse.
45. George Coryndon Begbie, London (1837), Begbies.
46. C S Beecroft & Co, London (1842), Touche Ross & Co.
47. William Edwards, London (*c.* 1843), Clark Whitehill and Arthur Andersen.
48. Jeremiah Harridge, London (pre–1846), Neville Russell.
49. W H Williams & Co, Bristol (1846), Price Waterhouse.
50. Holmes Dudley & Co, Newcastle upon Tyne (1847), Ernst & Young.
51. William Mathison, Liverpool (1847), Langton Morland.
52. Wm Henry Grey, London (pre–1848), Arthur Andersen.
53. Henry Chatteris, London (1848), Touche Ross & Co.
54. John Stanley Blease, Liverpool (1849), Blease, Lloyd & Co.
55. William Marshall, Leeds (1849), KPMG Peat Marwick.
56. Mason & Son, London (*c.* 1850), Ernst & Young.
57. William Edmonds, Portsea (1850s), Grant Thornton.
58. Joseph Sawyer, London (pre–1851), Clark Whitehill.
59. Alexander Morris & Son, Manchester (1852), Morris Gregory.
60. Taylor & Mellors, Nottingham (1854), Price Waterhouse and Mellors, Basden & Co.
61. F Charlton & Co, Birmingham (1854), Ernst & Young.
62. Thomas Coke Squance, Sunderland (1855), KPMG Peat Marwick.
63. Thomas Heaps, Liverpool (1856), Lithgow, Nelson & Co and Pannell Kerr Forster.
64. Henry Baldock Kingsford, London (1857), Spain Brothers & Co.
65. Lovewell Blake, Great Yarmouth (1858), Lovewell Blake.
66. Wykes & Co, Leicester (1859), KPMG Peat Marwick.
67. Murray & Child, Bury (pre–1860), BDO Binder Hamlyn.
68. Thomas Bowden Sons & Nephew, Newcastle upon Tyne (*c.* 1860), Ernst & Young.
69. John Mather, Manchester (*c.* 1860), Ernst & Young.
70. John Gordon, senior, Leeds (1860s), Touche Ross & Co.
71. Butcher & Litton, Manchester (1863), Touche Ross & Co.
72. David Smith, Manchester (1863), Touche Ross & Co.
73. Edward Whittaker, Southampton (1863), Price Waterhouse.
74. James Wood Sully & Alfred Allott, Sheffield (1865), J & A W Sully & Co, Sully & Co and Griffiths, Miles, Sully & Co.
75. Camm & Corbidge, Sheffield (1865), Grant Thornton.

Howitt (1966, p. 236) also gives the following as a founder firm, although, from the evidence available, it does not seem to meet the criterion:

Henry Kendrick, London (1870), Hard Dowdy.

REFERENCES

Statutes

1824 Bankruptcy Act (5 Geo. 4 c. 98)
1825 Bankruptcy Act (6 Geo. 4 c. 16)
1831 An Act to Establish a Court in Bankruptcy (1 & 2 Will. 4 c. 56)
1842 Relief of Insolvent Debtors Act (5 & 6 Vict. c. 116)
1844 Joint Stock Companies Act (7 & 8 Vict. c. 110)
1845 Companies Clauses Consolidation Act (8 & 9 Vict. c. 16)
1849 Bankrupt Law Consolidation Act (12 & 13 Vict. c. 106)
1855 Limited Liability Act (18 & 19 Vict. c. 133)
1856 Joint Stock Companies Act (19 & 20 Vict. c. 47)
1862 Companies Act (25 & 26 Vict. c. 89)
1867 Railway Companies Act (30 & 31 Vict. c. 127)
1868 Regulation of Railways Act (31 & 32 Vict. c. 119)
1869 Bankruptcy Act (32 & 33 Vict. c. 71)
1879 Companies Act (42 & 43 Vict. c. 76)
1883 Bankruptcy Act (46 & 47 Vict. c. 52)
1900 Companies Act (63 & 64 Vict. c. 48)
1903 Revenue Act (3 Edw. 7 c. 46)
1919 Sex Disqualification (Removal) Act (9 & 10 Geo. 5 c. 71)
1948 Companies Act (11 & 12 Geo. 6 c. 38)
1967 Companies Act (c. 81)
1989 Companies Act (c. 40)

Government committees

1867 Report from the Select Committee on Limited Liability Acts; with the Proceedings, Minutes of Evidence, Appendix, and Index; (329.) X. 393.

1877 Report from the Select Committee appointed to inquire into and report on the operations of the Companies Acts, 1862 and 1867, and to whom the Companies Acts Amendment (No. 2) Bill was referred; with the Proceedings, Minutes of Evidence, Appendix, and Index; (365.) VIII. 419.

Books, articles, and other printed sources

Bagnall, Sarah and Robert Lea (1992) 'Price War-torn Big Six Hit by Audit Fee Crunch', *Accountancy Age*, 22 October, p. 1.

Balogh, T (1947) *Studies in Financial Organization*, Cambridge, University Press.

Boys, Peter (1988) 'When Small Means Successful', *Accountancy*, Vol. 101, No. 1134, February, pp. 112–13.

— (1989) 'What's in a Name – Firms' Simplified Family Trees: Arthur Young', *Accountancy*, Vol. 103, No. 1145, January, p. 102.

Briston, Richard and Moyra Kedslie (1985) 'Must Smaller Firms Continue to Lose Out?', *Accountancy*, Vol. 96, No. 1099, March, pp. 163–4.

Brown, Richard (1905) *A History of Accounting and Accountants*, London, Frank Cass & Co (New impression 1968).

[Burton, J C (ed.)] (1948) *Arthur Young and the Business he Founded (Personal Reminiscences)*, New York, Arthur Young & Company.

Chalmers, A W (1883) Inaugural Address to the Liverpool Chartered Accountants' Students' Association in *The Accountant*, 10 March, pp. 12–14.

Comins & Co Centenary, 1890–1990 [1990] London, Comins & Co.

Cooper, Ernest (1886) 'Chartered Accountants as Auditors of Companies', *The Accountant*, 13 November, pp. 644–9

— (1921) 'Fifty-seven Years in an Accountant's Office', in *Proceedings of the Autumnal Meeting of the Institute of Chartered Accountants in England and Wales*, London, Gee & Co, pp. 41–73. (Reprinted New York and London, Garland Publishing, 1982.)

Cooper, V R V (1966) *Manual of Auditing*, London, Gee & Co.

Cornwell, S V P (1991) *Curtis Jenkins Cornwell & Co.: A Study in Professional Origins, 1816–1966*, New York and London, Garland Publishing.

Cypert, Samuel A (1991) *Following the Money: The Inside Story of Accounting's First Mega-merger*, New York, American Management Association.

DeMond, C W (1951) *Price, Waterhouse & Co. in America: A History of a Public Accounting Firm*, New York, Price Waterhouse & Co. (Reprinted New York, Arno Press, 1980.)

Edey, H C and Prot Panitpakdi (1956) 'British Company Accounting and the Law 1844–1900', in A C Littleton and B S Yamey (eds.) *Studies in the History of Accounting*, London, Sweet & Maxwell. (Reprinted New York, Arno Press, 1978.)

Edwards, J R (ed.) (1980) *British Company Legislation and Company Accounts, 1844–1976*, New York, Arno Press, 2 Vols.

Eldridge, H J (1911) 'The History of Book-keeping and the Growth of the Accountancy Profession', *Associated Accountants' Journal*, October, pp. 177–207.

Ernst & Ernst: A History of the Firm (1960) Cleveland, Ohio, Ernst & Ernst.

Etor, John R (1980) 'Edward Thomas Jones (1767–1833), Public Accountant', paper given at the Third International Congress of Accounting Historians, London.

Fiftieth Anniversary, 1898–1948 (1949) Lybrand, Ross Bros. & Montgomery. (Reprinted in *The Early History of Coopers & Lybrand*, New York and London, Garland Publishing, 1984.)

[Foye, Arthur B *et al*] (1970) *Haskins & Sells: Our First Seventy-five Years, 1895–1970*, New York, Haskins & Sells. (Reprinted New York and London, Garland Publishing, 1984.)

Gower, L C B, J B Cronin, A J Easson and Lord Wedderburn of Charlton (1979) *Gower's Principles of Modern Company Law*, 4th ed., London, Stevens & Sons.

[Hardie, Sir Charles] [1988] *Dixon Wilson Centenary, 1888–1988: A Brief History*, London, Dixon Wilson.

Hill Vellacott: An Historical Account of their Development since 1788 [1988] Hill Vellacott.

A History of Cooper Brothers & Co., 1854 to 1954 (1954) London, Batsford for Cooper Brothers & Co. (Reprinted New York and London, Garland Publishing, 1986.)

A History of the Chartered Accountants of Scotland from the Earliest Times to 1954 (1954) Edinburgh, The Institute of Chartered Accountants of Scotland. (Reprinted New York and London, Garland Publishing, 1984.)

Hopkins, Leon (1980) *The Hundredth Year*, Plymouth, Macdonald & Evans.

Howard Smith Thompson & Co, 7th November 1867 to 7th November 1967: The First 100 Years [1967] Howard Smith, Thompson & Co.

[Howitt, Sir Harold *et al* (comps.)] (1966) *The History of the Institute of Chartered Accountants in England and Wales, 1880–1965, and of its Founder Accountancy Bodies, 1870–1880: The Growth of a Profession and its Influence on Legislation and Public Affairs*, London, Heinemann. (Reprinted New York and London, Garland Publishing, 1984.)

Jeremy, David J (ed.) (1984–86) *Dictionary of Business Biography: A Biographical Dictionary of Business Leaders Active in Britain in the Period 1860–1980*, London, Butterworth, 5 Vols.

Jones, Edgar (1981) *Accountancy and the British Economy, 1840–1980: The Evolution of Ernst & Whinney*, London, Batsford.

Jones, Edward Thomas (1796) *Jones's English System of Book-keeping by Single or Double Entry* ... , Bristol, printed by R Edwards. (Reprinted New York, Arno Press, 1978 and London, Scolar Press, 1980.)

[Kettle, Sir Russell] (1958) *Deloitte & Co., 1845–1956*, Oxford, Oxford University Press for Deloitte, Plender, Griffiths & Co. (Reprinted New York and London, Garland Publishing, 1982.)

Kilpatrick, James (1942) *Deloitte, Plender, Griffiths & Co.: Some Notes on the Early Days of the Firm*, London, Wyman & Sons.

Letts, Stanford A [1980] *MacIntyre Hudson, May 1880–May 1980*, MacIntyre Hudson.

[Littler, Mark *et al*] (1974) *The First Sixty Years, 1913–1973*, Chicago, Arthur Andersen & Co.

[Medlam, Wilfred *et al*] [1980] *A History of Pannell Fitzpatrick & Co*, Pannell Kerr Forster.

Morrison, Kenneth (1980) 'PMM in the Past: The Founders', *PMM Platform*, summer, pp. 24–5.

— (1981) 'PMM in the Past: The First PMM Office', *PMM Platform*, spring, pp. 24–5.

Murray, A and R N Carter (1895) *A Guide to Income-Tax Practice*, London, Gee & Co.

Murray, David (1930) *Chapters in the History of Bookkeeping, Accountancy & Commercial Arithmetic*, Glasgow, Jackson, Wylie & Co. (Reprinted Osaka, Nihon Shoseki, 1977 and New York, Arno Press, 1978.)

[Osbourn, F C and R T Bell (comps.)] (1954) *Fifty Years: The Story of the*

Association of Certified and Corporate Accountants, 1904–54, London, The Association of Certified & Corporate Accountants.

Our Merger (1989) Coopers & Lybrand and Deloitte Haskins & Sells.

Parker, R H (1980a) 'Accounting Historians' Guide to London', insert in *Accounting and Business Research*, Vol. 10, No. 37A, Special Accounting History Issue.

— (ed.) (1980b) *British Accountants: A Biographical Sourcebook*, New York, Arno Press.

— (1980c) 'Those First Councillors ... a Golden Heritage', *Accountancy*, Vol. 91, No. 1041, May, pp. 36–42.

— (1986) *The Development of the Accountancy Profession in Britain to the Early Twentieth Century*, The Academy of Accounting Historians.

Pixley, Francis W (1881) *Auditors: Their Duties and Responsibilities under the Joint-Stock Companies Acts and the Friendly Societies and Industrial and Provident Societies Acts*, London, Effingham Wilson. (Reprinted New York, Arno Press, 1976.)

Richards, Archibald B (1981) *Touche Ross & Co., 1899–1981: The Origins and Growth of the United Kingdom Firm*, London, Touche Ross & Co.

Richards, G E (comp.) (1950) *History of the Firm: The First Fifty Years, 1850–1900*, Price Waterhouse & Co.

Robertson, D W (1949) 'Turquand, Youngs, McAuliffe & Co.', *The Arthur Andersen Chronicle*, July, pp. 142–9.

Rules and Regulations of the Society of Accountants in England (1875) London, The Society of Accountants in England.

Russell Limebeer: A London Firm of Chartered Accountants [1978] London, Russell Limebeer.

Sinclair, Prior (1946) 'The Certified Public Accountant on the Threshold of his Second Half Century', in *Fiftieth Anniversary, 1898–1948*, pp. 129–37.

Singleton-Green, Brian (1992) 'Incorporation: Non-Event of the Decade', *Accountancy*, Vol. 109, No. 1186, June, p. 23.

Sowerby, Tom (1985) *The History of the Chartered Institute of Public Finance and Accountancy, 1885–1985*, London, The Chartered Institute of Public Finance and Accountancy.

Stacey, Nicholas A H (1954) *English Accountancy, 1800–1954: A Study in Social and Economic History*, London, Gee & Co.

Stewart, Jas. C (1977) *Pioneers of a Profession: Chartered Accountants to 1879 – Being Biographical Notes on the Members of the Scottish Chartered Societies, 1854 to 1879*, Edinburgh, Scottish Committee on Accounting History, The Institute of Chartered Accountants of Scotland. (Reprinted New York and London, Garland Publishing, 1986.)

Swanson, Theodor (1972) *Touche Ross: A Biography – The Life and Services of a Multinational Partnership in the Expanding Profession of Accounting and Management Consulting*, Touche Ross & Co. (Reprinted New York and London, Garland Publishing, 1990.)

Waller, David (1990) 'The Accountants Shuffle Again', *Financial Times*, 11 July, p. 23.

Winsbury, Rex (1977) *Thomson McLintock & Co – The First Hundred Years*,

London, Seeley, Service & Co for Thomson McLintock & Co.
Wise, T A (1982) *Peat, Marwick, Mitchell & Co.: 85 years*, Peat, Marwick, Mitchell & Co.
Woolf, Arthur H (1912) *A Short History of Accountants and Accountancy*, London, Gee & Co. (Reprinted Osaka, Nihon Shoseki, 1974 and New York and London, Garland Publishing, 1986.)
Worthington, Beresford (1895) *Professional Accountants: An Historical Sketch*, London, Gee & Co. (Reprinted New York, Arno Press, 1978.)

Periodicals

Accountancy (July 1980), (August 1986), (July 1989), (August 1989), (February 1990), (April 1990), (July 1990), (August 1990), (July 1992).
Accountancy Age (3 August 1973), (27 July 1979), (2 July 1992).
The Accountant (October 1874).
C&L Journal (June 1979) 125th Anniversary Issue, No. 31 [Coopers & Lybrand].
Deloittes Newsletter (1 May 1974) Special Merger Issue [Coopers & Lybrand].
L. R. B. & M. Journal (January–March 1958) Vol. 39, No. 1 [Coopers & Lybrand]. (Reprinted in *The Early History of Coopers & Lybrand*, New York and London, Garland Publishing, 1984.)
The Reporter (December 1987) No. 50 [Price Waterhouse].

Accountants' archives: their nature and use

PETER BOYS AND WENDY HABGOOD

Accountancy is part of the service sector of the economy, offering professional expertise in a number of varied areas. These include both recurring work, such as auditing and taxation, and non-recurring work, for example investigations and management consultancy. Some firms specialise in one particular area, such as insolvency, while larger firms are divided up into specialist departments. The nature of the various services offered means that, on the whole, records relate to the work of, and the fees generated by, accountants. At the turn of the nineteenth century, when the earliest firms were established, there was little need for large amounts of capital to purchase fixed assets, although office accommodation had to be acquired. Today the need for capital is much greater, partly for equipment such as computers, but more especially for working capital purposes.

The records held by a firm of chartered accountants may conveniently be divided into three groups: the partnership's records, that is, those dealing with the internal affairs of the practice; the firm's records relating to work performed for clients; and clients' corporate and financial records held by the firm on its clients' behalf. The records listed in this volume comprise predominantly partnership records, both those which have been retained by the firms and those deposited in local record repositories. Clients' records have mostly been excluded from the survey at the request of the firms involved.

The survival rate of accountants' records is generally low. Many records, not surprisingly, have fallen victim to destruction at the time of mergers, of which there have been many in recent years, when consolidation of office premises often takes place. Conversely, in some firms which have merged, the interest displayed by particular partners in their firms' histories has ensured the survival of some of the profession's earliest records. It is significant, however, that the largest volume of records has emanated from smaller firms which have not been subject to multiple takeovers or amalgamations and have remained in the same premises for a substantial period. In many cases the survival of records has been largely fortuitous; few firms of chartered accountants have formal procedures for identifying, and preserving permanently, records of historical importance and only one firm surveyed, Price Waterhouse, has centralised archives administered by an in-house archivist.

Firms of chartered accountants have always been constituted as sole traders or partnerships and, unlike companies, have not been required to keep records for regulatory purposes, apart from the obvious one of taxation. There are few statutory requirements governing the retention of partnership records or of those documents relating to work performed for clients. There is, however, a need to keep certain records for specific periods so that a firm can defend itself against any charges of negligence. Recommended retention periods of records in the offices of practising accountants, for administrative or statutory purposes (such as the Statute of Limitations and taxation legislation) are included in P S D Shohet, C Swinson and Ian Herman, 'Business Documents – Management and Retention', *Accountants Digest*, No. 285, (summer 1992), a guide intended for companies developing records management systems. In this digest, the retention periods are listed as follows: books of the practice, retain indefinitely; time records, five years; general office correspondence, five years; audit working papers, six years (or eleven years if thought necessary for future evidence in court); permanent working papers and files, indefinitely; information relating to clients' chargeable assets and gifts, indefinitely; other tax papers, including correspondence, seven years, then return to client. Clients' corporate and financial records remain the property of the clients and have their own statutory retention periods. The form which the records, particularly the financial ones, take has varied in line with changes in technology and the tremendous growth in the size of accountancy practices. Thus, in most firms, hand-written books of account have been transferred first to mechanically operated, and then to computerised, accounting systems. Nevertheless, a number of firms still maintain their records on a hand-written basis. Although the form of the records may have changed and become more complex, their basic content has remained the same.

Partnership and dissolution agreements

The main document in terms of the administration of the practice is the partnership agreement. These legally binding agreements set out such information as the term of the partnership, the capital and profit sharing ratios, the names of the partners and that of the firm, what was to happen in the event of the death of a partner and other working conditions, such as the amount of time partners must devote to the business. These documents are particular to the firms concerned and, consequently, their content varies considerably. Partnership agreements of national firms may relate either to the whole firm or to local or regional practices. The largest of firms may also hold international agreements.

Partnership agreements have survived in large numbers, undoubtedly because of their legal nature. Most firms will have one or more such agreements; in smaller practices one may have been drawn up only in recent years after a decision to put the partnership on a more formal footing. Some firms hold long series of partnership agreements; see, for example, the entry relating to *Howard Smith, Thompson & Co.*

Agreements for the dissolution of partnerships and accompanying documents relate to the way in which the practice is to be divided among the partners. These may include lists of annual audits and clients, analyses of partners' fees, schedules of debtors and work-in-progress, valuations of partners' share of the business, correspondence relating to matters in dispute and inventories of office furniture (see, for example, *Comins & Co*). Other documents may be drawn up, providing details on the purchase of goodwill by some partners from another, for example when a partner retires.

Minutes

Partnership minutes, in any formal sense, are a relatively modern type of record and were rarely kept in any but the larger firms. Minutes of partners' meetings record decisions on technical accounting matters as well as on general matters of internal administration and finance. Minutes of a large firm may include those of its committees, its international firm and its national, regional or local partners' meetings.

Papers relating to mergers

Records relating to successful mergers may include agreements to merge or to work together as associate firms, either on a national or international basis. Accompanying papers commonly include correspondence and sundry documents relating to such matters as clients, division of work, work-in-progress, valuation of the practice, goodwill, profits, salaries, general administration and the combined firm's choice of name. Papers relating to abortive mergers have also survived.

Diaries

Partners' professional diaries, in the form of notebooks or pre-printed volumes, provide a daily record of work undertaken for clients. The amount of detail varies; some provide only the name of the client followed by a brief note of the nature of the assignment, while others include a more detailed description of the work undertaken. Diaries may include the time taken on a job and act as an informal time record or as an *aide-mémoire* for billing purposes; see for example *Curtis, Jenkins, Cornwell & Co* and *F Geen & Co.*

Time records

Accountants have usually charged their clients for the number of hours spent on a particular assignment and therefore need to keep time records. These records are very diverse; not only do they vary between firms but also in the names used to describe them and the information they contain.

The most basic records, on a day-by-day basis, show the way in which partners and staff spent their time. These records, or time-sheets, maintained daily, weekly, or monthly, were used to summarise the time spent on a client-by-client basis. In most cases summaries were transferred, via time day books or journals, to time ledgers, so as to build up the total amount of time spent on a client's work.

The amount of detail in time records varies; they may give a description of the main category of the service provided (insolvency, debt collecting, auditing) and of the more detailed form of the work undertaken (drawing up accounts, attending a stocktake). The records can contain the number and grades of staff employed, both in total and on any particular type of work. The earliest series of time records providing detailed descriptions of the work performed for clients are those of *Begbies* and *Curtis, Jenkins, Cornwell & Co.*

Time records may generate other papers providing summary information, such as time ledger balances. This information is used to evaluate work-in-progress at the end of the firm's financial year, for statistical purposes and for analyses of time spent.

In addition to the number of hours spent on a client's work, these records provide information on the names, number and significance of clients, the nature of their business and the charge-out rates for staff and partners. Moreover, they provide information on employment conditions and practices, such as how many hours were worked each day, how many days per week and how many weeks per year, by partners and their staff.

Fees and billing records

The amount of time spent on a client's work has to be converted into monetary terms by multiplying the time by the appropriate charge-out or billing rate for the particular grade of staff, so that the client can be billed (or invoiced) for the services rendered. The bill (or invoice) is also known as a fee note. Some firms may keep copies of these, sometimes in bills (delivered) books, while others may maintain details of these fees in accounts, or fees, rendered books, which could record such things as the name of the partner responsible for that client's work, the nature of the work, the time charged and the amount of the bill rendered. Less detail in these records may be compensated for by more in the time records.

In a formal double-entry bookkeeping system, the book of prime entry for the recording of fees would be a fees or bills journal (or day book), which would list the clients to whom bills had been sent and their amount, together with other information such as the bill number, the nature of the work, the time charged, the date and the period to which the bill applied. These amounts would be posted to fees ledgers, also known as clients' or debtors' ledgers, usually maintained in alphabetical order by client. The amount of detail included in these books of account varies from firm to firm.

In addition to the time charged for work undertaken, it is usual for firms to recover exceptional expenditure incurred on a client's work such as travelling and hotel expenses. Firms therefore keep records of these expenses, for example in clients' disbursements books, so that they may be recharged to clients as part of the fee.

All these records may give rise to a number of subsidiary, *ad hoc*, records such as: lists of charge-out rates; summaries and analyses of fees, for example by category of work; time and fee comparisons; analyses of fees journals; papers relating to bad debts and fees lost; lists of work done and fees rendered to show surplus or deficit in the fee recovered; and valuations of debtors.

In some respects these records contain similar information to that found in time records, but will contain the added dimension of monetary amounts. Thus they specifically provide information on the charge-out rates of partners and staff, the names of clients and their relative importance to the firm in terms of the total income derived from each client, and the nature of the firm's work completed, and hence the total charges and relative importance of certain types of work to that firm.

Ledgers, journals, cash books

Records kept on the basis of double-entry bookkeeping will rarely if ever conform to the ideal world where all entries are recorded in a single nominal or general ledger, supported by entries in a single journal or day book. For one thing the number of transactions, especially for cash, was too great even in the earliest firms of accountants for such a simple system to be appropriate. Thus, there will usually be a series of cash books (each of which acts both as a book of prime entry and as a separate ledger account) and ledgers (as has already been seen, a separate ledger would be kept for amounts owed to the firm by clients), supported by a number of journals or books of prime entry.

Apart from a separate ledger for debtors, a general ledger would contain accounts for assets and liabilities and for the various types of expenses and income. Private ledgers are retained for the confidential transactions of the partnership such as the partners' capital accounts and their drawings accounts. Cash books record all cash transactions, receipts on the left and payments on the right in a traditional ledger system. Since, at some stage in their life, all transactions are reflected in the cash account, these records tend to be somewhat voluminous and are often subdivided; so, for example, there may be petty cash books, private cash books (used to enter the cash transactions for the private ledger) or separate cash received and cash payment books.

Journals similarly can be of various types (fees or bills, private), but their use for the recording of normal day-to-day transactions has gradually died out and today they are only used for the more unusual transactions, such as the recording of adjustments, particularly at the end of the firm's financial year, before posting them to the ledger.

Apart from providing further detail about the financial transactions of a firm, ledgers can also provide information on other early activities of a practice, such as debt collection (*Francis Nicholls White & Co*) and stockbroking (*Mundy, Brewer & Johnson*). Moreover, as most firms were initially run by sole practitioners, their accounting records often mixed business matters with items of a more personal nature. The early records of *Curtis, Jenkins, Cornwell & Co*, for example, include references to the purchase of a piano, the education of the founder's children and medical expenses, along with investments in property and other household expenditure, thus providing information on the life-styles of accountants in the nineteenth century.

Partnership accounts

The term accounts is used here to denote summary information which would be extracted from the more detailed books of account. In the earlier records balance sheets and profit and loss accounts may form specific ledger accounts in the private ledger, or may be separate documents. A balance sheet listing the liabilities and assets of a firm would contain information on, for example, the capital of the firm, the drawings of the partners, and the cost of leases and office furniture and fixtures. A profit and loss account shows the overall profitability of the partnership, which for a firm of accountants is essentially the difference between fees generated on the one hand and salaries and office and other expenses, for example professional indemnity insurance, on the other. These summary statements, usually produced on an annual basis, are supported in some cases by working papers giving the make-up of certain figures. Separate accounts for individual offices may have been retained. Accounts provide ready information on the overall development of a firm.

Partnership tax records

These records mostly contain correspondence between the firm and the Inland Revenue and computations for the assessment of taxation.

Correspondence

Correspondence forms a potentially bulky series of records and is of little long-term value to firms. Consequently, it has not survived in any great quantity. Letters received by the firm or copies of letters sent out are more likely to have survived if bound in letter books. These often provide information about the names of clients, fees, general office routine and technical aspects of an accountant's work. Partners may have kept confidential, or private, letter-books. Clients' correspondence files are mostly current and are not covered by this guide.

Staff records

Wages and salary books, which have survived in small quantities, provide useful information about employees' length of service as well as the weekly or monthly payments made. Summary information about salaries may also be drawn from the firm's ledgers, journals and cash books. Staff and clerks' registers or record books provide details of employment history, such as dates of starting and leaving and, perhaps, wages received and the home address. The holiday book (1868–1917) of *Peat, Marwick, Mitchell & Co* includes similar information about staff service over a long period in addition to dates of holidays taken.

Articles of clerkship set out the terms and conditions of employment between clerk and principal, and include such information as the premium paid to the principal for accepting the clerk (a practice generally abandoned after the Second World War), and the clerk's remuneration, if any, during the term of the articles. Articles were replaced by the student contract in 1973.

Other records include papers concerning pension schemes, attendance books (see *Coopers & Lybrand*) and, particularly in the larger firms, recruitment and training material.

Office and staff rules, which have survived for a number of firms, mostly for the period 1900 to 1930, shed light on early working conditions in an accountant's office. Office rules may include some detail on certain aspects of professional work; for example, those of *Hill Vellacott* show the required uniformity of marks or 'ticks' to be recorded in clients' books when conducting an audit.

Staff records provide not only specific details about individuals but also general information regarding the size and growth of a firm.

Premises records

Title deeds, leases and tenancy agreements relating to office premises are the most commonly surviving property records. Some may relate to buildings of particular historical importance, such as those of *Peat, Marwick, Mitchell & Co.* Photographs of exterior and interior views of offices, plans and inventories of office furnishings (drawn up, for example, when a partnership changes) may also have been preserved.

Partners' private records

Firms' records may include partners' personal audit appointments, documents relating to offices held within the Institute of Chartered Accountants in England and Wales or its district societies, and papers concerning public offices held or private work undertaken. There may also be family records including, perhaps, books of account, diaries, correspondence and photographs.

Manuals and technical material

Few firms would seem to have retained non-current records relating to the technical aspects of accountancy. Particularly since the turn of this century, legal disclosure requirements, case law, and, more recently, professional standards concerning accounting and auditing, have led to the need for accounting staff, when carrying out professional work, to be armed with technical material such as checklists to ensure that Companies Act requirements have been complied with; standard formats for the presentation of accounts; audit programmes setting out the detailed work to be carried out during an audit; and other technical manuals.

On the whole the larger firms are more likely to have produced this material. Technical publications exist for *Price Waterhouse* (1914 to date), and there are audit manuals for *Viney, Price & Goodyear* (pre-1919) and Cooper Brothers & Co, now *Coopers & Lybrand* (written after the Second World War). Audit instructions and an audit notebook (1919–20), audit procedure manuals (1931, 1950), and an audit programme (*c.* 1900) survive for *Peat, Marwick, Mitchell & Co.* The firm also holds a number of other audit programmes, tailored to specific clients, dating from the 1900s. These completed audit programmes are listed under the client section in the firm's guide entry.

Technical material is a valuable source for tracing the history of accounting, auditing, taxation and related matters. Unfortunately, firms may have destroyed such material to obviate the risk of using out-of-date information, unaware of its potential value to researchers.

Biographical and historical papers

Amongst a firm's records may be notes, scrapbooks and partners' reminiscences, often compiled on the occasion of the firm's centenary or other anniversary. A number of firms have had their histories or a partner's memoirs published. Early in-house journals or newsletters (see *Price Waterhouse*) also provide useful information about a firm's development.

Clients: working papers

By far the majority of records maintained by firms of accountants today will relate to clients. However, working papers are regarded by most firms as current (even though, exceptionally, they may include all past papers relating to a client) and are, therefore, not covered by this guide. The working papers of current clients are typically retained for approximately twelve years and then destroyed; those of companies or firms which have ceased to be clients are normally kept for about ten years. Working papers will consist of files containing schedules supporting the detailed work performed during an audit. A series of clients' working papers may show the development of auditing techniques and the way in which technical accounting problems have been resolved.

Clients: corporate and financial records

Firms may hold, or have acquired, records which belong to their clients, such as journals, cash books, ledgers, and share registers, all of which they may have written up or maintained on behalf of clients; alternatively, or in addition, there may be documents such as memoranda and articles of association, prospectuses and runs of companies' annual reports and accounts. A number of firms have deposited these records in local record offices.

In conclusion, and more generally, the records listed in this guide will provide source material not only for the study of histories of individual accountancy firms but also for further research into the technical developments of accounting, auditing, taxation and other related areas. In addition, the existence of such material will enable researchers to study the influence, if any, which accountancy firms have had on the development or location of industries in certain parts of the country. Alternatively, and perhaps more likely, the records may illustrate the influence which industries in certain regions have had on the development of accountancy firms.

The accounting archives survey

Following the decision of the Institute of Chartered Accountants in England and Wales to launch an Archive Rescue Appeal, through one of its charitable trusts, to finance an archive survey of member firms, the Archive Panel was set up in September 1990 to establish the survey's terms of reference and to supervise the project over its two-year span. The panel included representatives from the Institute, the Business Archives Council and Guildhall Library, and accounting academics. The initiative was particularly welcomed by the Business Archives Council and Guildhall Library, who recognised the need for such a survey to locate, and encourage the preservation of, historically valuable records which were at risk of being lost or destroyed. The current trend for mergers between accountancy firms of all sizes, often resulting in the consolidation of office premises, was seen to present the greatest threat to the survival of accounting archives.

The survey aimed to locate and list the archives, that is, records which were out of regular business use, of a selection of member firms practising in England and Wales, including, as far as possible, a wide cross-section in terms of age, size and geographical location. Priority was to be given to locating the records of the old-established firms, some of these having remained independent throughout their existence, but the majority having become, through amalgamation, part of today's 'top twenty' firms – Coopers & Lybrand, KPMG Peat Marwick, Price Waterhouse, Ernst & Young, Touche Ross & Co, Arthur Andersen, Grant Thornton, BDO Binder Hamlyn, Pannell Kerr Forster, Stoy Hayward, Kidsons Impey, Clark Whitehill, Robson Rhodes, Moore Stephens, Neville Russell, Moores Rowland, Baker Tilly, Haines Watts, Saffery Champness and Hacker Young (listed, in order of fee income, as published in *Accountancy*, July 1992, amended to incorporate the merger between Stoy Hayward and Finnie & Co in July 1992). Equally of interest were the records of client businesses, which the survey aimed to bring to light. Records of sole practitioners fell outside the survey's terms of reference.

Based on the selection criteria of practising firms with two or more partners and with a head office in England (including the Channel Islands) or Wales, the maximum number of firms which could have been invited to participate in the survey totalled approximately 3,700. Scottish firms, having their head offices in Scotland, and members, therefore, of the Institute of Chartered Accountants of Scotland, were not included in the survey. Likewise, no Irish firms were included.

At an early stage the survey was given wide general publicity. Articles were included in the professional journal *Accountancy* and other Institute publications, and publicity leaflets were distributed by post and personal visits. This was followed up by the targeting of particular firms, notably the oldest in the country and those known to hold significant archive collections. Over the course of the project, letters were sent to the senior partners of 1,000 firms seeking their firms' participation in the survey.

The top 150 firms were the first to be approached, many of these having contributed to the Archive Rescue Appeal launched in 1989, and, in addition, the few 'founder firms' still in practice. This term was used by Sir Harold Howitt in *The History of the Institute of Chartered Accountants in England and Wales, 1880–1965, and of its Founder Accountancy Bodies, 1870–1880* (Heinemann, London, 1966) to describe those firms which could claim continuous partnership descent from either a signatory to the royal charter or a member of the first council or which were over 100 years old in 1965. (A listing of founder firms is provided in Appendix III, p. 55).

Similarly, the twenty largest firms, which have grown to the size they are today largely through amalgamation with successful, well-established provincial practices, were considered likely to hold some of the earliest records of the profession.

Enquiries were subsequently made to a further 850 firms throughout England and Wales. The selection of suitable firms to contact was greatly facilitated by lists supplied by the administrators of the Institute's district societies. Whilst information about personal membership was readily available in the Institute's own records, tracing the origins of firms, through all their various name changes and mergers, proved to be a very complex and laborious task.

The majority of firms who replied to our enquiries were most cooperative in allowing access to their records for listing purposes; others, whilst sympathetic towards the aims of the survey, were unable to trace any surviving archives.

Without a doubt, locating the historical records of the largest firms and their predecessor firms presented the survey with its most challenging task. Information about archive holdings in the firms' main, central London, offices was generally accessible, but disappointing. It was not unusual for known collections, listed in firms' published histories, to have been mislaid, and at least two firms were unable to confirm that the archives had not been destroyed subsequent to publication. Fortunately, enquiries made to provincial offices were more fruitful and several very early, previously unlisted, collections of predecessor firms' records were discovered in this way.

The firms surveyed, almost without exception, allowed access only to the partnership's and not to clients' records. The natural caution of firms in protecting the confidentiality of their own and clients' financial affairs also, undoubtedly, accounts for the paucity of such material in record repositories (although, interestingly, solicitors have been depositing equally confidential material for a number of years). Written enquiries to local record offices revealed that relatively few collections had been received from firms of chartered accountants, other than in their capacity as liquidators. The majority of these collections comprise the records of past clients and defunct businesses for which the firms have acted. Firms' partnership records have not been deposited in any significant quantities, with the two notable exceptions of the collections of the Liverpool practice Chalmers, Wade, Impey, Cudworth & Co (now part of Kidsons Impey), which comprises the partnership's financial books from 1816 to 1959, and the Bristol firm Curtis, Jenkins, Cornwell & Co (now part of Coopers & Lybrand), whose deposited partnership records span the period 1819 to 1918.

All of the firms visited in the course of the survey were strongly advised to deposit their archives in their local record repositories. The listed records of most firms were generally scattered throughout one, or more, offices, and were, on the whole, of such a small quantity that there was every danger of them being mislaid or destroyed at some time in the future. Encouragingly, both clients' and partnership records have been deposited as a result of the survey, although most material has remained in the custody of the firms. However, it is hoped that the survey will have sufficiently raised firms' awareness of the historical value of their records that they will now take appropriate measures to preserve them. The survey has covered only a small proportion of English and Welsh accountancy firms and there are, undoubtedly, others which hold important archive material but do not appear in the guide. Firms wishing to preserve historical records in their care, or obtain advice on record retention, should contact the Business Archives Council, whose address is given in 'Useful Addresses' in the User's Guide, or their local record office.

User's guide

The findings of the accounting archives survey are described in two distinct sections. The first, and larger, of these comprises lists of records, and brief histories, of firms of chartered accountants in England and Wales. Scottish and Irish firms or offices have not been included in the survey. Firms whose only relevant records are those of client businesses already deposited in local record offices have also been excluded. The second section comprises entries for the Institute of Chartered Accountants in England and Wales and its constituent and predecessor bodies for which there are surviving records. The information is correct as of 31 December 1992.

ARRANGEMENT OF THE BOOK

Firms of chartered accountants: lists of records

Entries are included for a total of 182 firms. This figure includes practising firms and a number of 'defunct' firms whose names have become extinct as a result of mergers. Each entry includes the name and address of the firm, a list of its offices, a brief history, details of the records and their location, and a list of relevant historical publications.

The firms are arranged alphabetically by first name or initial under their full current titles or, in the case of defunct firms, under the style in use at the time of merger. In an entry for a defunct firm, the current name of the successor firm is supplied in brackets. All of these names, and other name changes which are recorded in the history section of each entry, are fully referenced in an extensive name index at the back of the book.

The address given is the present location of the firm's main, or only, office, or, if it is a defunct firm, the last known address at which it practised prior to merger. This is followed, where appropriate, by a list of the firm's other offices, details of which are included in the history section. In all cases, the names of overseas offices have been excluded.

The history section of each entry outlines the origins, locations and name changes of the firm. Wherever possible, details of mergers, including the names and founding dates of the firms involved and the names of the new firms formed, are also given. Information about clients has been included where available. It should be noted that these sections are not intended to be definitive and it has not been possible to standardise the detail provided in each one. In many instances the dates supplied are only approximate. The histories have been compiled mainly from information supplied by the firms, from the surviving records or from the published or privately published sources listed in the reference sections. Details of firms' addresses and partnership name changes have mostly been obtained from the Institute of Chartered Accountants in England and Wales, *Lists of Members* (London, 1881 on) and the Society of Incorporated Accountants and Auditors, *Lists of Members* (London, 1885–1957). Information about some of the earliest firms is contained in Sir Harold Howitt (ed.), *The History of the Institute of Chartered Accountants in England and Wales, 1880–1965, and of its Founder Accountancy Bodies, 1870–1880* (Heinemann, London, 1966).

The records section of each entry is headed by the location of the records in 1992, whether they were held by the firm's main office, a branch office, or in a public record repository. Changes in the addresses of all publicly funded record offices can be discovered through reference to the Royal Commission on Historical Manuscripts' *Record Repositories in Great Britain* (HMSO, London). In many entries, as a result of the division of collections, there is more than one location. These locations are numbered as Records (1), Records (2) and so on.

Within the records section, partnership records are listed first, followed by clients' records under a separate sub-heading. Partnership records are arranged in the following order: partnership agreements and related papers; minutes; diaries; papers relating to mergers and partnership matters; time records; accounts and tax files; fees and billing records; ledgers, journals, cash books and other financial records; correspondence; staff records; property records; and miscellaneous other records. Clients' records, which include the firm's working papers and records maintained by the firm on behalf of clients, are listed as follows: audit working papers; minute books and other corporate records; accounts; ledgers, journals, cash books and other financial records; and miscellaneous records. With few exceptions, the records listed relate to past, and not current, clients of the firm.

The publications section lists published or manuscript histories, leaflets and articles to which the reader should refer for more detailed information about the firm. Many of the publications were privately published and distributed and may not be found in the copyright libraries or public libraries. Most are, however, held by the library of the Institute of Chartered Accountants in England and Wales, in London, which may be visited by appointment (see address below). This section does not offer an exhaustive bibliography. A comprehensive list of published histories of firms is provided in Appendix II, p. 46.

The Institute of Chartered Accountants in England and Wales and its constituent bodies: lists of records

Record lists are included for the Institute; the Institute of Accountants, one of the Institute's founding bodies; three district societies which originated as founding bodies; and the Society of Incorporated Accountants, which amalgamated with the Institute (and the Scottish and Irish Institutes) in 1957. The records of the Society of Accountants in England, the fifth founding body, do not appear to have survived.

The entries are arranged chronologically by the date of foundation of the accountancy body. The histories and records of these bodies are summarised in the same way as those of the firms of chartered accountants. A comprehensive list of published histories of professional bodies is provided in Appendix I, p. 44.

ACCESS TO RECORDS

The records listed in this book are summaries of more detailed lists compiled by, or supplied to, the survey archivist. These lists are available for consultation at the library of the Institute of Chartered Accountants in England and Wales in London and the National Register of Archives at the Royal Commission on Historical Manuscripts (see addresses below).

It should be noted that the co-operation of firms and record offices with the survey should not be taken to imply that access to historical records will be allowed. Access to records held by firms is at the discretion of the firm concerned and can only be granted when records are not deemed to be confidential and when facilities exist to allow access to be given to researchers.

Researchers wishing to see records held by firms are advised to write, seeking permission, to the Senior Partner, unless otherwise stated, at the address given in the relevant records section. It is recommended that researchers give as full an explanation of their research interests as possible and that they respect any special conditions of access imposed by the firm.

Where records have been publicly deposited, researchers should write to the County or Chief Archivist at the repository named in the relevant records section. Some records in public repositories are governed by conditions of access and depositing firms may have imposed closure periods on certain classes of records. Researchers are advised to contact the appropriate repository well before making a visit. If, for any reason, a researcher cannot contact a firm mentioned in this book, he or she should write for advice to the Members' Registration Department of the Institute of Chartered Accountants in England and Wales in Milton Keynes (see address below). Researchers unable to contact a publicly funded record repository are advised to contact the Royal Commission on Historical Manuscripts (see address below).

USEFUL ADDRESSES

The Institute of Chartered Accountants in England and Wales, PO Box 433, Chartered Accountants' Hall, Moorgate Place, London EC2P 2BJ

The Institute of Chartered Accountants in England and Wales, Gloucester House, 399 Silbury Boulevard, Central Milton Keynes MK9 2HL

National Register of Archives, Royal Commission on Historical Manuscripts, Quality House, Quality Court, Chancery Lane, London WC2A 1HP

Guildhall Library, Aldermanbury, London EC2P 2EJ

Business Archives Council, Clove Building, 4 Maguire Street, London SE1 2NQ

ABBREVIATIONS: HISTORIES AND SUMMARIES OF RECORDS

c.	circa
Co	Company
dec'd	deceased
est.	established
ICAEW	The Institute of Chartered Accountants in England and Wales
incl.	including
(l)	leaflet
Ltd	Limited
(m)	microfilm
n.d.	no date
(p)	photocopy
plc	public limited company
(*qv*)	*quod vide* (which see)
re	referring to
Unpub.	unpublished
(w)	wanting, i.e. record series incomplete

Firms of chartered accountants: lists of records

A J DOWNS & CO (Kidsons Impey)

77A Beverley Road, Hull, Humberside

History: Founded by Alfred John Downs who set up in practice at Parliament House, Parliament Street, Hull, Humberside, in 1912, having previously been employed as clerk to Hodgson & Harris, now part of Kidsons Impey. In 1915 his practice became A J Downs & Co. He acquired an office in Louth, Lincolnshire, in 1938. In 1968 the firm moved to 77A Beverley Road, Hull. In 1974 it amalgamated with Kidsons, now part of Kidsons Impey.

Records: Kingston upon Hull City Record Office, 79 Lowgate, Hull HU1 2AA

Private ledgers 1912–52; cash books: 1914–41, private 1923–63; transfer ledgers 1958–67.

Clients: General Cemetery Co: records 1846–1972; **Hull Exchange Co**: minute books 1862–1970s.

A LESLIE WING & CO (Hawsons)

Stirling Chambers, Campo Lane, Sheffield

History: Started by William Wing at Market Place Chambers, Sheffield, South Yorkshire, in 1881, moving to 7 North Church Street in *c*.1888; King's Chambers, Angel Street, in 1903; and Stirling Chambers, Campo Lane, in 1909. The practice was renamed William Wing & Son, when Arthur Leslie Wing was admitted as a partner, in 1908; Wing, Richards & Holmes in 1933; and A Leslie Wing & Co in *c*.1945. In 1946 the firm merged with W G Hawson & Co (*qv*), to form W G Hawson, Wing & Co (*qv*) now part of Hawsons (*qv*).

Records: Hawsons, Pegasus House, 463a Glossop Road, Sheffield S10 2QD

Fees ledger 1924–44.

ALBERT GOODMAN

Mary Street House, Mary Street, Taunton TA1 3NW

Also at Chard

History: Albert Goodman started in practice as an accountant in September 1866 at 3 Hammet Street, Taunton, Somerset. An associate of the Society of Accountants from 1877, he was admitted as an associate member of the newly formed ICAEW in 1880. The name of his practice was changed to Albert Goodman & Son when he was joined in 1893 by his son, Clifford. Another son, Reginald, became a partner in 1900 in the newly opened London office in Broad Street House, Old Broad Street. At the same time his son-in-law, H Jeanes Pollard, became a partner in Taunton and the style Albert Goodman, Sons & Pollard was adopted. There were further name changes, to Albert Goodman, Sons, Pollard & Bruford in 1904, when John Bruford was made a partner, and to Albert Goodman, Sons, Pollard & Braybrooks in 1915, when Frederick Braybrooks joined the London office. This title was shortened to Albert Goodman & Co in 1935. In 1965 the London office moved to 56 Moorgate and merged with other practices to become Rowland, Goodman, Sewell, Hutchinson & Sheen, which, through further mergers, became part of Moores Rowland in 1989. The Taunton office remained independent and in 1971 acquired the Chard, Somerset, practice of Stuart & Co. The Chard office moved from 19/21 High Street to Essex House, Fore Street, in 1986. The Taunton office moved from Hammet Street to the present address in 1987. The firm also had an office in Station Road, Ilminster, Somerset, between 1975 and 1984.

Records: Albert Goodman, Mary Street House, Mary Street, Taunton TA1 3NW

Partnership agreements 1894–1935; Court of Appeal judgement, John Bruford's right to practise 1914; accounts book 1894–1936; accounts incl. working papers 1902–65; ledgers: general 1894–06, private 1922–59; cash books 1899–1906, *c*.1970–date; list of profits (London and Taunton) 1916–64; tax correspondence 1951–66; wages book 1941–44; lease, mortgage and sale particulars, 3 Hammet Street 1881, 1883.

ALEX PICOT & CO

Paragon House, 95/97 Halkett Place, St Helier, Jersey JE1 1BX

History: Believed to be the oldest accountancy firm in Jersey, it was founded by Charles G Roberts in *c*.1885, at 12 Hill Street, St Helier. Originally acting as agents for commissions, the firm was first described as 'accountants' in 1898 when it was practising at 24 Hill Street. In 1902 Roberts was succeeded by Charles Henry Brockhurst, who took Alexander E Picot into partnership in 1913, when the firm was restyled Brockhurst &

Picot. This was changed to Alex E Picot & Co in 1926, when Brockhurst retired. At around the same time, an office was opened in High Street, Guernsey (now a separate practice). Following Picot's death in 1945 his two sons, partners in the firm since 1935 and 1939, carried on the practice under the name Alex Picot & Co. In 1983 the firm moved from Hill Street to 31 Broad Street and to its present address in 1990. Long-standing clients of the firm include Ann Street Brewery Co Ltd and Le Riches Stores Ltd.

Records: Alex Picot & Co, Paragon House, 95/97 Halkett Place, St Helier, Jersey JE1 1BX

Partnership agreements 1915, 1967; accounts: Guernsey 1926–50, 1963–70, Jersey 1963–date; fees ledger 1960–date; private ledgers 1960–date; cash books 1964–date; letter book incl. copy profit and loss accounts (Guernsey) 1926–70; staff records 1957–date; salaries records 1957–date; 26 Hill Street: leases 1930, 1952, plans 1972; photographs: partners *c.*1925–date, Hill Street n.d.; press cuttings book 1956–date.

Clients: Le Riches Stores Ltd: accounts 1898–1970s; **St Clements Housing Association Ltd**: accounts 1940–45.

APSLEYS

Apsley House, Billet Street, Taunton TA1 3TX

Also at Exeter, Tiverton and Wellington

History: Started by James Goodland who began to practise as an accountant in Kilkenny House, Taunton, Somerset, in 1904, moving to Hammet Street, Taunton, in 1923. By 1912 he had opened a branch office in Station Road, Tiverton, Devon. This branch later moved to St Andrews Street, Tiverton. The name of the firm became Goodland & Bull when Stanley Bull became a partner in 1932. This was changed to Goodland, Bull & Co in 1936. The Tiverton office moved to Bampton Street in 1954. The Taunton office moved into Bridgwater House, Corporation Street, in 1957 and into Apsley House in 1985. During this period the firm merged with Robson Rhodes but it underwent a demerger eight years later in 1987. An office in Wellington, Somerset, was acquired in 1986 when Robson Rhodes merged with the practice Hounsell, Hutchins & Co of 10 South Street. After the demerger, the firm adopted the name Apsleys. An office was opened in Exeter, Devon, in 1988 at 10 Southernhay West. The Tiverton office expanded rapidly after the war, being based primarily on agricultural work, which continues to account for a large percentage of the office's work. The firm also has strong historical links with a number of independent schools in the south-west and South Wales.

Records: Somerset Record Office, Obridge Road, Taunton TA2 7PU

Partnership agreements 1939–date; partners' meeting minutes 1960–date; diaries 1984–date; report on the future development of the practice 1967; accounts 1959–date; fees ledgers 1949–date; private ledgers *c.*1935–79, 1987–date; cash books 1980–date.

ARMITAGE & NORTON (KPMG Peat Marwick)
Station Street Buildings, Huddersfield, West Yorkshire

Also at Blackpool, Bradford, Dewsbury, Edinburgh, Glasgow, Halifax, High Wycombe, Leeds, Leicester, London, Loughborough, Manchester and Preston

History: Started by Charles Payne *c.*1868 in John William Street, Huddersfield, West Yorkshire. By 1879 the practice was called Chadwick & Armitage, after William Armitage was made a partner, and it subsequently became Armitage, Clough & Co (1880); Armitage, Clough & Norton (1888), when George Pepler Norton joined the firm; and Armitage & Norton (1889). In 1885 the firm opened its first London office at 89 Gresham Street. This was followed by further offices in West Yorkshire at Bradford (Hustlergate) in 1893, Halifax (Somerset House) in 1903 and Leeds (1 East Parade) in 1904. In 1902 the main Huddersfield office moved to Station Street Buildings, which was purpose-built to the design of J Hatchard Smith, an eminent London architect, and is now the Huddersfield office of KPMG Peat Marwick. By 1900 most of the firm's work came from the wool textile industry in the West Riding of Yorkshire, Scotland and the west of England. The firm also had many clients in the engineering and chemical industries in Yorkshire and on the Lancashire side of the Pennines as far as Manchester. After the second world war Armitage & Norton extended its activities and started to undertake work for other industries, such as cotton and man-made textiles, engineering, farm machinery and construction; it also undertook investigation work for various financial institutions. The firm started to expand before the second world war and in 1937 merged with the Leeds practice of J W Close Hirst & Co, East Parade. In 1946 it merged with Sharpe & Sharpe, Market Place Chambers, Huddersfield. Other offices were opened in Edinburgh, Lothian, in 1950 and Preston (13/14 Chapel Street), Lancashire, in 1969. During the next ten years the firm expanded by acquiring practices in various parts of the country, including: Herbert Godkin & Co, Loughborough and Leicester, Leicestershire, in 1971; Tebb, Beevers & Co, Leeds, in 1973; Oldham, Holland & Co, London and High Wycombe, Buckinghamshire, in 1975; R L Thursz & Co, Blackpool, Lancashire, and Dunn Wylie & Co, London, in 1976. In October 1987 the firm merged with Peat Marwick McLintock, now KPMG Peat Marwick, with the exception of the London and Edinburgh offices, which became part of Saffery Champness, and the Leicester and Loughborough offices, which were acquired by the local resident partners.

Records (1): KPMG Peat Marwick, PO Box A10, Station Street Buildings, Huddersfield HD1 1LZ (enquiries to G H Smith, FCA)

Partnership agreements 1889–1951; papers, dissolution of the London partnership 1887–1908; accounts: Huddersfield 1885–1917, 1933–49, Bradford 1946–67, Dewsbury 1900–07, Halifax 1906–49 (w), Leeds 1905–49, London (agency) 1891–1922, London (office) 1930–36, 1940–50; ledgers: 1921–34, 1962–71, private 1887–*c*.1930, *c*.1940–60s; cash books 1877–1909, 1924–71; lists of audit clients incl. fees charged 1894–1942; fees lost list 1966–71; Bradford office: private cash book 1937–67, statements of profits and salaries 1936–43; Dewsbury office: clients' ledger balances 1889–99; historical notes n.d..

Clients: Huddersfield Equitable Permanent Benefit Building Society: balance sheets 1864, 1891, 1898, 1925; **Huddersfield Safe Deposit Ltd**: registers of renters, deposit books, visiting and time books 1891–1946; **The Mutual Fund**, Huddersfield: ledger 1941–68.

Records (2): Kirklees District Archives, Central Library, Princess Alexander Walk, Huddersfield HD1 2SU

Drawing of Station Street Buildings 1899; photographs: Gilbert P Norton n.d., George Peplar Norton n.d.

Clients: Directors' reports, memoranda and articles of association, prospectuses, minutes, annual reports and accounts, balance sheets, audit books, income tax papers, bankruptcy papers, correspondence, private ledgers, cash books, stock catalogues of various companies incl.: **Bairstow Sons & Co Ltd** 1902–40; **Bentley Silk Mills Ltd** 1892–99; **J P Brierley & Co Ltd** 1900–39; **John Broadbent & Son (Longwood) Ltd** 1916–36; **Tho Broadhead & Sons Ltd** 1899; **Brook Dugdale & Co Ltd** 1925–30; **Clarke, Sons & Co**, Abingdon 1905–10; **Crawshaw & Warburton Ltd** 1908–10; **Crowther, Bruce & Co Ltd** 1897–1933; **John Eccles Ltd** 1915–62; **Edwards & Rawson** 1900–28; **F C S Ltd** 1899–1923; **Fisher Firth & Co** 1914–53; **G M & Co Ltd** 1904–05; **Gledhill Bros & Co Ltd** 1913–37; **Hargreave & Nussey Ltd** 1901–22; **Holloway Bros Ltd** 1895–1913; **Kirkburton Dyeing Co** 1899; **F H McGrath & Co Ltd** 1925–35; **Martin & Sons** 1890–1918; **Russian Petroleum Co** 1910; **Scott Motorcycle Co** 1924–31; **J W & H Shaw Ltd** 1902–31; **Stothart Faulden** 1900–03; **Edward Sykes & Sons Ltd** 1920–27; **Taylor & Lodge** 1899–1900.

ARMITAGE & NORTON (Saffery Champness)
Hazlitt House, 28 Southampton Buildings, Chancery Lane, London

History: Originated as the London office of the Huddersfield, West Yorkshire, firm, started by Charles Payne in *c*.1868 and named Armitage & Norton (*qv*) in 1889. The London office, first opened at 89 Gresham Street in 1885, was restyled Armitage, Norton, Paton & Co in 1923; Armitage, Norton, Boyce & Co in 1930; and Armitage & Norton in *c*.1945. The office occupied 9 Old Jewry Chambers *c*.1885–1923; 7 Golden Square 1923–24; 25–31 Moorgate 1924–38; and Salisbury House, Finsbury Circus 1938–86. The office moved to 28 Southampton Buildings, Chancery Lane, in 1986. In 1975 the office amalgamated with Oldham, Holland & Co (est. 1895), London and High Wycombe, Buckinghamshire, and Dunn, Wylie & Co (est. *c*.1880), London. In 1987 Armitage & Norton merged with Peat Marwick McLintock, now KPMG Peat Marwick, except for the London and Edinburgh, Lothian, offices, which amalgamated with Saffery Champness.

Records: Saffery Champness, Fairfax House, Fulwood Place, Gray's Inn, London WC1V 6UB

Work-in-progress book 1931–37; monthly salaries book 1929–75.

ARTHUR GODDARD & CO

2 St John's Place, St John's Square, London EC1M 4DE

History: In 1882 Arthur G Goddard, an unqualified accountant, opened an office at 3 Ludgate Circus Buildings, London. He was admitted to the ICAEW in 1887 and continued to practise as Arthur Goddard & Co at the same address until 1890, when he moved to St George's House, Eastcheap, London. A further move to 46 & 47 London Wall, London, took place in 1898. Goddard was killed in a hansom cab accident in 1913, after which his son took over the practice. In 1966 the firm merged with Longcrofts of 54 New Broad Street, London, and in 1978 with Dendy Neville & Co of 39–41 New Broad Street, London. Both of these resulted in demergers, in 1976 and 1983 respectively. The firm moved to Capel House, New Broad Street, London, after the first merger and to the present address in 1987. Clients of the firm have included several housing societies established during the 1970s.

Records: Arthur Goddard & Co, 2 St John's Place, St John's Square, London EC1M 4DE

Partnership agreements 1976–date; fee books 1935–58, 1963–66; private ledgers 1959–74.

ATKINSON, FINCH & CO

Central Chambers, 45/47 Albert Street, Rugby CV21 2SG

History: Started by William George Atkinson, in 1895, an associate member of the ICAEW, practising at 8 Albert Street, Rugby, Warwickshire. By 1909 he was in practice at 42 Albert Street. In 1929 he was joined by Arthur J Finch, a certified accountant. The firm moved to its present address in *c*.1960. In the early days it undertook agency work for the Commercial Union Assurance Co Ltd and has had a long association with the Northern Assurance Co Ltd and with working men's clubs in the area.

Records: Atkinson, Finch & Co, Central Chambers, 45/47 Albert Street, Rugby CV21 2SG

Partnership accounts 1906–date; agents' commission ledgers 1899–1963.

Clients: Kenilworth Conservative Club: accounts and working papers 1940–date; **Rugby Conservative Club**: accounts and working papers 1940–date; **The Rugby Lions**: accounts and working papers 1927–date; **Rugby United Railwaymen's Club**: accounts and working papers 1927–date.

BAGSHAWS (Moore Stephens)
3 St Helen's Place, London

Also at Guildford

History: Founded in the 1850s by William Edward Bagshaw who by 1865 was practising at 35 Coleman Street, London, under the style Bagshaw & Westcott. By 1867 the firm had been renamed Bagshaw, Westcott & Johnson. In 1876 he was practising under his own name and in 1878 he moved to 10 Moorgate. By 1880 he was practising under the style Bagshaw & Co. In 1881 the firm moved to St Michael's House, 1 St Michael's Alley, Cornhill. Bagshaw's two sons, William Hastings and Claud Edward, were admitted as partners in 1891 and 1903 respectively. By 1919 the firm had moved to 6 Crosby Square, Bishopsgate, and it subsequently moved to 63 & 64 New Broad Street in *c*.1920 and to 3 St Helen's Place in *c*.1945. The style of the firm was changed to Bagshaws in 1987. An office was opened in Guildford, Surrey, in 1988. The firm has always specialised in the area of shipping insurance work and the audit of shipowners, protection and indemnity associations, including Britannia Steam Ship Insurance Association Ltd, London Steam-Ship Owners' Mutual Insurance Association Ltd, West of England Ship Owners' Mutual Insurance Association (London) Ltd, United Kingdom Mutual Steam Ship Assurance Association (Bermuda) Ltd, and Liverpool and London Steamship Protection and Indemnity Association Ltd. In May 1991 the firm amalgamated with Moore Stephens, London.

Records: Moore Stephens, St Paul's House, Warwick Lane, London EC4P 4BN

Partnership agreements: 1891, 1903, 1981, dissolution 1908; partners' meeting minutes 1988; partnership files 1985–89; accounts, some incl. working papers, 1956–89; income tax papers 1944–82 (w); clients' ledger sheets 1950–80 (w); fee notes 1970s–80s; ledgers: 1910–53, incl. profit and loss accounts and balance sheets 1910–46, sheets 1962–80 (w), private 1854–1916, incl. balance sheets 1872–83, 1951–67, 1980s; cash books 1854–71, 1882–1917; office cash book incl. salaries 1966–74; cash books incl. fees journals 1957–86; trial balances 1919, 1932, 1988; work-in-progress sheets 1980s; W E Bagshaw's: annual analysis of personal expenditure 1866–1915, memorandum book re ships and protection associations 1877–78, investments ledger 1912–20, family ledger 1916–37, executors' account book incl. estate duty affidavits, notes re UK stocks held 1917–50; wages books 1946–65, 1975–88; salaries books/sheets 1973–83; papers: articled clerks 1962–83 (w), staff, employment, etc., 1969–81; leases, tenancy agreements, 3 St Helen's Place 1946–86.

BAILEY, PAGE & CO (Bailey, Page & Roper)
Coopers Building, Church Street, Liverpool, Merseyside

History: Originated as the practice Thornton & Co, Queen Assurance Building, Dale Street, Liverpool, Merseyside, which James Page and Reginald Bailey purchased in 1923. In 1963 Bailey, Page & Co moved to Lombard Chambers, Bixteth Street, Liverpool, and in 1978 to Coopers Building, Church Street. In the early 1980s the firm began an association with Michael Roper & Co, also of Coopers Building, Church Street, which led to a full merger in January 1988. The new firm, styled Bailey, Page & Roper, merged with Edward Denton & Son (*qv*) in 1991. Bailey, Page & Co were the first accountants to the Beatles and Gerry and the Pacemakers.

Records: Bailey, Page & Roper, Norwich House, Water Street, Liverpool L2 9XR

General ledger 1923–29; staff record book *c.*1940–65.

BAKER ROOKE (Baker Tilly)
Clement House, 99 Aldwych, London

Also at Billinghurst, Bradford, Bromley, Crawley, Guildford, Leeds, Stratford-upon-Avon, Sturminster Newton and Yeovil

History: Formed in 1975 as Baker, Rooke & Amsdons following the merger of Baker, Rooke & Co (*qv*) with Amsdons, Cossart & Wells (est. *c.*1900), London, and renamed Baker Rooke in 1982. In 1988 Baker Rooke amalgamated with Howard, Tilly & Co, comprising Howard, Howes & Co (est. 1870) and Brown, Peet & Tilly (est. pre–1880), to form Baker Tilly.

Records: Baker Tilly, 2 Bloomsbury Street, London WC1B 3ST

Partnership agreements 1975–85; minutes: partners' meetings 1974–83, national 1981–88, executive committee 1981–84, constitutional committee 1976–80; photographs, partners 1970s.

BAKER, ROOKE & CO (Baker Tilly)
Clement House, 99 Aldwych, London

History: Formed in 1966 when Baker, Todman & Co (*qv*) amalgamated with the London firm Rooke, Lane & Co, comprising Chas. W Rooke, Lane & Co (est. 1901) and N H Stubbs & Co (est. 1939). In 1975 Baker, Rooke & Co amalgamated with the London firm Amsdon, Cossart & Wells (est. *c*.1900) to form Baker, Rooke & Amsdons. This firm was renamed Baker Rooke (*qv*) in 1982. In 1988 it became part of Baker Tilly.

Records: Baker Tilly, 2 Bloomsbury Street, London WC1B 3ST

Partnership agreements 1969–75; partners' meeting minutes 1966–74.

BAKER, TODMAN & CO (Baker Tilly)
Canada House, Norfolk Street, London

History: Founded as J A Berger & Co in 1923 at 72 Avenue Chambers, Southampton Row, London, and subsequently renamed Berger, Baker & Co in 1925 and Baker Todman & Co in 1929. The firm moved to 70–75 Avenue Chambers, Southampton Row, in 1928 and to Canada House, Norfolk Street, in 1932. In 1966 Baker, Todman & Co amalgamated with Rooke, Lane & Co to form Baker, Rooke & Co (*qv*), now part of Baker Tilly.

Records: Baker Tilly, 2 Bloomsbury Street, London WC1B 3ST

Partners' meeting minutes 1937–61.

BARBER, HARRISON & PLATT
2 Rutland Park, Sheffield S10 2PD

History: Formed in 1970 as a result of the merger between Jarvis Barber & Sons (*qv*), Ransom Harrison & Lewis (*qv*), and Sissons, Platt & Co, 9 Broomhall Road, Sheffield, South Yorkshire.

Records: Barber, Harrison & Platt, 2 Rutland Park, Sheffield S10 2PD

Partners' meeting minutes 1970–86; tax files 1970–80.

BARNETT, WESTMACOTT & CO (Comins & Co)
43/44 Broad Street, London

History: In 1906 the firm was practising as Whale, Barnett & Co at 43 Bishopsgate Street, London. Ernst Edward Barnett qualified as a chartered accountant in 1903 and worked as clerk to W B Peat & Co in London, a predecessor firm of Peat, Marwick, Mitchell & Co (*qv*), before joining Whale Barnett & Co in 1906. The firm moved to 80 Bishopsgate, in 1910, to 7 Union Court, Old Broad Street, in 1912, and to 59/60 Broad Street Avenue, Blomfield Street, in 1934. Following a merger, in 1965, with Alex

Parkes, Westmacott & Co (est. *c.*1906), the firm became Barnett, Westmacott & Co. In 1972, it merged with Charles Comins and Co to form Comins & Co (*qv*).

Records: Comins & Co, 22 St Andrew Street, London EC4A 3AN

Partnership accounts and tax files 1955–72; fees ledger 1970–72; private ledgers 1940–71; correspondence 1969–72; salaries books 1963–65.

BARRON & BARRON

Bathurst House, 86 Micklegate, York YO1 2HN

Also at Easingwold, Selby and Thirsk

History: Started by Thomas Henry Barron, formerly a City Treasurer of York, who was in practice at 1 Minster Gates, York, North Yorkshire, in 1899. By 1905 he was in partnership with his son, Arthur Henry Barron, under the name of Barron & Barron. The firm opened an office in London (1 Crane Court, Fleet Street) in 1956. This office was sold in 1961. In 1970 the York office moved to 54 Micklegate and, in 1984, to its present address. It opened offices in the North Yorkshire towns of Thirsk (21 Millgate) in 1990 and Selby (5 The Crescent) and Easingwold (Market Square) in 1991.

Records: Barron & Barron, Bathurst House, 86 Micklegate, York YO1 2HN

Draft partnership agreement 1951; partners' meeting minutes 1972–date; papers, sale of London practice, incl. valuation, 1961–62; calculation of partners' share of work-in-progress 1955–58; work programme book 1968–71; accounts and working papers 1959–date; charges day book 1970s–80s; bills day book 1972–81; bills delivered book 1970s–80s; nominal ledgers 1939–85; cash books: 1919–63, 1969–71, 1974–date, private 1971–84; disbursements day book 1910–date; correspondence: tax 1939–date, staff pension scheme 1953–date; staff recruitment file 1947–55; inventory and valuation, 1 Minster Gates 1952; papers, London office furniture 1952; photograph, Arthur Barron *c.*1930.

Clients: Buena Tierra Mining Co Ltd: share issue notes 1946; **The Exploration Co Ltd**: share certificate 1904; **Joseph Frank & Son Ltd**, timber merchants: liquidation papers 1934–49; **Rotherford & Co Ltd**, coal merchants: liquidation papers 1934–49.

BEGBIES

6 Raymond Buildings, Gray's Inn, London WC1R 5BP

History: Started in 1837 by George Coryndon Begbie in an office at 63 Coleman Street, London. The early practice dealt mainly with insolvency work, but accounting and audit work was accepted as early as the 1840s and by 1855 a considerable audit practice had been built up. In 1855 Begbie enlarged the partnership by promoting George Robinson, a former clerk. The name of the firm was changed to Begbie & Robinson and then, in 1860, to Begbie, Robinson & Hockley when Frederick Hockley was made a partner. In 1870 the firm moved to 3 Raymond Buildings, London, where it remained until 1987, when it moved to its present address. Partnership name changes since 1870 include: Begbie, Robinson & Wright (1888); Begbie, Robinson & Co (1904); Begbie, Robinson, Cox & Knight (1920); and Begbie, Pickering & Co (1970). The last name change resulted from a merger with Clarke, Pickering & Co of 23 Bedford Row, London. This partnership lasted until 1982, when the firm's name was shortened to Begbies. Over the years the firm has had offices in Tonbridge (Bank Street), Kent, and Watford (St Albans Road), and Hemel Hempstead (The Marlowes), Hertfordshire. The last of these to be closed was Hemel Hempstead in 1970. Clients of the firm have included the *Illustrated London News*, the *Illustrated Times* and the *Penny Illustrated Paper*. The firm continues to specialise in insolvency work.

Records: Begbies, 6 Raymond Buildings, Gray's Inn, London WC1R 5BP

Partnership agreements 1859–69; partners' meeting minutes 1970; time ledgers 1837–41, 1871–1908, 1940–68; time day books 1848–52, 1854–57, 1863–80; time account book incl. monthly time summary 1965–67; balance sheet and profit and loss account book 1855–72; clients' ledger 1931–70; fees analysis books 1930s–60s; fees and time comparisons 1968; bill books 1855–1900, 1927–70; private ledgers 1914–72; cash books 1968–70; private cash books *c.* 1920–50; branch office expenses accounts 1930–34; bank passbooks 1907–30; office and staff correspondence, annual salary sheets 1940–70; list of clients 1950; photographs: partners 1887–1930, 150th anniversary celebrations 1987; historical notes 1938; George Robinson: drawings account book 1857–60, private ledgers 1862–89, cash book 1857–74, family papers incl. estates receiver's book 1827–41, deeds re lands in Stockport 1765–1905, Mrs Robinson's account books 1889–95.

Anon., *Begbie, Robinson, Cox and Knight: A Hundred Years of Accountancy, 1837–1937* (London, the firm, 1938)

Peter Boys, 'When Small Means Successful', *Accountancy*, Vol. 101, No. 1134 (1988), pp. 112–13

BELL & COMPANY

64 Harpur Street, Bedford MK40 2ST

History: The Bedford practice of Bell & Company was founded by Norman Bell who, in 1922, following a brief period of employment with Deloitte, Plender, Griffiths & Co in Canada, became a partner in Ashley,

Butterworth & Co of Bristol, Avon, and Biggleswade, Bedfordshire. Bell was introduced to the firm by Stanley McCombie who, following a chance meeting on a train, invited him to purchase a share in the Biggleswade practice in Market Chambers, The Square. Shortly after becoming a partner, Bell established Butterworth & Bell's first Bedford office at 15a St Paul's Square. This was moved to 8 St Paul's Square in 1924. The firm also acquired offices in London in 1922, Bridgwater, Somerset, in 1923 and Weston-super-Mare, Somerset, in 1925. In 1928 a major split occurred when Butterworth took over the offices in Weston-super-Mare and Bridgwater whilst the Biggleswade and Bedford offices were carried on by Bell and McCombie as Bell, McCombie & Co. In 1932 the firm amalgamated with Watts, Knowles & Co, which had offices in the Hertfordshire towns of Baldock (High Street), Letchworth (Midland Bank Chambers), Royston (7 Melbourn Street) and Welwyn Garden City (35 Bridge Road). Through a merger with Stanley McCombie's practice it acquired an office at 17 Market Place, Hitchin, Hertfordshire. After this the firm practised under the style Bell, Watts, McCombie & Knowles until 1942 when it became Bell, McCombie & Co once again. The practice established in Bedford moved to larger premises in Lime Street, High Street, in 1938. Whilst at its previous address in St Paul's Square Bell's secretary Vera Burton, who had joined the firm in the early 1920s, studied for, and passed, the ICAEW's examinations. She qualified in 1935, being one of the first 100 female chartered accountants, and was immediately made a local partner in the Bedford office. Shortly after the Second World War the firm underwent a second reorganisation when the Biggleswade and Bedford practices split off from the rest of the firm. Finally, Bedford, by far the largest practice, separated from the Biggleswade office which then became J W Austin & Co. Bell and Burton continued the Bedford practice under the name of Bell & Company. In 1958 the practice was taken over by Sam E Clear whose daughter, and then son, subsequently became partners in the firm. Between 1939 and 1958 the size of the firm doubled and since then has more then doubled again. In 1991 the firm moved to larger premises in Harpur Street.

Records: Bell & Company, 64 Harpur Street, Bedford MK40 2ST

Partnership agreements 1935, 1950; assignment of lease and sale of goodwill, Luton practice 1931; memorandum of purchase from retiring partners 1958; specimen set of accounts 1938, 1948; fees book 1922–26; fees receipts book 1941–62; private ledger 1938–58; salaries books 1932–date; historical notes n.d.

BERRY, WEEKS & BROOKING (Brooking, Knowles & Lawrence)
Northgate Place, Staple Garden, Winchester, Hampshire

History: A firm styled Weeks, Green & Co was in practice at 6 East Park Terrace, Southampton, Hampshire, before the Second World War. By

1946, this practice had moved to 21 Cumberland Place, Southampton, and an office had been established at 3a City Road, Winchester, Hampshire, under the style Berry, Weeks & Green. The Winchester office moved to Staple Garden in 1951. In 1963 the firm was restyled Berry, Weeks & Brooking. In 1968 it merged with Lawrence, Mayes & Co (*qv*) and Brooking, Holmes & Co (*qv*), both of Basingstoke, Hampshire, to become Brooking, Lawrence & Co, now Brooking, Knowles & Lawrence.

Records: Brooking, Knowles & Lawrence, Clifton House, Bunnian Place, Basingstoke RG21 1JE

Partnership accounts 1962–68.

BLOOMER HEAVEN

33 Lionel Street, Birmingham B3 1AB

History: Founded in 1877 when Joseph Lewis commenced practising as an accountant at 35 Paradise Street, Birmingham, West Midlands. He was joined in 1893 by Harry Howard Bloomer and the practice became Joseph Lewis & Bloomer. During the next thirty years the practice underwent a number of name changes, including: Joseph Lewis, Bloomer and Ford (1900); Bloomer, Ford & Page (1912); Bloomer, Ford & Co (1913); Bloomer, Ford & Mansell (1921); and, when Harold Heaven became a partner in 1926, Bloomer, Heaven & Co. The firm occupied 40 Bennetts Hill from 1912; 75 & 77 Colmore Row from 1924; and Waterloo House, 20 Waterloo Street, from 1926. From the mid–1940s to the 1950s the firm had a second office in Henley-in-Arden, Warwickshire, at 120 High Street. The Birmingham office moved to Dilworth House, 190 Broad Street, in 1952. There followed a series of amalgamations with small local practices, including: H F Adams & Co (87–89 Edmund Street) in 1956; McKenzie & Co (109 Colmore Row) in 1964; Stone, Watson & Co (177 Corporation Street) in 1973; John Lewis & Co (21 Bennetts Hill) in 1980; Rubery & Co and E Bramwell & Co (both of 77 Greenfield Road, Harborne) in 1982; H M Madeley & Co (271 Hagley Court, Edgbaston) in 1985; and Goodkin & Co (61/71 Cornwall Street) in 1985. The firm moved in 1966 to the Post & Mail House, Colmore Circus, and in 1988 to the present address.

Records: Bloomer Heaven, 33 Lionel Street, Birmingham B3 1AB

Partnership agreements *c.*1960–date; partners' meeting minutes *c.*1980–date; private ledger and cash book 1894–1900; private ledgers *c.*1950–date; cash books *c.*1960–date; photograph, H H Bloomer *c.*1920.

BOOTH AINSWORTH

Ashfield House, 12 Ashfield Road, Cheadle SK8 1BE

Also at Stockport

History: Started in 1880 at 14 Brown Street, Manchester, Greater Manchester, by Edward Lawton, a founder member of Manchester Institute of Accountants, and renamed Edward Lawton & Son in 1893. The practice was subsequently carried on by Edward Ainsworth and was renamed Edward Ainsworth & Son in 1953. In 1959 it amalgamated with the Cheadle, Greater Manchester, practice of Frank Booth (*qv*) and became Booth Ainsworth & Co. The firm moved to its present address at the time of the merger and acquired an office in Marple (23 Stockport Road), Greater Manchester, in 1969. In November 1991 this office was moved to St Petersgate, Stockport, Greater Manchester.

Records: Booth Ainsworth, Ashfield House, 12 Ashfield Road, Cheadle SK8 1BE

Salaries books 1958–63.

BOOTH WHITE

6 Raleigh House, Admirals Way, Waterside, London E14 9SN

Also at Bristol, Chatham, Chester, Ipswich, Llandudno, Liverpool, Preston, Sidcup, Southend-on-Sea and Watford

History: Formed in 1967 as Booth White & Co as a result of a merger between Parkin S Booth & Co (*qv*), insolvency accountants, Liverpool, Merseyside, and London, and Francis Nicholls White & Co (*qv*), insolvency accountants, London. The new firm moved to 1 Wardrobe Place, Carter Lane, St Paul's, London, in 1967 and to the present address in 1989. Its name was shortened to Booth White in 1989. The Liverpool office of the firm still practises under the name Parkin S Booth & Co.

Records: Guildhall Library, Aldermanbury, London EC2P 2EJ

Partnership accounts 1967–71; income tax computations 1971, 1972.

BOURNER BULLOCK

Sovereign House, 212/224 Shaftesbury Avenue, London WC2H 8HQ

History: Originated as the London office of Bourner, Bullock & Co (*qv*), founded by Thomas Bullock and Charles Bourner in Newcastle-under-Lyme, Staffordshire, in 1889. The London office was opened at 10 Throgmorton Avenue in 1890. In 1900 this office was reformed as a separate partnership and in 1903 was renamed Bourner, Bullock, Andrew & Co. The firm occupied Bush Lane House, Cannon Street, from 1895 until 1964. It then moved to Marcol House, 289–293 Regent Street, and in 1980 to its present offices. The firm's name was shortened to Bourner Bullock in 1979.

Records: Bourner Bullock, Sovereign House, 212/224 Shaftesbury Avenue, London WC2H 8HQ

Partnership agreements 1921–61; register of work 1896–1918; profit and loss accounts 1900 on; articles of clerkship 1889–1914; office inventory 1941.

BOURNER, BULLOCK & CO (KPMG Peat Marwick)
Albion Street, Hanley, Staffordshire

Also at Congleton, Leek and Stoke-on-Trent

History: Founded by Thomas Bullock who became a Fellow of the ICAEW in 1880. By 1889 he was practising at Nelson Place, Newcastle-under-Lyme, Staffordshire, under the style Bullock & Bourner, Arthur Charles Bourner having been admitted as a partner. This style was changed to Bullock, Bourner & Thomson in *c.*1890 and to Bourner, Bullock & Co in 1893. By 1890 the firm had offices in Birmingham (104 Colmore Row), West Midlands; Hanley (Albion Street) and Longton (Courier Chambers), Staffordshire; and London (10 Throgmorton Avenue). With the establishment of the main office in Hanley in 1893, the firm expanded rapidly and offices were opened in Congleton (12 West Street), Cheshire, in 1910 and Leek (50 St Edward Street), Staffordshire, in 1923. In 1900 the London office, at Bush Lane House, Cannon Street, was reformed as a separate partnership which became Bourner, Bullock, Andrew & Co in 1903 and is now known as Bourner Bullock (*qv*). In 1964 Bourner, Bullock & Co, by then the largest firm in the Potteries, merged with Peat, Marwick, Mitchell & Co (*qv*), now part of KPMG Peat Marwick.

Records: KPMG Peat Marwick, Festival Way, Stoke-on-Trent ST1 5TA

Balance sheets and profit and loss accounts and drafts 1892–96, 1898; draft accounts 1899; appointments of Thomas Bullock as official receiver in bankruptcy for North Staffordshire 1883, 1893; historical notes 1964.

BRIGHT GRAHAME MURRAY
124–130 Seymour Place, London W1H 6AA

History: Founded by Leo Grahame and Sydney Bright who started to practise as Bright, Grahame & Co at 88 Fenchurch Street, London, in 1934. They moved to larger premises at 46A Finsbury Square four years later. During the Second World War the firm expanded considerably and in 1947 Grahame was joined in partnership by Cyril Murray. The name of the firm was changed to Bright, Grahame, Murray & Co, a title which it retained until 1985 when the present style was adopted. The firm moved in 1950 from the City to 61 Portland Place and to 22 Dorset Street in 1969. A merger with Alfred N Emanuel & Co of Richmond House, Dean Street, London, took place in 1970 and four years later a further move was made to the present offices.

Records: Bright Grahame Murray, 124–130 Seymour Place, London W1H 6AA

Fees journal 1934–50; private ledgers 1946–78; journals 1963–71; cash books 1963–82; staff registers 1952–81; mortgage, 22 Dorset Street 1969.

BROOKING, HOLMES & CO (Brooking, Knowles & Lawrence)
Lloyds Bank Chambers, Basingstoke, Hampshire

History: The firm was, until 1959, the Basingstoke, Hampshire, office of A C Brading & Co (also of London, Bournemouth, Dorset, and Reading and Newbury, Berkshire) which originated as Brading, Milne & Co in Alton, Hampshire, in the 1930s. In 1968 Brooking, Holmes & Co merged with Lawrence, Mayes & Co (*qv*), Basingstoke, and Berry, Weeks & Brooking (*qv*), Winchester, Hampshire, to become Brooking, Lawrence & Co, now Brooking, Knowles & Lawrence.

Records: Brooking, Knowles & Lawrence, Clifton House, Bunnian Place, Basingstoke RG21 1JE

Partnership agreements 1949–59; accounts 1948–68; private ledgers 1949–68.

Clients: Working paper files 1948–68.

BROOMFIELD & ALEXANDER
Pendragon House, Caxton Place, Pentwyn, Cardiff CF2 7XE

Also at Blackwood, Newport and Pontypool

History: In 1912 Samuel Broomfield, a certified accountant, arrived in Newport, Gwent, from Liverpool, Merseyside, and set up in practice at 84 High Street. His first clients were acquired by visiting shopkeepers and businesses in the Welsh valleys and he continued this practice into the 1930s, keeping a record of each visit and its outcome. In 1920 he was joined in partnership, at 81 High Street, Newport, by John Alexander, a chartered accountant from Manchester, Greater Manchester, who remained in the north and acted on a consultancy basis. Alexander left the practice in 1934. Offices were opened in Blackwood (York Chambers, High Street) in 1923 and in Pontypool (15 Commercial Street), Gwent, in 1928. The Cardiff, South Glamorgan, office was opened in 1991.

Records: Broomfield & Alexander, Pendragon House, Caxton Place, Pentwyn, Cardiff CF2 7XE

Partnership accounts and working papers 1923–date; diary of business introductions 1912–30s; wages: book 1919–23, summary 1935–42; historical notes n.d.

BRYDEN, JOHNSON & CO
1–4 King's Parade, Lower Coombe Street, Croydon CR0 1AA

History: The practice of Bryden, Fedden & Co was set up by A B Bryden, a Scottish chartered accountant, and F G Fedden at 23 Bucklersbury, London, in 1897. In 1922, when the firm was at 108a Cannon Street, Bryden was joined in partnership by Stanley Johnson. The firm became Bryden, Johnson & Co and continued to practise at Cannon Street until 1933 when it moved to Laurence Pountney Lane. There followed moves to other offices at 39 St James's Street (1935), 13 Southampton Place (1943), Cambridge Circus (1968) and the present address (1975). Past clients of the firm include Dumfries Motor Co, McDougall & Bonthron, barge owners and lightermen, BTP plc, chemical manufacturers, and the Aluminium Plant & Vessel Co.

Records: Bryden, Johnson & Co, 1–4 King's Parade, Lower Coombe Street, Croydon CR0 1AA

Partnership agreements 1897–date; partners' meeting minutes 1988–date; private ledgers 1953–73; journals 1952–78; cash books 1949–83; cash received book 1962–79; wages books 1944–73; salaries sheets 1973–7; historical notes 1927–44.

C HERBERT SMITH & CO (Ernst & Young)
82 Colmore Row, Birmingham

History: Founded by Charles Herbert Smith, clerk to A J Williams & Co, 77 Colmore Row, Birmingham, West Midlands. In 1903 Smith was admitted as a partner and the practice was renamed A J Williams, Smith & Co and moved to 82 Colmore Row in the following year. Its name became C Herbert Smith & Co in 1905. In 1908 the practice amalgamated with H H Russell, Birmingham, and became C Herbert Smith & Russell (*qv*) which, through a succession of mergers, is now part of Ernst & Young.

Records: Archives Division, Birmingham Central Library, Chamberlain Square, Birmingham B3 3HQ

Private ledger 1905–08.

C HERBERT SMITH & RUSSELL (Ernst & Young)
Devonshire House, 40–42 Great Charles Street, Birmingham

History: Formed in 1908 through the merger of the Birmingham, West Midlands, practices of C Herbert Smith & Co (*qv*) and H H Russell. Following the merger, the firm occupied offices in Phoenix Chambers, 82–84 Colmore Row. Early clients of the firm included Best & Lloyd, manufacturers of gas light fittings. In 1927 the firm took over the practice of Powell,

Jerome & Co (est. 1821), 15 Newhall Street, Birmingham, and, as a result, acquired the audits of Joseph Lucas Ltd, electrical component manufacturers, and Mitchells & Butlers Ltd, brewers. The firm moved to Eden Place Chambers, 71 Edmund Street, in 1934. In 1962 the firm merged with Whinney, Smith & Whinney, now part of Ernst & Young.

Records: Archives Division, Birmingham Central Library, Chamberlain Square, Birmingham B3 3HQ

Private ledgers incl. balance sheets and profit and loss accounts 1908–46; tax papers, balance sheets, profit and loss accounts, ledger balances, lists of debtors and creditors 1945–63.

Edgar Jones, *Accountancy and the British Economy 1840–1980: The Evolution of Ernst & Whinney* (London, Batsford, 1981)

C J RYLAND & CO (KPMG Peat Marwick)
4 Berkeley Square, Clifton, Bristol, Avon

Also at Weston-super-Mare

History: Started by C J Ryland *c.*1886 at Cardwell Chambers, Marsh Street, Bristol, Avon. By 1909 the practice was known as C J Ryland & Co. In 1928 it moved to 16 & 18 Clare Street and remained there until 1962 when it moved to 4 Berkeley Square. It opened an office at 13 Meadow Street, Weston-super-Mare, Avon, in 1950. In 1967 it merged with Grace, Darbyshire & Todd (*qv*), also of Bristol, to form Grace, Ryland & Co, now part of KPMG Peat Marwick.

Records: Bristol Record Office, 'B' Bond Warehouse, Smeaton Road, Bristol BS1 6XN

Private ledger 1909–25.

CHALMERS, IMPEY & CO (Kidsons Impey)
6 Long Lane, London

Also at Birmingham, Bradford, Glasgow, Lerwick, Liverpool and Warrington

History: Formed in 1961 as Chalmers, Wade, Impey, Cudworth & Co and renamed Chalmers, Impey & Co in 1965, as a result of the merger between Chalmers, Wade & Co (*qv*) and Impey, Cudworth & Co (est. 1870s), Edgbaston, West Midlands, and London. In 1985 Chalmers, Impey & Co merged with the national firm Hodgson Harris (est. 1870s) and Poulsoms (est. 1924), Liverpool, Merseyside; Wilmslow, Cheshire; St Albans, Hertfordshire; and Manchester, Greater Manchester, to form Hodgson Impey, now part of Kidsons Impey.

Records: Liverpool Record Office and Local History Department, City Libraries, William Brown Street, Liverpool L3 8EW

Staff register and time book 1963–70.

CHALMERS, WADE & CO (Kidsons Impey)
5 Fenwick Street, Liverpool, Merseyside
Also at Birmingham, London, Manchester, Yeovil, Wells and Weymouth

History: Founded by Joseph Redish who set up in practice in Liverpool, Merseyside, in 1796. His practice was restyled Redish & Bird in 1803; Redish, Bird & Eden in 1807; Redish, Bird, Eden & Co in 1813; Redish, Bird & Redish in 1816; Redish & Bird in 1821; Redish, Bird & Price in 1837; Redish & Bird in 1839; Redish, Bird & Marsden in 1841; Bird & Marsden in 1843; George Marsden in 1847; Marsden, Pearson & Wade in 1870; Chalmers & Wade in 1877; and Chalmers, Wade & Co in 1886. In 1880 the firm was practising at 7 Fenwick Street and moved to 5 Fenwick Street in 1881. Antony Wigham Chalmers, who became a partner in 1877, was a founding member of the Incorporated Society of Liverpool Accountants and a petitioner for the charter of the ICAEW and a member of its first council. The firm opened offices in London in 1896; Wells and Yeovil, Somerset, in 1922; Shaftesbury, Dorset, in 1925; Sturminster Newton and Weymouth, Dorset, in 1928; Birmingham, West Midlands, in 1935; and Manchester, Greater Manchester, in 1960. In 1961, Chalmers, Wade & Co amalgamated with Impey, Cudworth & Co (est. 1870s), Edgbaston, West Midlands, and London to form Chalmers, Wade, Impey, Cudworth & Co, now part of Kidsons Impey.

Records: Liverpool Record Office and Local History Department, City Libraries, William Brown Street, Liverpool L3 8EW

Time ledgers 1903–24; accounts rendered books 1877, 1913–37; ledgers 1816–49, 1861–62, 1905–37, 1948–59; journals 1908–59; cash books 1819–48, 1862–1902 (w), 1907–59; balance books 1895–1904, 1915–26; interest and dividend book 1916–21; staff record books 1956–61.

CHAMPNESS, COWPER & CO (Saffery Champness)
7 Portland Place, London

History: Formed in 1973 through the merger of J H Champness, Corderoy, Beesly & Co (*qv*) and Somerset, Cowper & Co (*qv*). In 1982 Champness, Cowper & Co merged with Safferys (est. 1855), London, Margate, Kent, Woking, Surrey, and Guernsey, Channel Islands, to form Saffery Champness.

Records: Saffery Champness, Fairfax House, Fulwood Place, Gray's Inn, London WC1V 6UB

Partnership agreements 1974–79.

CHANTREY, BUTTON & CO (Chantrey Vellacott)
Africa House, 64–78 Kingsway, London

Also at Croydon and Watford

History: Formed in 1920 by the amalgamation of Chantrey, Chantrey & Co (est. *c.*1896), 61 & 62 Lincoln's Inn Fields, London, and Howard Button, Hamp & Co (est. 1889), 49 Queen Victoria Street, London. Chantrey, Button & Co occupied 61 & 62 Lincoln's Inn Fields until 1928 when it moved to Africa House, Kingsway, London. Offices were opened in Watford, Hertfordshire, in 1964 and Croydon, Surrey, in 1969. In 1972 the firm acquired the practice Wm F Smart, Son & Bloor (*qv*). In 1984 the firm merged with Wood, King & Co, formerly Wood & Co (*qv*), 1 Old Burlington Street, London, and became Chantrey Wood King, now part of Chantrey Vellacott.

Records: Chantrey Vellacott, Russell Square House, 10-12 Russell Square, London WC1B 5LF

Partners' meeting minutes 1920–29.

CHARLES BAKER & CO (KPMG Peat Marwick)
39 Bennetts Hill, Birmingham, West Midlands

Also at London

History: Established by Charles Baker who set up in practice in Burlington Chambers, New Street, Birmingham, West Midlands, in *c.*1875. By 1877 he was practising with Arthur Henry Gibson at 7 Waterloo Street, under the name of Baker & Gibson. The practice moved to 39 Bennetts Hill in 1881. By 1888 the practice was styled Baker, Gibson & Co and had a London office, known as Baker Gibson & Fiedler, at 19 & 21 Queen Victoria Street. In 1894 the name of the firm was changed to Charles Baker & Co. In 1921 the firm was acquired by Thomson McLintock & Co (*qv*), now part of KPMG Peat Marwick.

Records: Archives Division, Birmingham Central Library, Chamberlain Square, Birmingham B3 3HQ

Salaries book 1895–1904, 1919–43.

COMINS & CO
22 St Andrew Street, London EC4A 3AN

Also at Ashford

History: Established by Charles Comins and William Albert Schultz as Schultz & Comins in 1890 at 46 Cannon Street, London. In 1895 the partners opened an office in New York, USA, being only the sixth British firm to do so. In 1901 the London office moved to 50 Cannon Street. The New York office was closed in 1909. The partnership of Schultz, Comins & Co, as the firm had been styled since 1903, was dissolved in 1909, to create 2 separate firms, W A Schultz & Co (renamed W A Scott & Co in 1914) and Charles Comins & Co, which continued to practise at the same address. In 1965 they were reunited as Charles Comins & Co. The new firm merged with the City firm of Barnett, Westmacott & Co (*qv*), 59/60 Broad Street Avenue, London, in 1972 and moved to its present address in 1974. The firm then adopted the style Comins & Co. A merger, with the West End practice Goodman, Myers, Smith & Co (*qv*), Roxburghe House, Regent Street, London, in 1978, brought to the firm many clients in the entertainment business. An office was opened in Ashford, Kent, in 1978.

Records: Comins & Co, 22 St Andrew Street, London EC4A 3AN

Partnership agreements 1890–1980; partners' meeting minutes 1967–date; papers, merger with Barnett, Westmacott & Co 1973; accounts 1947–date; ledgers: accounts (Charles Comins & Co) n.d., general 1972–76, private 1960–70; index to clients' fees 1950; correspondence and papers, partnership dissolution 1896, 1909; wages book 1976–77; office leases: 50 Cannon Street 1901–02, Ashford 1978–79; photographs, partners 1970s.

Anon., *Comins & Co Centenary* (London, the firm, 1990) (l)

COOK SUTTON & CO (James & Cowper)

Orbit House, 64/65 St Mary's Butts, Reading, Berkshire

Also at Henley-on-Thames

History: Formed on 1 July 1935 when Goodman Talfourd-Cook entered into partnership with Ralph Sutton, who had purchased his practice, two years before qualifying, in 1931, under the name Cook Sutton & Co at 16 Friar Street, Reading, Berkshire. Sutton died on the same day but Talfourd-Cook continued the practice under the same name, as a sole practitioner, until 1952. In 1937 the practice moved to 6/8 Blagrave Street and in 1951 to 64/65 St Mary's Butts. A practice was established in Nairobi, Kenya, in 1956. In 1965 the firm acquired part of the practice of Tarry, Wood & Co, Henley-on-Thames, Berkshire. In 1991 it amalgamated with James & Cowper (*qv*), Newbury, Reading and Wantage, Berkshire.

Records: James & Cowper, Wesley Gate, 68/82 Queens Road, Reading RG1 4BP (enquiries to B Talfourd-Cook, FCA)

Agreement, purchase of practice of Ralph W Sutton & Co by Talfourd-Cook 1931 (p); fees rendered books 1935–54; cash books 1935–45.

COOPER-PARRY, HALL, DOUGHTY & CO (Cooper-Parry, Prior & Palmer)
102 Friar Gate, Derby, Derbyshire

Also at Ashbourne, Burton-on-Trent, Long Eaton and Uttoxeter

History: Formed in 1929 through the amalgamation of Hart & Cooper-Parry (est. *c.*1918), 43 Wardwick, Derby, Derbyshire; Wilshire, Hall & Co, 24 The Strand, Derby; and Hodgson, Reeve & Co, 43 Wardwick, Derby. In 1965 Cooper-Parry, Hall, Doughty & Co merged with Watson, Sowter & Co (*qv*) to form Cooper-Parry, Watson, Sowter & Co, now Cooper-Parry, Prior & Palmer.

Records: Cooper-Parry, Prior & Palmer, 102 Friar Gate, Derby DE1 1FH

Partners' meeting minutes 1942–45; office rules 1929.

COOPERS & LYBRAND (Coopers & Lybrand)
Plumtree Court, London

Also at Aberdeen, Birmingham, Blackburn, Bournemouth, Bristol, Cambridge, Cardiff, Edinburgh, Glasgow, Irvine, King's Lynn, Leeds, Leicester, Liverpool, Maidstone, Manchester, Middlesbrough, Newcastle upon Tyne, Milton Keynes, Northampton, Norwich, Nottingham, Plymouth, Reading, Sheffield, Southampton, Swansea and Uxbridge

History: Founded by William Cooper who left Quilter, Ball & Co in 1854 and set up in practice at 13 George Street, London. In 1858 his brother, Arthur, became a partner and they continued in practice as W & A Cooper until 1861, when the firm was renamed Cooper Brothers & Co. This name was retained until 1973 when the firm became Coopers & Lybrand. Both Arthur and Ernest Cooper played an active part in the formation of the ICAEW in 1880. Arthur was a member of its first council and its president 1883–84; Ernest was president 1899–1901. In 1877 the firm moved to 14 George Street. From the beginning the firm's business flourished; it became well-known in the City and by 1864 had made visits abroad. By 1900 the firm acted for a wide range of clients at home and abroad, including banks, iron and steel manufacturers, the engineering industry, insurance, tea, mines, land, finance and exploration companies, shipping companies, breweries, railways, hospitals and schools. The firm opened its first provincial office, in Liverpool, Merseyside, in 1920, and opened overseas offices in Brussels, Belgium, in 1921; Paris, France, in 1930; New York, USA, in 1926; and Montreal, Canada, in 1936. By 1945 there were eight offices and 250 staff worldwide. After the Second World War, major changes in the firm were led by Henry Benson (grandson of Francis Cooper), and John Pears (a partner in the firm from 1926). Specialist departments of taxation, investigation and management accounting were created within the firm, and the regional and international practices were expanded. Cooper's *Manual of Auditing*, which was to become a definitive textbook for the profession, was issued in 1946. The firm acquired more provincial offices through amalgamations with two old-established firms: Alfred Tongue & Co (est. in 1860 by David Chadwick, first president of the Manchester Institute of Accountants), Glasgow, Strathclyde, and Sheffield, South Yorkshire, in 1950; Aspell, Dunn & Co (est. 1903), Leicester, Leicestershire, in 1952; Carter & Co (est. in 1857 by Edward Carter, a member of the first council of the ICAEW), Birmingham, West Midlands, in 1960; and Curtis, Jenkins, Cornwell & Co (*qv*), Bristol, Avon, in 1966. In 1957 Cooper Brothers & Co in the UK, Lybrand, Ross Bros & Montgomery in the USA, and McDonald Currie & Co in Canada, formed the international firm Coopers & Lybrand, with seventy-nine offices in nineteen countries. In 1959 the London office moved to Abacus House, 33 Gutter Lane. In 1973 the style of the firm was changed from Cooper Brothers & Co to Coopers & Lybrand. The firm merged with the insolvency practice W H Cork, Gully & Co (est. 1896) in 1980. In 1985 it moved to Plumtree Court. Partners in the firm who have been presidents of the ICAEW include: John Pears (1960–61); Brian Maynard (1977–78); Brian Jenkins (1985–86), and Philip Couse (1989–90). In 1990 the firm merged with Deloitte Haskins & Sells (*qv*) to form Coopers & Lybrand Deloitte, now known as Coopers & Lybrand.

Records: Coopers & Lybrand, Plumtree Court, London EC4A 4HT

Partnership agreements 1928 on; draft agreement, Arthur and Francis Cooper 1879; international agreements 1957 on; partners' meeting minutes 1966 on; accounts (London) 1874; account book 1932; ledgers: 1854–1970 (w), private 1870–1938 (w); cash books: 1865, 1932 on, private 1870, 1938 on; registers of securities 1879–1936 (w); index to estates 1854; audits: register 1856–1930, lists 1856, 1898; letter books: 1947–50, private 1870–92, 1947–58; extracts from letters from colleagues in the field 1914–18; list and photographs of partners 1861–1969; salaries books 1920, 1940–46; attendance book 1920; leases: Manchester office 1939, 1965, Glasgow office 1964; papers, conferences 1950s on; photographs: 14 George Street 1861–1959, Paris dinner 1881, partners, office premises, conferences *c.* 1939–date, centenary celebrations 1954; audit manual *c.* 1946; list of London accountants compiled from trade directories incl. biographical notes *c.* 1874–79.

Anon., *A History of Cooper Brothers & Co, 1854 to 1954* (London, Batsford for the firm, 1954)

Anon., *The Early History of Coopers & Lybrand* (New York and London, Garland Publishing, 1984)

Peter Boys, 'What's in a Name – Firms' Simplified Family Trees: Coopers & Lybrand', *Accountancy*, Vol. 103, No. 1147 (March 1989), p. 97

J R Edwards, 'Sir Francis D'Arcy Cooper', in David J Jeremy (ed.), *Dictionary of Business Biography*, Vol. 1 (London, Butterworth, 1984)

Edgar Jones, 'Henry Alexander Benson', in David J Jeremy (ed.), *Dictionary of Business Biography*, Vol. 1 (London, Butterworth, 1984)

Edgar Jones, 'Arthur Cooper', in David J Jeremy (ed.), *Dictionary of Business Biography*, Vol. 1 (London, Butterworth, 1984)

Edgar Jones, 'Ernest Cooper', in David J Jeremy (ed.), *Dictionary of Business Biography*, Vol. 1 (London, Butterworth, 1984)

C&L Journal, 125th Anniversary Issue, No. 31 (June 1979)

CRANE CHRISTMAS & CO (Kingston Smith)
70 Old Broad Street, London

History: Founded by Ernest George Palmer and Raymond Crane as Palmer & Crane, 3, 4 & 5 Queen Street, Cheapside, London, in 1895. The practice was restyled Crane, Christmas & Co in 1903, when Frederick Herbert Cooper Christmas became a partner. The firm moved to 54 Gresham Street in 1896; 46 & 47 London Wall in 1909; and 70 Old Broad Street in 1954. In 1971 Crane, Christmas & Co merged with Callingham, Brown & Co (est. 1908), 38 Finsbury Square, London, to form Callingham, Crane & Co, later Callingham Crane. In 1991 the City office of Callingham Crane merged with Kingston Smith, London, Hayes, Upminster, and Croydon, London, and St Albans, Hertfordshire. The Leatherhead, Surrey, office of Callingham Crane continues as an independent firm.

Records: Kingston Smith, Devonshire House, 146 Bishopsgate, London EC2M 4JX

Private ledger 1895–1931.

CREASEYS
12 Lonsdale Gardens, Tunbridge Wells, Kent TN1 1PA

Also at Tonbridge

History: Founded by Robert George Mackie Creasey and Thomas Edward Crabb who were practising in 1868 at St Clements House, 27 Clements Lane, London, under the name Crabb & Creasey. In 1880 Crabb left the firm to practise in Essex Street, Strand, Creasey remaining at the Clements Lane address until 1886 when he moved to 8 & 9 Martin's Lane. The name of the practice was changed to Creasey & Sons when the latter was joined, in 1896, by his two sons. One son left the firm in 1902 and the name was changed to Creasey & Son. Percy Wickenden was made a partner in 1907 and was placed in charge of the newly opened office in Mount Pleasant, Tunbridge Wells, Kent, in 1908. At the same time the style Creasey, Son & Wickenden was adopted. The name was retained until 1984 when it was shortened to Creaseys. The London office remained in Martin's Lane until 1923 when it moved to 84 Chancery Lane. In the same year another office was opened, in High Street, Tonbridge, Kent. The Tunbridge Wells office moved to its present address in 1928. In 1934 the firm acquired the Chatham, Kent, practice of Charles Ferrier Dempster. The partnership continued to expand after the Second World War, having an office in Bexhill, East Sussex, between 1952 and 1958 and opening an office in Sevenoaks, Kent, in 1970. The London office amalgamated with Josolyne, Miles & Cassleton Elliott in 1970. Creaseys opened another London office between 1986 and 1988. In January 1988 the Tunbridge Wells and Tonbridge offices separated from those of Sevenoaks and Chatham to become two distinct firms. Tunbridge Wells and Tonbridge retained the name Creaseys, whilst Sevenoaks and Chatham reverted to Creasey, Son & Wickenden.

Records: Creaseys, 12 Lonsdale Gardens, Tunbridge Wells TN1 1PA

Partnership agreements 1935–date; dissolution agreement and papers 1948; partners' meeting minutes 1936, 1939, 1946–date (w); accounts: 1935–date, drafts 1933–34, 1939, Chatham 1944–54, London *c.* 1944–56, 1987–88, Tonbridge 1945–date; working papers *c.* 1935–date; tax files 1956–66; ledgers: nominal 1919–40, private 1919–41, Chatham 1935–38; cash books: 1947–date, cheque 1910–date, petty 1878–84; disbursements books 1948–73; clients' ledger balances agreement 1934; rents receivable ledger 1956–69; investment register 1902–23; railway investments ledger sheets 1897, 1899, 1907; correspondence: between offices 1946–87, possible merger 1949–50, partners' 1940–44; partner's valuation of book debts and work-in-progress 1952; articles of clerkship 1920–date; partners' personal papers 1884–1967; insurance agency appointments 1917–49; officers' declarations of secrecy 1936–51; staff pensions records 1935–67; employment contracts 1920–55; wages books 1915–40; mortgages, leases, offices 1933–63; office inventories *c.* 1939, 1941, 1965; insurance policies 1928–64; contracts: electricity supply 1928, telephones 1908, 1928, office equipment 1927–51; photographs: partner 1920s, staff *c.*1940.

Clients: F Allcorn: private ledger 1959–61; **Thomas and Clara Armstrong**: trust account, papers and correspondence 1944–54; **Armstrong Brown**: private ledger 1959–72; **Arnold Fooks Chadwick & Co**: private ledger 1957–76; **Barrett of Battle Ltd**: inventory and valuation of letter printing plant and machinery 1943, deed of surrender 1947, other records 1943–64 (m); **T Bates and Sons Ltd**: minutes 1936–66, private ledger 1923–65, other records 1946–67 (m); **Winifred M Blaker**: working papers 1948–49; **Beacon Hotel Crowborough Ltd**: liquidators' timetable 1937; **William T Bean**: probate documents 1904–08, papers re estate 1935; **Berry & Berry**: ledger accounts 1905–79, other records 1947–date (m); **J H Bishop Ltd**: family wills 1920, 1924; **Mrs L and J H Brinkhurst**: private ledger 1955–61, other records 1961–80 (m); **Browne, Crosskey & Harris Ltd**: draft pension scheme 1947, insurance policies 1954–66, tenancy agreement re garages in Lewes, East Sussex 1956, 1959, other records 1953–74 (m); **Buggs & Sons**: private ledger 1953–62, other records 1957–date (m); **A Burslem & Sons (Masons) Ltd**: register of members, etc. 1932; **Ellis Carr, Miss Ada Carr & Mrs Katherine Wallis**: share dividend certificates 1919–30, bank passbooks 1926–32, lists of investments and securities 1921–29, bank paying-in books and letters 1919–23, other records 1950–60 (m); **E B Champernowne**: private ledger 1946–58; **Lewis Edward & John Lewis Clay**: partnership deed 1949; **R H & R W Clutton**: private ledger 1952–70, pensions fund 1957–71, other records 1957–date (m); **Drs Cogan, Symons and Gibbs**: private ledger 1951–67, other records 1950–73 (m); **Mrs M C Couldrey**: receipt for capital concerning Naomi Carr Trust 1938, other records 1928–75 (m); **Crosskey, Harris & Teasel Ltd**: leases re properties in Lewes, East Sussex 1938, 1949, other records 1939–70 (m); **Crowborough Beacon Golf Club Ltd**: memorandum and articles of association 1896; **John Davidson**: private ledger 1952–66, other records 1946–72 (m); **Robert Carter Dowson**: family papers 1932–76; **Maude Caroline Dowson**: records 1927–79 (m); **Edwards & Martin Ltd**: memorandum and articles of association 1963, other records 1977–date (m); **Edwards & Martin (Roofing) Ltd**: memorandum and articles of association 1965; **J J Gayler**: private ledgers 1958–70; **Hall's Bookshop**: records 1939–date (m); **Hemsley (Builders) Ltd**: share certificate 1957; **Hernden Farms Ltd**: private ledger 1949–55; **W B Hewitt**: private ledger 1951–69; **E R Hickmott & Sons Ltd**: register of members, etc. 1959–date, minute book 1959–date, articles of association 1959, other records 1967–date (m); **W T Hollamby & Co**: partnership deed 1947; **Dr B B Hosford**: share and dividend register 1945–74; **C F Irish & Sons Ltd**: register of members, etc. 1936, 1966, share certificate book 1936–73, memorandum and articles of association 1936, minute book 1936–80, annual returns 1937–69; **Henry Wood Johnson**: papers 1923–57; **D C Jones**, Heathfield: private ledger 1944–65, other records 1975–date (m); **H Kemp (Ashphalte) Ltd**: agreement of sale and appointment of managing director 1937, other records 1968–date (m); **H J & F J Moat**: private ledger 1928–70; **Mount Pleasant Congregational Church**: miscellaneous papers 1941–43; **Mrs K Newington**: private ledger 1934–65; **Oswald Field Ltd**: share certificate book 1947–74, register of members, etc. 1947–74, minute book 1947–77; **Payne & Son (Silversmiths) Ltd**: share certificate book 1937–date, share transfers, etc. 1937–date, register of members, etc. 1937–date, private ledger 1954–date, memorandum and articles of association 1937, annual returns 1950–date, other records 1970–date (m); **Picton Children's Trust**: private ledger 1949–54; **W J Piper & Son**: private ledgers 1938–60; **Percy G Pratt Ltd**: directors' account book 1957–60; **Punnett & Sons**: register of members, etc. 1915–49; **Royal Victoria Sussex Hotel**: leases 1887, 1895, letters concerning repairs 1906, 1930; **St Ermin Hotel**, Madeira Park: wages book 1943–48, bills 1943–44; **Amy Santer**: probate of will 1953; **Silverdale Garage (H J Harper)**: account book 1950–58; **South of England Mutual Plate Glass Insurance Co Ltd**: minute book 1898–1930; **Soultney Hall Hotel Ltd**: certificate of incorporation 1936; **J R Stedman Ltd**: memorandum and articles of association 1947; **Thomas Oliver and Elizabeth Sarah Stidolph**: probate of will and final accounts 1915, 1954; **Swain, Gunner & Swain Ltd**: inventory and valuation of Forge and Furnace farms, Bedgebury, Kent 1944–45; **Ernst Aubry Sweetman**: administration account 1932; **B H Thorpe & Co Ltd**: share certificate 1953; **Trade Protection Chamber Ltd**: leases 1958, 1960; **Tunbridge Wells Mutual Plate Glass Co Ltd**: certificate of incorporation 1882; **Tunbridge Wells Nurseries Ltd**: steering committee minutes 1956; **Tunbridge Wells Permanent Building Society**: transfer of engagements to Hastings and Thanet Building Society 1958; **Tunbridge Wells & Southern Eastern Counties Agricultural Society**: ledger 1953–67; **Tunbridge Wells Bowling & Tennis Grounds Ltd**: founders' certificates receipt book 1923–27, certificate of incorporation 1923, other records 1970–date (m); **Tunbridge Wells Squash Racket Club**: private ledger 1947–70; **Tunbridge Wells, Tonbridge & District Chamber of Commerce Ltd**: miscellaneous papers 1912–21; **Universal Trust Ltd,** London: directors' report 1944; **Gordon Urquhart and Mrs K G Addinsell**: schedule of deeds re properties in Harrow and Tunbridge Wells 1905–39; **R Wallace & Co**: private ledger 1940–66; **W J P Walter**: share register 1933–77, private ledger 1929–80, minute book 1933–80; **Mrs Katharine Wallis**: stocks and shares book *c.* 1895–1923, executors' accounts 1930; **Ward Adams & Co Ltd**: certificate of incorporation, register of members 1958; **Ward Wharfage Ltd**: certificate of incorporation 1949; **White & Co Ironmongers Ltd**: register of members 1935–36, papers 1943–59; **Mrs R Wickham**: bank deposit book 1937–57, other records 1922–86 (m); **Williams, James, Clifton & Co Ltd**: articles of association 1926, share valuation certificate 1963; **Wood & Wallis Ltd**: minute book 1932–75.

CURTIS, JENKINS, CORNWELL & CO (Coopers & Lybrand)
Eagle House, St Stephen's Street, Bristol, Avon

Also at Cirencester, London and Newport (Gwent)

History: Founded by Robert Fletcher who started practising as an accountant in 1816, opening his first office at 10 Queen's Square, Bristol, Avon, in 1819. He moved, later the same year, to 2 Queen's Square and, in 1820, to New Buildings in Small Street, the centre of the financial and banking sector of the city. His practice flourished and by 1821 he had three permanent members of staff undertaking general accountancy, executorship and bankruptcy work for clients in Bristol; London; Liverpool, Merseyside; Cheltenham, Gloucestershire; and Wales. In 1823 Fletcher moved to Small Street Court and in 1830 to Exchange Chambers. In 1839 he entered into partnership with William Vaughan Jenkins, his son-in-law, and John Curtis, a member of the firm's staff since 1823. The practice then became Robert Fletcher & Co and, in 1845, Curtis, Jenkins & Co. Fletcher retired in 1857. Clients of the firm in the nineteenth century included the Bristol & Birmingham Railway Co, the Bristol Blind Asylum, the Bristol & Exeter Railway Co, the Bristol & Gloucestershire Railway Co, the *Bristol Mercury*, Bristol Steam Navigation Co, Bristol Waterworks Co, the Cambrian Brewery, the City Corporation, the Clifton Suspension Bridge Trust, Colthurst & Harding, the Guardian Assurance Agency, the London and Bridgewater Shipping Co, the Nailsea Colliery Co, the law firm Osborne Ward, Ricketts, Wills & Co (later WD & HO Wills, tobacco manufacturers), White Oak Colliery, and William Lewton Clarke, solicitor. In 1907 the firm moved to offices at 44 Corn Street. Its name was changed to Curtis, Jenkins, Cornwell & Co in 1920, when Stanley William Cornwell became a partner. Offices were opened in London (Trafalgar Buildings, 1 Charing Cross) in 1921; Newport (Llandone Estate Buildings, Field Road), Gwent, in 1954; and Cirencester (Dollar St House), Gloucestershire, in 1960. The Bristol office moved to Eagle House, St Stephen's Street, in 1959. In 1966 the firm merged with the national accountancy firm Cooper Brothers & Co, later Coopers & Lybrand (*qv*).

Records: Bristol Record Office, 'B' Bond Warehouse, Smeaton Road, Bristol BS1 6XN

Professional diary incl. daily work record, time charged 1838; time books (some fee details) 1820, 1821, 1828, 1836, 1843–57, 1862–67, 1876–77; ledgers: 1819 (draft), 1820–36, 1836–40, incl. outstanding balances 1840–56, private 1883–1908; cash books 1819 (draft), 1819–27, 1831–39; copy out-letters 1843–57; salaries book 1912–18; extracts from diary of 'E F S', life on board the *True Briton* 1870; biographical notes, Fletcher family, Ashley Lodge, Ashley Hill n.d.

Clients: Barnes Estate: appointments of trustees incl. schedules of investments 1894, 1909, accounts 1884–1909; **Bristol Juvenile Organisations Committee**: lease of St Matthew Moorfields School 1920, agreement, right of way 1921, tenancy agreement, Cardwell Chambers, Marsh Street

1919; **Burleigh Estate**: deeds, copy wills 1799–1900; **Alice Cole's Charity**, St Leonard's parish: accounts of receipts and disbursements 1648–1823, extract from Alice Cole's will 1604/5, list of feoffees 1659, orders and rules of Free School, St James' Back n.d.; **Franklyn, Morgan & Davey**, tobacco and snuff manufacturers: partnership agreements 1873–98, correspondence, partnership, papers 1880–87, leases 1873, 1880; **Gloucestershire Society**, relief of poor: declaration of trust 1830; **Harvey Estate**: deeds, probate documents, residuary accounts 1786–1890; **Humphris Farm**, Oxenton, Gloucestershire: tenancy agreements 1867, 1909, report on state of repair and cultivation of farm 1909; **Edna and Vera May Trust Fund**: correspondence, accounts, statements, papers 1916–29; **Merchant Tailors' Charity**: grant of messuage, shops and land for building a hall for the Guild of the Fraternity 1402; **St Philip's Bridge Co Ltd**: share certificate 1839; **Unemployed Welfare Association**: correspondence, papers, appointment of R A Dicketts 1933–34; **Ware Estate**: probate documents, papers 1851–1911.

S V P Cornwell, *Curtis Jenkins Cornwell & Co: A Study in Professional Origins, 1816–1966* (New York/London, Garland Publishing, 1991)

DAFFERN & CO

Queens House, Queens Road, Coventry CV1 3DR

History: Started by Thomas Mason Daffern who set up in practice in 1896 as an incorporated accountant, stockbroker, insurance agent and rent-collector in Economic Chambers, Little Park Street, Coventry, West Midlands. From *c.*1875 to 1895, whilst he was employed as secretary of the Leigh Mills Co Ltd, Daffern became involved with the Coventry Permanent Economic Building Society, an association which the practice still maintains. In 1919 he was succeeded by his son, Thomas Wells Daffern, and the firm was renamed Daffern & Co. In 1925 it moved to 19/20 High Street along with the Building Society and Daffern's other businesses. In November 1940 the offices suffered severe bomb damage in the major air raid on Coventry and new premises were found at 29 Warwick Road. The firm remained there until 1975, when it moved to the present Queens House premises. In 1962 an office was opened at 12 The Parade, Leamington Spa, Warwickshire. Early major clients included: British Piston Ring Co Ltd, W H Jones & Son Ltd, builders; Coventry Radiator & Presswork Ltd; J G Gray Ltd, builders; Coventry Motor Fittings Ltd; E Harris & Son, builders; Atkins & Turton Ltd, grocers; Edward O'Brien Ltd, cycle manufacturers; E Wooton Ltd, hat manufacturers; Glenn & Co Ltd, sweet makers; Foleshill Brick & Tile Co Ltd; Wormells, slate manufacturers; Garlicks Ltd, builders; T F Wilkinson & Co Ltd, loom manufacturers; and Kelly & Son, builders.

Records: Daffern & Co, Queens House, Queens Road, Coventry CV1 3DR

Partnership agreements 1930–74; accounts schedules 1932–33, 1939–80; ledgers: 1919–61, incl. accounts 1920–51, cost 1897–*c.*1944, nominal 1961–date; cash books 1919–38; weekly wages book 1913–15; historical notes n.d.

Clients: Copies of accounts 1901–date (m) from 1926.

DAVID OWEN & CO
17 Market Place, Devizes SN10 1BA

Also at Marlborough

History: Started by David Owen, secretary of the Wiltshire Friendly Society, who set up in practice in the society's offices at Bank Chambers, Devizes, Wiltshire, in 1890. By 1909 he was practising with his son, Ralph David Owen, under the style David Owen & Co. The firm acquired an office in Marlborough, Wiltshire, in 1937 and had an office in Trowbridge, Wiltshire, between 1966 and 1978. In 1978 the Devizes office moved to 17 Market Place.

Records (1): David Owen & Co, 17 Market Place, Devizes SN10 1BA

Partnership agreements 1968–date; monthly salaries books 1942–52; office: inventory 1955, lease 1957.

Clients: W E Chivers & Sons Ltd, builders: directors' meeting minutes 1933–39, ledgers: 1928–55, private 1915–17, 1938–76, impersonal 1923–60; **Wadworth & Co**, brewers: ledgers: private 1885–1902, rents 1937–43, 1950–54.

Records (2): Wiltshire County Record Office, County Hall, Trowbridge BA14 8JG

Clients: papers 1920–31.

DAVIES & CRANE
5 Winckley Street, Preston PR1 2AA

History: Founded *c.* 1872 by Henry Davies who set up in practice in Winckley Street, Preston, Lancashire. Henry Bee was taken into partnership in *c.* 1873 and the style Davies & Bee was adopted. Bee left the firm and, in 1882, Davies and Thomas Henry Crane, who was practising in Southport, Merseyside, amalgamated names, becoming Davies & Crane in both Preston and Southport. Both offices continued to practise independently. The Southport firm also practises as Davies & Crane (*qv*). In 1975 the firm opened an office at 15 Milbourne Street, Blackpool, Lancashire. This office was closed in 1989. Clients of the firm have included Leyland Motors

Ltd, Trustee Savings Bank (North West Section), a number of coalmines in Wigan, Greater Manchester, and gunpowder factories around Barrow-in-Furness, Cumbria.

Records: Davies & Crane, 5 Winckley Street, Preston PR1 2AA

Partnership agreement 1946; private ledgers 1924–date; appointment of Henry Davies as agent of Northern Assurance Co 1868; deeds, plans, 5 Winckley Street 1804, 1990.

Clients: Bispham Conservative Club: share register 1925; **Leyland Motors Ltd**: records 1920s on; **Preston Victoria Permanent Benefit Building Society**: rules 1873, 1878, 1883.

DAVIES & CRANE

Hoghton Chambers, Hoghton Street, Southport PR9 0TB

History: Founded by Thomas Henry Crane who set up in practice at 33 London Street, Southport, Merseyside, in 1880 and by Henry Davies who was trading in Preston, Lancashire, as Davies & Bee. In 1882 Crane & Davies amalgamated names, becoming Davies & Crane in both Preston and Southport, although both offices continued to practise independently. The Preston firm also practises under the name Davies & Crane (*qv*). The Southport firm moved to 211 Lord Street in *c.* 1890; 399 Lord Street in 1906; and the present address in 1928.

Records: Davies & Crane, Hoghton Chambers, Hoghton Street, Southport PR9 0TB

Partnership agreements 1924–date; nominal ledgers 1924–date; articles of clerkship 1914–70s.

DEAN & SON (Dean Statham)

Bank Passage, Stafford, Staffordshire

Also at Newcastle-under-Lyme

History: Founded *c.*1880 by George Dean, an incorporated accountant who had been on the audit staff of the London & North Western Railway Company. By 1897 he was practising at 9 St Mary's Grove, Stafford, Staffordshire. In 1903 he was joined by his son, Walter James Dean, who was admitted to partnership in 1909, when the practice became Dean & Son. The firm moved to 18 Market Square in the 1920s, to 4 Market Square in 1930, and to Bank Passage in 1965. In 1963 it opened an office at 13 Brunswick Street, Newcastle-under-Lyme, Staffordshire. In 1970 the firm amalgamated with Reginald Statham & Co (est. 1934), Northcote Chambers, 13a King Street, Newcastle-under-Lyme, and formed Dean Statham.

Records (1): Dean Statham, Bank Passage, Stafford ST16 2JS

Partnership accounts: 1913–32, draft 1909–38; working papers 1909–39.

Records (2): Staffordshire Record Office, County Buildings, Eastgate Street, Stafford ST16 2LZ

Clients: Amies Ltd, boot and shoe factors and retailers: general ledger 1919–30; **Artus Productions**: general ledger 1947; **J Ashton**: general ledger 1938–45; **Attwoods Garage**, Stafford: general ledger 1928–30; **Auriol Builders Ltd**: cash book 1935–39; **G H Austin & Sons Ltd**, Knightley Garage, coach operators, Woodseaves, Staffordshire: general ledger 1948–55; **J & W A Averill**, aerated water manufacturers, Stafford: private ledger 1922–24; **John Bagnall**, agricultural engineer, Stafford: private ledger 1923–34; **W G Bagnall Ltd**, locomotive manufacturers, Stafford: private ledger 1889–1924; **Barton & Riley**, shoe manufacturers, Stafford: private ledger 1899–1908; **Board of Arbitration & Conciliation for the Boot & Shoe Trade of Stafford & District**: quarterly meeting minutes 1920–46; **C Brassington & Co Ltd**, motor dealers, Stafford: sales journal 1938–53, purchase journal 1939–54; **Brocton Garage Ltd**, Brocton, Staffordshire: general ledger 1953–60; **William Campbell**, sweetshop owner, Stafford: general ledger 1913–31; **A A Cleland**, boot and shoe retailer, Stafford: general ledger 1934–37; **James Clewlow & Sons**, shoe makers, Stafford: general ledger 1922–26; **Mrs E Colclough**, children's clothing and fancy goods, Stafford: general ledger 1925–34; **Colwich Brick & Tile Co**, Colwich, Staffordshire: general ledger 1921–36; **P T Dale**, ironmongers, Stafford: private ledger 1920–53; **Dr D J Corke**, physician, Rugeley, Staffordshire: private ledger 1919–23; **Dickenson & Sons**, ironmongers, Stafford: cash book *c.*1940–62, sales journal 1936–65; **P Dodd**, farrier: general ledger 1930–38; **James Dyche Ltd**, shoe manufacturers, Stafford: shareholders' meetings minutes 1947–54, share certificates register 1947; **G Dyke & Son**, builders and contractors, Stafford: private ledger 1923–27; **James Elliott**, dec'd, Stafford: executors' accounts ledger *c.*1929–40; **F Espley & Sons**, builders and contractors, Stafford: private ledger 1916–33, general ledger 1916 on; **W & J Eymer**, chemists and opticians, Stafford: general ledger 1919–24; **J W Follows**, draper, Stafford: day book 1925–29; **Forebridge Shoeing Forge Ltd**, Stafford: directors' meeting minutes 1917–23, general ledger 1917–30; **Sarah Fowke**, Penkridge: executors' accounts 1921–36; **W F Fowke**, chemists, Stafford: general ledger 1927–28, private ledger 1927–28; **W F Fowke** dec'd: probate documents, family papers 1869–1940, cash book 1936–41; **Ralph Gee & Son Ltd**, transport contractors, Rugeley: general ledgers 1924–35, 1934–37, 1946–52, nominal ledger 1938–42, private ledgers 1929–32, 1937–38, cash books 1935–41, 1948–51; **W Gwennap (Agricultural) Ltd**, engineeers, Stafford: general ledger 1950–59; **Halden & Haywood Ltd**, printers and stationers, Stafford: general ledger 1913–38; **D Hatfield Ltd**, chemist, Stafford: general ledger 1927–30, annual general meeting minutes 1932; **Heels Ltd**, shoe heel manufacturers, Stafford: nominal ledger 1924; **G Hill & Co**, coal and coke merchants, Stafford: general ledger 1919–34; **David Hollins & Co Ltd**, shoe manufacturers, Stafford: shareholders', directors' and annual general meetings minutes 1907–1931; **E J Hurlestone**, printers and stationers, Eccleshall: general ledger 1932–35; **W J Jeffs & Co**, drapers, Stafford: cash book *c.*1968; **R Keighley**, ladies' outfitter, Stafford: private ledger 1917–1918; **Lowe, Derryman & Co**, agricultural merchants: general ledger 1929–30; **W A Malkin & Sons**, millers, Standon, Staffordshire: private ledgers 1903–42; **W Marson**, JP, Stafford: accounts 1908–18, executors' accounts 1926–34; **Mason & Marson**, shoe manufacturers, Stafford: private ledger 1907–19, general ledgers 1914, 1916–19, *c.*1926–34; **Midland Auto Electrical Co**, Lichfield, Staffordshire: general ledger 1948–49, analytical accounts 1948–49; **Modern Jewellers Ltd**, Stafford: private ledger 1930–31; **National Association of Corn & Agricultural Merchants Staffordshire branch**: monthly meeting minutes 1939–53; **North Stafford Garage Ltd**, Stafford: cash book 1946–53; **Oakey & Wooding**, agricultural engineers, Stafford: private ledger 1929–34; **A W H Peach**, shoe manufacturer, Stafford: private ledger 1930–31; **Porter & Arnold**, architects and surveyors, Stafford: private ledger 1929–31; **E R Poulston Ltd**, coal merchants, Stafford: general ledger 1908–30; **Proudlock's Taxis**, Stafford: cash book 1959–60; **G Sandy**, builder and shopfitter: private ledger 1920–23; **Scarlett Bros**, painters, decorators, locksmiths, Stafford: general ledger 1922–31; **Shoe Findings Ltd**, suppliers of sundries to shoe manufacturers (later cardboard box manufacturers), Stafford: general ledger 1916–24; **F Silvester**, baker and confectioner, Stafford: private ledger 1920–28; **J Slater**, grocer, Eccleshall: private ledger 1951–61; **James & Samuel Smallwood**, builders and contractors, Stafford: general ledger 1922–47; **William Smallwood**, builders, Stone, Staffordshire: general ledger 1901–21; **Stafford & District Association of Boot & Shoe Manufacturers**: minutes 1877–80, 1896–1944; **Stafford & District Humane Burial Society**, registers of members 1835, 1859–28, minutes 1911–32, entrance books 1890–1929, annual statements of benefits and payments 1849–1936; **Stafford Entertainments Ltd**, cinema proprietors: cash takings and analysis books for various cinemas, Stafford 1930–40, cash takings and analysis book 1940–47; **Stafford Master Bakers Association**: quarterly meeting minutes 1942–50; **Stafford Mutual Plate Glass Insurance Association Ltd**: rough minutes 1901–38, cash book 1923–40; **W & J Wallace Ltd**, boot manufacturers, Rochdale, Lancashire: directors' meetings minutes 1902–33, register of members 1902–35, nominal ledgers 1928–32, cash book *c.*1922–23; **Watkins & Co (Eccleshall) Ltd**, grocers and corn merchants: register of members and directors 1953, share certificate register 1953; **Wooliscroft & Co**, garage proprietors, Uttoxeter, Staffordshire: private ledger 1934–39.

DELOITTE HASKINS & SELLS (Coopers & Lybrand)
128 Queen Victoria Street, London

Also at Aberdeen, Belfast, Birmingham, Bristol, Cambridge, Cardiff, Croydon, Edinburgh, Gloucester, Leeds, Liverpool, Manchester, Newcastle upon Tyne, Norwich, Nottingham, Reading, Southampton and Swansea

History: Founded by William Welch Deloitte who opened his first office at 11 Basinghall Street, London, in 1845, having previously worked in the office of the official assignee in bankruptcy of the City of London. In 1855 the practice moved to 4 Lothbury and became Deloitte & Greenwood in 1857 when Thomas Greenwood was taken into partnership. The firm was renamed Deloitte, Greenwood & Dever when Henry Dever became a partner in 1862; Deloitte, Dever, Hollebone & Co in 1867; Deloitte, Dever, Hollebone & Griffiths in 1869; and Deloitte, Dever, Griffiths & Co in 1873. Deloitte also linked up with James Halliday to form Deloitte & Halliday in Manchester, Greater Manchester, although this partnership was dissolved in 1877. From the outset the firm flourished, becoming auditor to many of the leading railway companies as well as other important undertakings throughout the country, such as docks, collieries and ironworks. Deloitte was also active in the formation of the ICAEW in 1880; he was a member of the first council of the Institute of Accountants in London, in 1870, and of the ICAEW's first council, and was its president 1888–89. The firm's first branch office was opened in New York, USA, in 1890. In 1902, William Plender (Sir William Plender from 1911) became senior partner of the firm. During the First World War he undertook a wide range of public activities, including membership of government committees dealing with the organisation of the telegraph service; liquor trade finance; metropolitan munitions; military service; enemy debts; and company law amendment. In 1905 the firm moved its headquarters to 5 London Wall Buildings under the name Deloitte, Plender, Griffiths & Co. Following the First World War, the firm expanded in the UK and abroad. Overseas, agency arrangements with the US firm Haskins & Sells (est. 1886) allowed the opening of firms in France, Belgium, Italy, Canada, Cuba and Mexico; a merger with Haskins & Sells in 1952 led to the opening of offices in Switzerland, Spain and Portugal. In the UK, the firm established branch offices in Cardiff, South Glamorgan, in 1912; Truro, Cornwall, in 1920; Swansea, West Glamorgan, in 1923, and Manchester in 1949. In 1918 an amalgamation took place with the old-established practice Welton & Bond (est. 1833), London. In 1969 the firm merged with Tribe, Clarke & Co (est. 1780), Bristol, Avon. This was followed by other mergers including: Winter, Robinson, Sisson & Benson (*qv*), Newcastle upon Tyne, Tyne and Wear, in 1969; Graham, Smart & Annan (est. 1904), Glasgow, Strathclyde, and Edinburgh, Lothian, in 1973; and the Scottish firm Kerr, MacLeod & Co and Harmood Banner & Co (est. 1805), London, Liverpool, Merseyside, Portsmouth and Southampton, Hampshire, Chester, Cheshire,and Wrexham, Clwyd, and Manchester, in 1974. In 1971 the firm's name was changed from Deloitte, Plender, Griffiths & Co to Deloitte & Co, and in 1978 to Deloitte Haskins & Sells. The firm moved to 128 Queen Victoria Street in 1974. Deloitte Haskins & Sells and its predecessor firms have produced several presidents of the ICAEW: William Welch Deloitte (Deloitte, Dever, Griffiths & Co) 1888–89; Thomas Abercrombie Welton (Welton, Jones & Co, later Welton & Bond) 1891–92; John George Griffiths (Deloitte, Dever, Griffiths & Co) 1897–99; John Sutherland Harmood-Banner (Harmood Banner & Son, later Harmood Banner & Co) 1904–05; William Plender (Deloitte, Plender, Griffiths & Co) 1910–12, 1929–30; William Cash (Cash, Stone & Co) 1921–23; Arthur Edwin Cutforth (Deloitte, Plender, Griffiths & Co) 1934–36; Gilbert Shepherd (Gilbert Shepherd, Owen & Co) 1947–48; Sir Russell Kettle (Deloitte, Plender, Griffiths & Co) 1949–50; Charles William Boyce (Boyce, Welch & Co) 1951–52; Donald Victor House (Harmood Banner, Lewis & Mounsey) 1954–55; Robert Pearson Winter (Winter, Robinson, Sisson & Benson) 1963–64; Wilfrid Guy Densem (Deloitte, Plender, Griffiths & Co) 1964–65, and David Gordon Richards (Deloitte Haskins & Sells) 1979–80. In 1990 the firm merged with Coopers & Lybrand (*qv*), to form Coopers & Lybrand Deloitte, now known as Coopers & Lybrand.

Records (1): Coopers & Lybrand, Plumtree Court, London EC4A 4HT

Partnership agreements 1953 on; international agreements 1967–90; minutes 1974 on; time ledger 1845–46; letter books 1910–11, 1922–27; presidential speeches: W W Deloitte 1888, John Griffiths 1898, 1899; staff register 1914; salaries books 1876–94; roll of honour 1915.

Records (2): Guildhall Library, Aldermanbury, London EC2P 2EJ

Time record book 1936–39.

Peter Boys, 'What's in a Name – Firms' Simplified Family Trees: Deloitte Haskins & Sells', *Accountancy*, Vol. 103, No. 1148 (April 1989), pp.118–19

M F Bywater, 'William Quilter', in David J Jeremy (ed.), *Dictionary of Business Biography*, Vol. 4 (London, Butterworth, 1985)

R P T Davenport-Hines, 'Sir John Sutherland Harmood-Banner', in David J Jeremy (ed.), *Dictionary of Business Biography*, Vol. 3 (London, Butterworth, 1985)

J R Edwards, 'William Plender', in David J Jeremy (ed.), *Dictionary of Business Biography*, Vol. 4 (London, Butterworth, 1985)

Edgar Jones, 'William Welch Deloitte', in David J Jeremy (ed.), *Dictionary of Business Biography*, Vol. 2 (London, Butterworth, 1984)

Sir Russell Kettle, *Deloitte & Co, 1845–1956* (Oxford, Oxford University Press for the firm, 1958)

James Kilpatrick, *Deloitte, Plender, Griffiths & Co: Some Notes on the Early Days of the Firm* (London, Wyman & Sons, 1942)

DENNING & CO (Grant Thornton)
8/16 Park Street, Bristol, Avon

History: Founded by Frederick Denning who was in practice in Bristol, Avon, under the style Denning, Smith & Co in 1864. By 1881 he was practising as Denning & Co at Shannon Court, Corn Street, and subsequently moved to 36 Baldwin Street in 1914; 10 Park Street in *c.*1945; and Central Chambers, 8/16 Park Street, in 1959. In 1964 the firm acquired offices in Bath, Avon, Chippenham and Trowbridge, Wiltshire, and Minehead and Taunton, Somerset. In 1968 the Bristol office of Denning & Co amalgamated with the national firm Thornton Baker & Co which became Grant Thornton (*qv*) in 1986.

Records: Bristol Record Office, 'B' Bond Warehouse, Smeaton Road, Bristol BS1 6XN

Ledgers: 1883–1901, 1913–47 incl. profit and loss accounts and balance sheets, private 1864–1901.

DRURY, THURGOOD & CO
71 Mark Lane, London EC3R 7RD

History: In 1878 Harry Voce Thurgood started working as a clerk with James Waddell & Co in Queen Victoria Street, London. He left in 1883 and a year later joined the firm of Drury & Elliott, 11 Queen Victoria Street. In 1897 he started to practise in his own name but by 1899, after the death of Elliott, he had joined Frank Drury as a partner. He carried on the practice as Drury, Thurgood & Co after Drury's retirement in 1901. The name of the firm has remained unchanged since then, except during 1909–18 when it was known as Drury, Thurgood, Hatfield & Co. For many years the firm acted for several tea companies as the natural successor to James Waddell & Co and Drury & Elliott. The firm took offices in Dashwood House at 69 Old Broad Street during the Second World War after its offices in Queen Victoria Street were bombed. The firm moved to Leith House at 47 Gresham Street upon merging with Reads, Cocke & Watson, now Reads & Co (*qv*), in 1964 and has practised from its current address at 71 Mark Lane, London, since 1987. The combined firm continues to practise under the names of both Reads & Co and Drury, Thurgood & Co.

Records: Drury, Thurgood & Co, 71 Mark Lane, London EC3R 7RD

Partnership agreements: 1908–36, dissolution 1901, 1918; time ledger 1964–68; accounts 1928–78; tax file 1971–80; clients' ledgers: 1936–68, balances 1966; fees journals 1936–74; private ledgers 1926–76; cash books 1938–75; trial balances 1942–46, 1951; weekly salaries book 1942–45; office leases: Dashwood House 1960, Leith House 1965; photographs, partners *c.*1900–45.

E NOEL HUMPHREYS & CO

6 Hunter Street, Chester CH1 2AU

History: Started by Edward Noel Humphreys who set up in practice under his own name at 37 Pepper Street, Chester, Cheshire, in 1893, having formerly worked as clerk to Wakefield & Enock, 16 Corn Exchange Chambers. The firm became E Noel Humphreys & Co in 1921. It moved to Grosvenor Chambers, 6 Newgate Street, in 1894; 9 & 11 Old Bank Buildings, Eastgate, in 1895; and 6 Hunter Street in 1966.

Records: E Noel Humphreys & Co, 6 Hunter Street, Chester CH1 2AU

Partnership accounts 1894–97; fees ledgers 1928–70; accounts rendered book 1939–70; private ledgers 1893–97, 1930–43, 1952–65; private correspondence 1925–33; salaries books 1935, 1937–38.

EDWARD DENTON & SON (Bailey, Page & Roper)

410 Tower Building, 22 Water Street, Liverpool, Merseyside

Also at Runcorn

History: Founded by Edward Denton who was practising under the name Edward Denton & Son at 77 Dale Street, Liverpool, Merseyside, in *c.*1881. The name of the firm was subsequently changed to Denton, Son & Welch, following a merger with Wilmot, Welch & Co, Liverpool and Crewe, Cheshire, in 1920 and to Edward Denton & Son in 1927. William Denton, Edward's son and a partner in the firm from the 1890s until 1920, was Lord Mayor of Liverpool 1936–37, and became Deputy Lieutenant of Lancashire in 1937. The firm moved from Dale Street to 16 Manchester Street in 1890, and then to Westminster Chambers, 3 Crosshall Street, in *c.*1893; 7 Sweeting Street in 1898; 30 Exchange Street East in 1934; 1 Marybone in 1956; 373 Sefton House, Exchange Flags, in 1974; Drury House, 19 Water Street, in 1977; and 410 Tower Building, 22 Water Street, in 1982. It had offices in Crewe (Temple Chambers) 1922–28 and Chester (33 Nicholas Street), Cheshire, 1949–54 and opened an office in Runcorn (54 High Street), Cheshire, in 1961. In January 1991 the firm merged with Bailey, Page & Roper and moved to Norwich House, Water Street, Liverpool.

Records: Bailey, Page & Roper, Norwich House, Water Street, Liverpool L2 9XR

Partnership agreements: 1934–66, draft dissolution 1927; balance sheets and accounts 1890–92, 1922–67 (w); fees ledgers 1906–53; list of fees paid 1947; ledgers: general 1920–48, private 1900–20, property (rent) 1893–1954; balances: trial 1889, 1931, general ledger 1952–54; dividend book 1900–22; correspondence: clients 1882–91, partnership matters 1968–81; weekly salaries books 1927–48; tenancy agreement, offices 1933; plans, 48–58 Renshaw Street n.d.; Denton family papers: 1891–1970, Edward Denton, Soho Street Baptist Chapel 1878–1927, Major William Denton 1908–37; William Denton, private account book 1938–41.

Clients: Major T T Vernon: balance sheet and statement of private account 1913, 1914; **Southport Cafe Co**: balance sheet, directors' report and correspondence 1890–91.

EDWARD MOORE & SONS (Moores Rowland)
4 Chiswell Street, London

Also at Bury St Edmunds, Cardiff, Chelmsford, Colchester, Croydon, Edinburgh, Epping, Kingston-upon-Thames, Northampton and Walsall.

History: Founded by Edward Moore who began to practise as a public accountant in 1866 at East India Chambers, Leadenhall Street, London, under the name of Moore & Wallis's Mercantile Agency, having previously been employed by Stubbs Mercantile Agency. In 1880 he took his son, Edward Cecil, into partnership and the practice became Edward Moore & Son, operating from offices at 3 Crosby Square. Sir Edward Cecil Moore was Lord Mayor of London 1922–23 and president of the ICAEW in 1923. The style of the firm was changed to Edward Moore & Sons in 1891 when another son was admitted to partnership. The firm moved to Thames House, Queen Street Place, in 1922, and to 4 Chiswell Street in 1968. It had an office in Paris, France, from 1920 to *c.* 1945 and from 1965 was once again represented overseas. Branch offices were opened in Northampton, Northamptonshire, in 1972; Kingston-upon-Thames, Surrey, in 1975; and Bury St Edmunds, Suffolk, Chelmsford, Essex, Edinburgh, Lothian, and Glasgow, Strathclyde, in 1978. The firm amalgamated with a number of practices, including McCann, Bentley & Co, London (1970); Wilson, Bigg & Co, London (1971); Boty, Cox, Crawford & Ridley, Croydon, Surrey (1975); and Herbert, Pepper & Rudland, Walsall, West Midlands (1984). In January 1985 Edward Moore & Sons merged with Rowland Nevill, New Broad Street, London, formed in 1976 through the merger of Rowland & Co and Nevill, Hovey, Gardner & Co (*qv*), to form Moores & Rowland, now Moores Rowland.

Records (1): Guildhall Library, Aldermanbury, London EC2P 2EJ

Charges registers 1922–32; ledgers 1909–26; private cash books 1912–23,

1926–40; charges account balance for work completed 1909; out-letter books 1866–69; monthly salaries books: 1909–28, summaries 1929–55; weekly salaries books 1942–45, 1948–51; valuation and inventory, 3 Thames House 1923; circulars 1866, 1880; historical notes n.d.

Clients: London Parcels Delivery Co: minute book 1837–46.

Records (2): Moores Rowland, Clifford's Inn, Fetter Lane, London EC4A 1AS

Partnership agreement 1877; London partners' meeting minutes 1980–84.

EDWARD THOMAS PEIRSON & SONS
39 High Street, Market Harborough LE16 7NU

History: Originated as the Market Harborough, Leicestershire, office (opened 1938) of the Coventry, West Midlands, firm established by Edward Thomas Peirson in 1853 and renamed Edward Thomas Peirson & Son in 1888, and Edward Thomas Peirson & Sons in 1913. Peirson was a member of the first council of the ICAEW in 1880. The Market Harborough practice first occupied 44 High Street, moving to 39 High Street in 1944. In 1967 the Coventry office of Edward Thomas Peirson & Sons amalgamated with Leech, Evans & Co (est. 1923), Coventry and London, to form Leech, Peirson, Evans & Co, now part of Kidsons Impey. The Market Harborough practice became completely independent of the firm in 1971. Its name has remained unaltered since 1938. Long-standing, early clients of the firm included W Symington & Co, manufacturers of soups and table creams, and Market Harborough Land Society whose obligations were taken over by Market Harborough Building Society in 1963.

Records (1): Edward Thomas Peirson & Sons, 39 High Street, Market Harborough LE16 7NU

Partnership agreement 1960; nominal ledger incl. details of fees, 1957–84; letter from Buckingham Palace to E T Peirson expressing gratitude for his supervision of the Soldiers' and Sailors' Families Association's accounts 1916; illuminated scroll presented by the City of Coventry to E T Peirson as auditor of the Corporation 1918.

Clients: W Symington & Co Ltd: profit and loss account and balance sheet 1908 (p); letter from the company regarding its sales figures 1916 (p).

Records (2): Leicestershire Record Office, Long Street, Wigston Magna, Leicester LE8 2AH

Clients: Market Harborough Land Society: minutes 1894–1964, building committee minutes 1903–37, street committee minutes 1903–38, register of committee members 1948–63, share transfer forms book 1913–27, rules 1920, annual returns 1930–48 (w), accounts 1932–64, investors'

accounts 1912–29, 1934–64, weekly accounts for houses and investors 1955–62, ledger 1947–63, stamps cash book 1962–64, sundries cash book 1962–64, statement of borrowing power 1895, correspondence, accounts 1878–1893, 1948, 1954–61, 1964, returns 1936–37, annual balance sheet and report 1940, rules and proposed changes 1940, 1960, dissolution of the Society 1958–64, papers, accounts and property of the Society 1878–93, specifications and plans, Nelson Street offices 1950, title deeds and property papers 1819–1935, loan agreements 1930, deeds registers and correspondence 1953–62.

EDWARD THOMAS PEIRSON & SONS (Kidsons Impey)
13 Eaton Road, Coventry, West Midlands

History: Founded by Edward Thomas Peirson who started in practice in Coventry, West Midlands, in 1853. A member of the first council of the ICAEW, by 1880 Peirson was practising at 46 Jordan Well. In 1888 the firm changed its name to Edward Thomas Peirson & Son, when Sidney Thomas Peirson joined, and moved to 17 Hertford Street. The style was changed to Edward Thomas Peirson & Sons in 1912. An office was opened in Market Harborough, Leicestershire, in 1938. In 1951 the Coventry office moved to 13 Eaton Road. In 1967 this office amalgamated with Leech, Evans & Co (est. 1923), 45 Warwick Road, Coventry, and London, to form Leech, Peirson, Evans & Co. In 1988 this firm merged with Hodgson Impey, now part of Kidsons Impey. The Market Harborough firm continues to practise under the name Edward Thomas Peirson & Sons (*qv*).

Records: Coventry City Record Office, Mandela House, Bayley Lane, Coventry CV1 5RG

Ledgers: 1909–63, private 1941–63; cash books 1937–62; registers of fire policies 1904–13, 1942–50; general insurance books 1939–52; list of cash books, ledgers and papers given for salvage 1942; photograph, centenary luncheon n.d.

EDWARDS & KEEPING
Unity Chambers, 34 High East Street, Dorchester DT1 1HA

History: Alfred Rendell Edwards started practising as an accountant in *c.*1894 at 16 Cornhill, Dorchester, Dorset, having previously worked as clerk to a local solicitor. Borough treasurer of Dorchester and secretary to the Dorset Friendly Society, he was admitted to the Society of Incorporated Accountants in 1904. He was joined in 1908 by his son Alfred Harman Edwards and in 1912 the practice became Edwards & Edwards. That style was retained until 1969 when it became Edwards & Keeping. In 1983 the firm moved to its present address from 22 High East Street which it had occupied since 1924.

Records: Edwards & Keeping, Unity Chambers, 34 High East Street, Dorchester DT1 1HA

Partnership agreements 1925–date; partners' meeting minutes 1949–date; accounts 1924–date; private ledgers 1947–date; journal 1905–13; cash books 1930–date; correspondence of A R Edwards 1890–1920s; lists of clients 1950s–date; inventory, 22 High East Street 1955.

EDWIN GUTHRIE & CO (KPMG Peat Marwick)
71 King Street, Manchester, Greater Manchester

Also at London

History: The firm of Thomas, Wade & Guthrie was practising at 32 Brown Street, Manchester, Greater Manchester, in 1875, moving to 71 King Street *c.*1885. By 1887 the firm had an office at 10 Tokenhouse Yard, London. Charles Henry Wade and Edwin Guthrie were leading accountants in Manchester. In 1878 they formed the Accountants' Incorporation Association and were petitioners for the royal charter of the ICAEW in 1880 and members of its first council. In 1883 Guthrie established the first British accountancy firm in New York, USA, styled Barrow, Wade, Guthrie & Co. In 1895 Wade left the Manchester firm and Guthrie continued to practise as Edwin Guthrie & Co. In 1955 the firm merged with Peat, Marwick, Mitchell & Co (*qv*), now part of KPMG Peat Marwick.

Records: KPMG Peat Marwick, 7 Tib Lane, Manchester M2 6DS

Partnership half-yearly accounts with working papers 1911–26; sundry accounts incl. salaries lists, private ledger balances, lists of audits and fees, draft accounts 1875–1908; income tax files 1914–25; cash books: 1910–14, private 1895–1911; letter books 1875–91; list of clients 1955; staff pension scheme records 1935–*c.*1955; photograph, Edwin Guthrie *c.*1900.

M F Bywater, 'Edwin Guthrie', in David J Jeremy (ed.), *Dictionary of Business Biography*, Vol. 2 (London, Butterworth, 1984)

T A Wise, *Peat, Marwick, Mitchell & Co: 85 Years* (New York, the firm, 1982)

ELLACOTT STRANKS & CO
Beechfield House, 38 West Bar, Banbury OX16 9RX

History: Started by Geoffrey Ellacott, a sole practitioner in High Street, Banbury, Oxfordshire, from 1954 until 1957. The firm became Ellacott, Stranks & Co when H Moreton Stranks became a partner in 1963. It moved to its present address in 1970. The firm specialises in agricultural work mainly in Oxfordshire, Northamptonshire, Warwickshire, Berkshire, Buckinghamshire, Worcestershire and Gloucestershire, but also in Kent, Cornwall, Wales and Scotland.

Records: Ellacott Stranks & Co, Beechfield House, 38 West Bar, Banbury OX16 9RX

Partners' diaries incl. time charged 1965–88; time ledgers 1980–date; accounts 1954–57, 1960s–date; fees ledgers 1958–71; cash books 1962–70.

ERNEST FRANCIS & SON

Somerset House, Blagrave Street, Reading RG1 1QB

Also at Basingstoke

History: Started by Ernest Francis who was practising with Samuel Preston under the style Preston & Francis, accountants and estate agents, at 150 Friar Street, Reading, Berkshire, in 1887. From 1888 Francis carried on the practice under his own name at the same address. Following a move to 38 Friar Street in *c.*1890 the auctioneering side of the practice ceased. Francis became a member of the ICAEW in 1896. In 1921 Francis was joined in partnership by his son, Oswald, and the firm was restyled Ernest Francis & Son. The firm moved to 172 Friar Street in 1897 and subsequently to 8 The Forbury in 1934, and the present address in 1972. An office was opened in Basingstoke, Hampshire, in 1956.

Records: Ernest Francis & Son, Somerset House, Blagrave Street, Reading RG1 1QB

Partnership agreements 1928–date; accounts 1945–date; nominal ledgers 1940–date; wages books 1957–66; tenancy agreement, 8 The Forbury n.d.; articles of clerkship 1911; photograph, Samuel Preston *c.*1880.

EVERETT, CHETTLE & CO

34/36 Gray's Inn Road, London WC1X 8HR

History: Started by Ralph Marven Everett in 1903 at 18 Bishopsgate, London, and moved to Winchester House, Old Broad Street, in 1908. The style of the firm was changed to R M Everett & Co in 1921 and Everett, Chettle & Co in 1929. The firm moved to 14 Leadenhall Street in 1935 and to 35/37 Chiswell Street in 1955. In 1981 it merged with Frazer, Dargue & Co (*qv*), also of 35/37 Chiswell Street. The firm moved to its present address in 1987.

Records: Everett, Chettle & Co, 34/36 Gray's Inn Road, London WC1X 8HR

Partners' meeting minutes 1929–54; clients' ledgers 1950–date; ledgers 1976–date; journal 1969 on; cash books 1970–date.

Clients: Wm Duncumb Ltd: particulars of shares 1921–33, summary of shares and dividends 1933–41, family dividend account 1949–50; **Wilson & Whitworth Ltd**, printers and stationers: out-letter books 1892–1911, 1917–35, trading accounts and balance sheets 1898, 1907, share summary 1875–99, inventory of trade fixtures 1898.

F GEEN & CO

68 Liverpool Road, Stoke-on-Trent ST4 1BG

History: One of the oldest accounting firms in Stoke-on-Trent, Staffordshire, it was started by Frederick Geen who commenced practising as an accountant in 1884 at Glebe Buildings, having previously been employed in the audit office of the North Staffordshire Railway Co and a number of local potteries. Amongst his employees were John Sandland, who joined the practice in *c.*1888 and subsequently qualified as an incorporated accountant, and Frederick Carder, who joined in 1907 after qualifying as a chartered accountant. In 1896 Geen was admitted as a Fellow of the ICAEW and a year later he moved into the present, purpose-built, offices. Throughout his life he had extensive business connections and was also an active councillor and alderman. He was elected Mayor of the new county borough in 1911 and remained in office until 1913. Following Geen's death in 1915 the practice was purchased from his executors by his partners, Carder and Sandland, who adopted the style F Geen & Co. Carder, who was admitted to partnership in 1915, remained with the firm until 1973. During this time he had a major interest in many colliery companies and became involved in negotiations for nationalisation of the industry in 1946. In the 1930s he bought the Buildwas Park estate in Shropshire.

Records: F Geen & Co, 68 Liverpool Road, Stoke-on-Trent ST4 1BG

Partnership agreements 1915–date; partners' meeting minutes 1980–date; diaries incl. time charged 1924–51, 1972–74; assignment of share and interest in the firm 1936; accounts and working papers 1915–date; tax computations 1926–37; work-in-progress sheets 1931; list of services and fees 1949–52; ledgers: general 1941–47, private 1915–date; private cash book 1919–63; register of deeds and documents 1912–*c.*1979; registers of securities purchased and sold 1955–62; correspondence: staff matters *c.*1945–59, clients' *c.*1930–80; articles of clerkship and employment contracts 1915–71; monthly salaries books 1915–72; scrapbook of circulars and press cuttings 1958–65; photographs, partners *c.*1920–date; historical notes 1915.

Clients: Beecham's Pills Ltd: prospectus, balance sheets 1928; **J W Beswick Ltd**, pottery manufacturers: private ledgers 1906–44; **Brereton & Hayes Collieries**: balance sheets and working accounts 1881–89; **Bucknall Saw Mills Ltd**: minutes 1960–80; **Buildwas Park Estate**: deeds and tenancy agreements 1913–22, 1947–52, estate valuation 1947, sale particulars of Buildwas Abbey estate 1954, cash book 1970; **J Cadman & Co Ltd,** timber merchants: minutes, private ledger, cash book, 1944–81; **Charles Keeling Ltd**, protective clothing manufacturers: private ledgers 1942–72; **Crown Staffordshire Porcelain Co Ltd**: minutes 1923–63; **English China Clays Ltd**: prospectus, balance sheets 1931; **Madeley Collieries Ltd**: prospectus, balance sheets 1924; **J & G Meakin Ltd,** pottery manufacturers: memorandum and articles of association 1951, lists of shareholders 1955–56, abstract of accounts 1934–53, annual accounts 1952–56; **Merryhill Colliery Co Ltd**: memorandum and articles of association 1942, minutes 1942–80; **Newcastle (Staffs) Motor Co Ltd**: minutes 1946–63, photograph, premises *c.*1930; **Odhams Press Ltd:** prospectus, balance sheets 1930; **E R Poulston Ltd**, coal merchants: minutes 1947–80; **Royal Crown Derby Co**: liquidation papers and related correspondence 1930–40; **Skoda Works:** prospectus, balance sheets 1930; **Stafford Coal & Iron Co:** prospectus, balance sheets 1930; **Wesley Abbey**, Staffordshire, chemical works: particulars of sale and plans 1901–33; **Norton & Biddulph Collieries**: plan 1949.

F W POPPLEWELL & SON

48 & 50 Mosley Street, Manchester, Greater Manchester

Also at Buxton, New Mills and Southport

History: Founded by Francis Wilkinson Popplewell, a fellow of the Manchester Institute of Accountants (est. 1871), who started practising at Bridgewater Buildings, Albert Square, Manchester, Greater Manchester, in *c.*1850. By 1880 he was practising with his son, Alfred Paul, under the style F W Popplewell & Son. The firm moved to 87 Mosley Street in *c.*1887; 2 Marsden Street, Pall Mall, in 1894; 2 St James's Square in 1902; and 48 & 50 Mosley Street in 1935. The firm had offices in Stockport, Greater Manchester, 1918–20; New Mills, Derbyshire, 1920–59; Buxton, Derbyshire, 1923–59; and Southport, Merseyside, 1931–59. The firm appears to have ceased practising in 1959.

Records: Manchester Central Library, Archives Department, St Peter's Square, Manchester M2 5PD

Ledgers 1851–68; day books 1866–83; cash book 1863–68; articles of clerkship 1900; F W Popplewell's personal accounts 1905–09.

FERGUSON MAIDMENT & CO

Sardinia House, Sardinia Street, Lincoln's Inn Fields, London WC2A 3LZ

History: Founded by Alexander Fletcher Ferguson who went to Bombay, India, in 1889 as chief accountant in the merchant firm of Ritchie, Stewart

& Co. Whilst there he became a successful accountant in his own right and, in 1893, left the firm to set up in practice as A F Ferguson & Co. The firm prospered in Bombay and other Indian cities. In London it was represented for some years by Viney, Price & Goodyear (*qv*), now part of BDO Binder Hamlyn. However, Ferguson was concerned about the firm's lack of experience in Indian affairs and left India in 1912 to open an office in London at 27 Old Jewry. After being joined by one of the partners of the Indian practice in 1925 the London office adopted the name Ferguson, Gilchrist & Co and moved to 10 & 12 Walbrook, London. These offices were damaged during the blitz and the firm moved temporarily to 6a Sun Street, Hitchin, Hertfordshire. More permanent accommodation was found after the Second World War at 27 Old Broad Street, London. In 1954 the London office became known as Ferguson, Rowland & Davies and shortly after moved to Bush Lane House, Cannon Street, London. In 1981 the UK firm merged with Maidment & Co (formerly part of Maidment, Penney, Quick & Co) and its name changed to Ferguson, Maidment & Co. At the same time it moved to its present address.

Records: Ferguson Maidment & Co, Sardinia House, Sardinia Street, Lincoln's Inn Fields, London WC2A 3LZ

Partnership agreements 1929, 1981–date; partners' meeting minutes 1981–date; private ledgers 1981–date; journals 1981–date; cash books 1981–date; reminiscences of A F Ferguson 1941.

Clients: Oriental Gas Co Ltd, Calcutta: minute book 1854–78, journal 1911–86.

Anon., *A F Ferguson & Co, Chartered Accountants, India: History of the Firm* (Unpub., *c.*1965)

FINNIE, ROSS, WELCH & CO (Stoy Hayward)

Petershill House, 31 St Paul's Churchyard, London

Also at Glasgow and Leeds

History: Formed in 1936 as a result of the merger between the Scottish firm Finnie, Ross & Co and George Morris, Welch & Co (est. 1891), London. Finnie, Ross, Welch & Co merged with Franklin, Wild & Co (*qv*) in 1974 to form Finnie, Ross, Wild & Co. In 1984 this firm became part of Finnie & Co, now part of Stoy Hayward.

Records: Stoy Hayward, 8 Baker Street, London W1M 1DA

Partners' meeting minutes 1940–74; accounts 1946–74.

FORRESTER BOYD

26 South St Mary's Gate, Grimsby DN31 1LW

Also at Louth and Scunthorpe

History: Formed in 1935 through the merger of Robson Boyd (est. 1910) and Forrester & Forrester (est. 1900), both of Grimsby, Humberside. The firm has occupied its present offices since 1935. Over the years it has merged with a number of local practices, including: W Munro & Co in 1962; Cross & Co in 1972; and Kirmans & Co, Grimsby and Louth, Lincolnshire, and Wm E Stockwood & Co in 1991.

Records: Forrester Boyd, 26 South St Mary's Gate, Grimsby DN31 1LW

Partnership accounts 1935–date; private ledgers 1935–date; private cash books 1965–date.

FRANCIS CLARK

23 Devon Square, Newton Abbot TQ12 2HU

Also at Exeter, Plymouth, Tavistock and Torquay

History: The practice began in 1919 when Francis S Clark opened an office at 1A Union Street, Newton Abbot, Devon, after returning from Salisbury, Southern Rhodesia (Zimbabwe), where he had been practising as a certified accountant. By the time he was joined by Francis Cundy in 1937 his office had moved to 67A Queen Street, Newton Abbot. A separate farm accounts department was set up in 1942. After Francis Clark's retirement in 1946, Francis Cundy was joined by Stanley Kennard, who had acquired some offices in Newton Abbot to continue his London practice during the war. An office was opened in Alphington Street, Exeter, Devon, in 1955 and in 1965 the Newton Abbot office moved to the present premises in Devon Square. Offices were opened at 138 Union Street, Torquay, Devon, in 1968 and 8–10 Whimple Street, Plymouth, Devon, in 1981. In 1979 the firm formed an association with Pannell Fitzpatrick & Co, now Pannell Kerr Forster, which lasted until 1987. It practised under that firm's name until 1985 when it reverted to the name Francis Clark. In 1986 the firm merged with two West Devon practices: Robins (est. 1946), Tavistock (Russell Street) and Plymouth (6 The Crescent) and Rice, Nancarrow & Co (est. 1984), Plymouth (Houndiscombe Road) and Saltash (73 Fore Street). The Torquay office moved to 58 The Terrace in 1976 and the Houndiscombe Road premises replaced 8–10 Whimple Street as the Plymouth office of Francis Clark in 1986.

Records: Francis Clark, 23 Devon Square, Newton Abbot, Devon TQ12 2HU

Partners' meeting minutes 1953–date; accounts 1937–date; fees ledger 1925–31.

FRANCIS NICHOLLS WHITE & CO (Booth White)
73 Cheapside, London

History: Originated *c.* 1858 as Robinson, Nicholls & Co of 13 Old Jewry, London. In 1863 the name was changed to Francis Nicholls & Co; in 1866 to Nicholls & Leatherdale; and in 1885 to Francis Nicholls White & Co. From its beginnings, the firm practised as accountants dealing mainly with insolvency matters; it also acted as proprietors of a debt collection business known as the British Mercantile Agency (est. 1855) and of a number of trade associations formed as specialised branches of the Agency. The practice continued at premises at 13/14 Old Jewry Chambers until 1924 when it moved to 73 Cheapside. In 1954 it moved to 19 Eastcheap. In 1967 the firm amalgamated with Parkin S Booth & Co (*qv*), insolvency accountants, Liverpool, Merseyside, and London and became Booth White & Co, now Booth White (*qv*). The Liverpool office continued to practise under the name Parkin S Booth & Co.

Records: Guildhall Library, Aldermanbury, London EC2P 2EJ

Audit charges book 1899–1931; private ledgers 1868–88, 1932–55; private journal 1899–1912; details of annual net profit and distribution of drawings 1904–17; list of clients and fees n.d.; staff record book 1911–49.

Clients: BMA Ltd: ledger *c.* 1922–32, membership information booklets 1915; **Cooper Craig's Ltd**, drapery trade protection office: debt information slips 1910–38, cash payments book (incl. BMA Ltd) 1933–68, membership information booklets *c.* 1925; **Cricene Co**, Regent Street, London: liquidation record book 1920; **Alfred Gerrard & Charles Wm Birch,** chemists: partnership agreement 1898; **Monger & Marchant Ltd**, Cheney Lane, London: liquidation record book 1934; **Paper Trade Protection Association**: Trade Advisory Committee minutes 1922–32, membership information booklets 1915; **E F Suckling**, chemist, Linton, Cambridge: liquidation record book 1919–21; **Wholesale Chemists, Druggists & Allied Traders' Association**: Trade Advisory Committee minutes 1925–39, membership information booklets *c.* 1925.

FRANK BOOTH (Booth Ainsworth)
Midland Bank Chambers, Ashfield Road, Cheadle, Greater Manchester

History: Started by Frank Booth at Midland Bank Chambers, Ashfield Road, Cheadle, Greater Manchester, in 1934. This practice amalgamated with Booth Ainsworth & Co, now Booth Ainsworth (*qv*), in 1959.

Records: Booth Ainsworth, Ashfield House, 12 Ashfield Road, Cheadle SK8 1BE

Ledger 1935–56; cash books 1934–56.

FRANK C BEVAN & CO (Bevan & Buckland)
Albion Chambers, Cambrian Place, Swansea, West Glamorgan

History: Founded by Frank Cecil Bevan who set up in practice at Post Office Chambers, 9 Wind Street, Swansea, West Glamorgan, in 1902. The practice was restyled Frank C Bevan & Co in 1921. It moved from Wind Street to Metropolitan Bank Chambers, Castle Square, in 1908; to 62 & 63 Exchange Buildings in 1914; and to Albion Chambers, Cambrian Place, in 1979. The firm amalgamated with Sidney H Buckland & Son in 1985, following which it was restyled Frank C Bevan & Buckland, and with two partners of Pritchard, Read & Co (*qv*) in 1988. The firm's name was changed to Bevan & Buckland in 1989. Early clients of the firm included ironmongery businesses, shipping and coal exporting agencies, and a number of colliery companies and landed estates.

Records: Bevan & Buckland, Russell House, 31 Russell Street, Swansea SA1 4HR

Time record book 1945–50.

FRANKLIN, WILD & CO (Stoy Hayward)
Regent Arcade House, 19–25 Argyll Street, London

History: Founded by George Franklin who started practising in Sheffield, South Yorkshire, in 1871. In 1880 he was in practice at 187 Norfolk Street ,moving to Imperial Chambers, Norfolk Row, in *c*.1888. In 1890 the style of the firm was changed to Franklin, Wild & Co. An office opened in London at 14/15 Broad Street Avenue in *c*.1890, which became a separate practice in the 1890s. The firm moved to 5, 6 & 7 Broad Street Avenue in 1893; 22 & 23 Broad Street Avenue in 1895; 22–28 Broad Street Avenue in 1909; 42–45 New Broad Street in 1922; and 19–25 Argyll Street in 1964. In 1974 Franklin, Wild & Co merged with Finnie, Ross, Welch & Co (*qv*), London, Glasgow, Strathclyde, and Leeds, West Yorkshire, to form Finnie, Ross, Wild & Co. In 1984, through a series of mergers, this firm became part of Finnie & Co, now part of Stoy Hayward.

Records (1): Stoy Hayward, 1a The Old Yard, Rectory Lane, Brasted, Westerham TN16 1JP

Partnership accounts book 1911–17; fees: ledgers 1905–31, journals 1946–73; bill books 1958–66; ledgers: 1891–1910, nominal 1905–51; journals 1891–1906, 1940–69; cash books: 1919–34, 1947–73, petty 1921–24, 1927; out-letter book 1934.

Records (2): Stoy Hayward, Kreston House, 8 Gate Street, London WC2A 3HJ

Bill book 1951–55.

FRAZER, DARGUE & CO (Everett, Chettle & Co)
35/37 Chiswell Street, London

History: Reginald Frederick Frazer set up in practice at 51 Evered Avenue, Rice Lane, Liverpool, Merseyside, in 1915. By 1918 he was practising at 19–20 Central Buildings, 41 North John Street, Liverpool, under the name R F Frazer & Co. In 1927 an office was opened in London at Bank House, 28 Broadway, Stratford, London. T W Dargue became a partner in the same year. In 1931 the Stratford office was renamed Frazer, Dargue & Co, the Liverpool office remaining as R F Frazer & Co. The London firm moved to 35/37 Chiswell Street in 1973 and merged with Everett, Chettle & Co (*qv*) of the same address in 1981.

Records: Everett, Chettle & Co, 34/36 Gray's Inn Road, London WC1X 8HR

Partnership agreements: 1952, 1957; draft dissolution 1957; general ledgers 1927–57; cash received book incl. journal and fees rendered 1927–71; cash books 1957–85; annual accounts summary 1929–51; tenancy agreement, licence to let, 28 Broadway 1931, 1958.

FRAZER, WHITING & CO (Littlejohn Frazer)
City Gate House, Finsbury Square, London

Also at Romford and Southend-on-Sea

History: Founded as Frazer, Bowman & Co in 1925 and subsequently renamed Frazer, Bowman, Wilson & Co in 1931 and Frazer, Whiting & Co in *c.*1945. The firm's first office was at 271–273 Oxford Street, London. It moved to Botolph Chambers, 119 Bishopsgate, in *c.*1933; 126 Bishopsgate in *c.*1945; and City Gate House, Finsbury Square, in 1970. Offices were opened in Romford, Essex, in *c.*1945 and Southend-on-Sea, Essex, in 1963. In 1986 Frazer, Whiting & Co amalgamated with the London firm Littlejohn de Paula, comprising R J Jeffreys (est. 1908), London, and Littlejohn, Wilson, McKnight & Co (*qv*), to form Littlejohn Frazer.

Records: Littlejohn Frazer, 1 Park Place, Canary Wharf, London E14 4HJ

Partnership agreement 1930; statements of accounts 1951, 1963 incl. working papers; copy income tax returns 1927–47; private ledgers, London office 1940–53, 1948–58.

FREEMAN, BREAM & CO (KPMG Peat Marwick)
Bank Chambers, Town Hall Square, Leicester, Leicestershire

History: Originated as Wilshere, Gimson & Co which was practising at 1 Welford Place, Leicester, Leicestershire, by *c.*1907. The partnership combined stockbroking with accountancy. Before the First World War,

Wilshere left and Gimson practised alone until 1918 when he sold the practice to Herbert William Driver and it was restyled Driver & Co. Freeman was taken into partnership in 1925. By this time the firm had moved to Town Hall Square. In 1926 the partnership was dissolved. Freeman took over the majority of the client list and took into partnership Clifford Bream, when the firm was renamed Freeman, Bream & Co. In 1967 the firm merged with Wykes & Co (est. 1859), Leicester, and Peat, Marwick, Mitchell & Co (*qv*), now part of KPMG Peat Marwick. Clients of the firm included Alfred Herbert Ltd, machine tool manufacturers, Faire Brothers Ltd, elastic manufacturers, and Chilprufe Ltd, clothing manufacturers.

Records: KPMG Peat Marwick, Peat House, 1 Waterloo Way, Leicester LE1 6LP

Partnership agreements: 1918, 1925, 1964, dissolution 1926; papers and correspondence, mergers with Wykes & Co and Peat, Marwick, Mitchell & Co 1964–68; accounts 1961–68; tax files 1961–67; fees journal 1965–67; private ledger 1946–69; cash book 1961–69.

GANE JACKSON SCOTT

62 Doughty Street, London WC1N 2LQ

History: Founded by Herbert Jackson who in 1867 left Deloitte, Dever, Hollebone & Co, later part of Coopers & Lybrand (*qv*), where he had been a senior clerk, to set up a practice in Basinghall Street, London. He was joined three years later by another clerk from Deloitte's, John Gane, with whom he started to practise in an office at 53 Coleman Street, London, under the name of Gane, Jackson & Co. In 1896, the firm, by then known as Gane, Jackson, Jeffreys & Wells, moved to 66 Coleman Street, London. John Gane became president of the ICAEW in 1905 and George Robert Freeman, who became a partner in 1903, was made president in 1925. The name Gane, Jackson, Jeffreys & Freeman was retained until 1963 when the firm amalgamated with Newport, Nelson & Co, 79 Bishopsgate, London, and became Gane, Jackson, Nelson & Freeman. In 1973, shortly after its merger with W T Walton & Son, the firm moved from City-Gate House, Finsbury Square, London, which it had occupied since 1952, to 55/59 Saffron Hill, London. It remained there until 1980 when it moved to the present address. The name Gane Jackson Scott was adopted in 1985.

Records: Gane Jackson Scott, 62 Doughty Street, London WC1N 2LQ

Private ledgers 1959–date; cash book 1956–date; staff rules 1909; photograph, George Robert Freeman 1925.

Clients: Becos Traders Ltd, Russia and Siberia: minute books 1915–91, directors' attendance book 1914–37, register of members and share ledger 1929–86, share transfer forms 1915–87, private ledger 1916–20.

GEO LITTLE, SEBIRE & CO

The Grove, Pipers Lane, Harpenden AL5 1AH

Also at Enfield and London

History: Founded by George Little who set up in practice in Moorgate, London, in 1904. In 1925 Geo Little, Sebire & Co was formed when Little took Charles Berisford Sebire into partnership. The offices in Moorgate were destroyed by enemy action in 1940. The firm then moved to Adelaide House, London Bridge, where it remained for thirty years. The London office at present occupies 26/28 Bartholomew Square. Offices were opened in St Albans, Hertfordshire, in 1926 and Edmonton, London, in 1949. Following expansion of the practice, larger offices were taken at Harpenden, Hertfordshire, in 1987. The Edmonton office moved to Enfield, London, in 1975.

Records: Geo. Little, Sebire & Co, 3 Cecil Court, London Road, Enfield EN2 6DL

Fees: book 1924–*c.* 1930, summary 1954–64; private ledgers 1950s–date; salaries books: monthly (Enfield) 1950–65, weekly (London) 1920s–30s; leases, 1950, 1953; photographs: George Little n.d., Charles B Sebire n.d; historical notes n.d.

GILCHRIST, TASH

Cleveland Buildings, Queens Square, Middlesbrough TS2 1PA

History: Founded in the 1870s by John Gilchrist who, by 1880, was practising at Exchange Place, Middlesbrough, Cleveland. The firm became Gilchrist & Tash in 1894 and Gilchrist, Tash & Wilson in 1922. In 1930 the firm amalgamated with the Middlesbrough firm Monkhouse, Sansom & Co and its associated office Sansom, Bell & Co, Darlington, County Durham. The Darlington office retained the name Sansom, Bell & Co whilst the Middlesbrough office was restyled Gilchrist, Tash, Wilson & Sansom. The firm moved from Exchange Place to 29 Wilson Street in 1910; Court Chambers, 17 Albert Road, in 1930; and Cleveland Buildings, Queens Square, in 1960. The firm was restyled Gilchrist, Tash in 1989.

Records: Gilchrist, Tash, Cleveland Buildings, Queens Square, Middlesbrough TS2 1PA

Partnership agreements: 1922, 1932, 1950, drafts 1955–date; accounts 1920–23, 1932–66, incl. working papers 1945–60; cash books 1971–79; correspondence: income tax 1947–53, staff pension scheme 1951; plans, Cleveland Buildings 1949, 1964.

GLOVER & CO
15 Netherhall Road, Doncaster DN1 2PH

History: Founded by Joseph Horner Glover, an incorporated accountant, in 1886. He set up offices at 6 Priory Place, Doncaster, South Yorkshire, in 1886 and around the same time acquired an office at 4 King Street, Wakefield, West Yorkshire. In 1894 he entered into partnership with George William Townend of Goole, Humberside, as Townend & Glover and, a year later, purchased part of the Goole practice at Carlisle Chambers, Carlisle Street. In 1910 this partnership was dissolved. Townend took the Goole office and Glover the Doncaster office, which he carried on as a sole practitioner until he retired in 1922. In 1923 the practice was purchased by Frederick Mills and Allan Greasby. Branch offices were opened in Stanhope House, Park Lane, London, in 1929 (closed 1932), and at 167 High Street, Scunthorpe, Humberside, in 1930. In 1944 the firm was reorganised; the Wakefield office became F W T Mills & Co and the Doncaster office, Glover & Co; the Scunthorpe office was sold to its branch manager in 1950. Glover & Co moved to 18 Priory Place, Doncaster, in 1950 and to 15 Netherhall Road in 1988.

Records: Glover & Co, 15 Netherhall Road, Doncaster DN1 2PH

Partnership agreements 1895–date; accounts 1895–1910, 1923–51, 1957–date; ledger 1884–1905; cash books: 1924–73, private 1944–46.

Clients: Stapleforth & Co: audit notebook, working papers, report, correspondence, bill 1898–99.

GOODMAN, MYERS, SMITH & CO (Comins & Co)
Roxburgh House, Regent Street, London

History: The firm was started in 1960 by Ellis Goodman who practised under his own name until 1962 when he was joined by Lawrence Myers. The firm styled Goodman, Myers & Co occupied 47 Albemarle Street, London, between 1962 and 1965. It then moved to Roxburgh House in Regent Street. The firm became Goodman, Myers, Smith & Co in 1969. In 1978 it amalgamated with Charles Comins & Co, now Comins & Co (*qv*), bringing to the new firm many clients from the entertainment business.

Records: Comins & Co, 22 St Andrew Street, London EC4A 3AN

Partnership agreements 1971–75; time ledger 1975–78; accounts 1967–68; fees day books 1964–69, 1978–79; private ledgers 1960–78; cash books 1962–67; expenses day book 1965–68; correspondence, Roxburgh House 1966–79; staff records 1966–78; salaries book 1973–78.

GRACE, DARBYSHIRE & TODD
19 Whiteladies Road, Bristol, Avon

History: Started by John Moxham, a Quaker, who set up in practice at 5 Exchange Buildings, Bristol, Avon, in 1818. He subsequently moved to 50 Broad Street in 1831, 35 Queens Square in 1832, and Bank Court, Corn Street, in 1834. In 1857 his practice was acquired by James Grace and James Grace, junior, who were also Quakers, and was carried on under the name James Grace & Son at Shannon Court, Corn Street. In 1861 the firm was restyled James & Henry Grace when James, junior, and his brother, Henry, took over the practice. This name was retained until 1920. In 1861 the firm moved to Bank Court, Corn Street, and in 1892 to 24 Clare Street. Between 1900 and 1914 it had an office at 34 Great St Helens, London. Members of the Grace family carried on the practice until 1920 when Gerald F Todd joined the firm, bringing his own practice into it, and Philip Darbyshire was also taken into the partnership. The name was then changed to Grace, Darbyshire & Todd. The firm moved to 6 Bridge Street in 1921, 41 Corn Street in 1930, and 19 Whiteladies Road in 1947. Early clients of the firm included: Bristol & Exeter Railway Co, Bristol United Gas Light Co, Bristol Waterworks, the Friends Provident Institution, the Trustees of *The Friend* (Joseph Storrs Fry, George Cadbury and Joseph Rowntree) and the City of Bristol. From the early days the firm has specialised in the area of investment and financial services and executorship and trusteeship work based on its Quaker connections in the west of England. In 1962 the Tyndall Funds were formed by the partnership as authorised unit trusts to provide managed investment for trust and client portfolios and later generally offered to the public. Gateway Supermarkets Ltd was another business created from a trust investment developed and managed by the partnership. In 1967 the firm merged with the Bristol firm C J Ryland & Co (*qv*) and became Grace, Ryland & Co. In 1969 the general practice of this firm was sold to Thomson McLintock & Co (*qv*), now part of KPMG Peat Marwick. The financial practice, including the management of the Tyndall Funds and Gateway Securities Ltd (Gateway Supermarkets), was absorbed by The West of England Trust Ltd, a private investment company which had a long association with the firm.

Records: The West of England Trust Ltd, 21 St Thomas Street, Bristol BS1 6JS (enquiries to H G M Leighton, FCA)

Partnership agreements: 1946–51, dissolution 1901; partners' meeting minutes 1895–1954; management meeting minutes 1965; notes, extension of partnership 1939; time record books 1864–94; account book 1857–58; fees record book 1859–63; private ledger 1860–74; 'dissected cash book' incl. capital account, private ledger special account, profit and loss accounts 1870–74; general ledger balances 1867–69; private ledger: transfers from trade expenses 1868, balances 1869–70; letter books 1858–1910; correspondence: staff outing 1911, time sheets, audit files 1925, partnership matters 1949–53, management meetings 1965–66; appointments as auditors *c.*1890–1946; office rules 1912, 1923; partners' personnel files 1940–60; staff bonus scheme papers 1950; office: manual 1926, inventory *c.*1950; paper on coal mine accounts, presented by Henry Ernest Grace to Bristol Chartered Accountants Students' Society 1898; personal and family papers incl. death certificate of James Grace, senior, 1858, marriage settlement of James Grace, junior, 1859, copy birth and marriage certificates of John Moxham n.d., James Edward Grace's arithmetic and note books 1884, *c.*1890; circulars, partnership changes 1857–1955; press cuttings, Grace partners 1892–1956; photographs: partners *c.*1855–90, 1957–60s, staff outings 1891, 1903, 1911.

Clients: Bristol & West Gloucestershire Building Society: liquidation papers 1885; **Joseph Storrs Fry**: will 1913; **Elizabeth Webster**: estate ledger 1874–75.

Anon., *A Short History of Grace, Darbyshire and Todd, Chartered Accountants of Bristol, 1818–1957* (Bristol, the firm, 1957)

Anon., *The Pedigree of Tyndall over 150 years, 1818–1974* (Bristol, The West of England Trust Ltd, 1974)

GRANT THORNTON

Grant Thornton House, Melton Street, Euston Square, London NW1 2EP

Also at Aylesbury, Banbury, Bath, Bedford, Birmingham, Bournemouth, Bradford, Brighton, Bristol, Bury St Edmonds, Cardiff, Cheltenham, Cleckheaton, Clydebank, Corby, Coventry, Crawley, Edinburgh, Glasgow, High Wycombe, Ipswich, Leeds, Leicester, Liverpool, Luton, Manchester, Milton Keynes, Newcastle upon Tyne, Northampton, Nottingham, Oxford, Petersfield, Plymouth, Poole, Portsmouth, Rushden, Ryde, Sheffield, Southampton, Warrington, Wellingborough, West London (Ealing), Witney and Worthing

History: Formed in July 1959 as Thornton Baker & Co and subsequently renamed Thornton Baker in 1978 and Grant Thornton in 1986. Thornton Baker & Co was the result of a merger between Thornton & Thornton (*qv*), London and Oxford, Oxfordshire, and Baker & Co (est. 1868), Leicester, Leicestershire, Bedford, Bedfordshire, Coventry, West Midlands, London, Northampton, Northamptonshire, Nuneaton, Warwickshire, Rushden, Northamptonshire, Spalding, Lincolnshire, and Wellingborough, Northamptonshire. Following the 1959 merger, Thornton Baker & Co expanded and established offices in every major city in the UK. The firm developed differently from other large firms, growing to become a national firm through amalgamations with many leading, often long-established, firms in the provinces and only acquiring a central London base in the 1960s. Thornton Baker & Co's constitution of 1964 defined the firm as 'a consortium of firms practising under the Thornton Baker name'. In the 1960s, thirty-four firms joined the consortium, including: Edmonds & Co (est. 1850s), Eastbourne and Brighton, East Sussex (1961); Percy Stembridge & Co, Birmingham, West Midlands (1961); Pettitt Madox, Portsmouth, Hampshire (1962); E M Owen and Bryce Hanmer, Liverpool, Merseyside (1962); Camm Metcalfe Best and Joshua Wortley, Sheffield, South Yorkshire (1962); Whitfield & Co, Leeds, West Yorkshire (1963); W Bolton & Co and Walton Watts & Co, Manchester, Greater Manchester (1963); Bolton Wawn, Newcastle upon Tyne, Tyne and Wear (1963); Henderson, Griffiths, Cardiff, South Glamorgan (1965); Williamson, Butterfield & Roberts, Bradford, West Yorkshire (1965); Baker Owen, Bristol, Avon (1965); Cattell & Chater, Kettering, Northamptonshire (1966); T G Shuttleworth & Son (est. pre-1880), Sheffield (1966); Clayton, Baker, Lickiss & Smith, Bournemouth, Dorset (1968); and Reynolds McCarran, Dublin, Eire (1969). In London, the firm's small City and West End offices were brought together in Lee House, London Wall, in 1962. After 1970, there were eighteen further mergers, including those with Martin, Currie & Scott, Edinburgh, Lothian (1971); Kidston, Jackson McBain (est. 1844), Glasgow, Strathclyde (1975); Jolliffe Cork & Co (est. 1896), London, Birmingham, West Midlands, Croydon, Surrey, Manchester, Greater Manchester, Southampton, Hampshire, Wakefield, West Yorkshire, and Watford, Hertfordshire; and Waugh Haines Rigby & Co, Cheltenham, Gloucestershire (1986). The firm became Grant Thornton in 1986, following a link with Alexander Grant in the USA. At the same time the firm became a founder member of the world-wide firm Grant Thornton International. The London office moved into Grant Thornton House in 1987. Arthur Green (formerly of Bryce Hanmer) was president of the ICAEW 1987–88 and Michael Lickiss (formerly of Clayton, Baker, Lickiss & Smith) was president 1990–91.

Records (1): Grant Thornton, Grant Thornton House, Melton Street, Euston Square, London NW1 2EP

Partnership agreements 1959–date; equity partners', council, policy board and executive meeting minutes 1959–date; international agreements and papers 1976–date; papers: mergers 1971–86, bids for client work 1971–date; time records 1971–date; fees records 1971–date; other financial records 1971–date; staff records 1971–date; title deeds, leases, plans of offices 1959–date; photographs, London office 1987–date.

Records (2): Grant Thornton, 1 Westminster Way, Oxford OX2 0PZ

Partners' meeting minutes: 1959, Oxford office 1965–85; partnership agreements, Oxford, Leicester, London, Birmingham and Bedford groups 1960; Oxford group: partnership papers 1965–79, analyses of fees 1970–74, accounts and working papers 1959–68, private ledger sheets 1959–66; private cash books 1959–67; leases and tenancy agreements, 9 King Edward Street 1959–75; copy schedules of branch fees 1925–59; history papers 1962–74; partners' reminiscences *c*.1965.

Records (3): East Sussex Record Office, The Maltings, Castle Precincts, Lewes BN7 1YT

Clients: Queens Hotel Brighton Ltd: ledgers 1927–47, 1952–55; cash book 1943–48; hotel receipt book 1973–45

Peter Boys, 'What's in a Name – Firms' Simplified Family Trees: Grant Thornton', *Accountancy*, Vol. 103, No. 1150 (June 1989), p. 98

Peter Hubbard, *Grant Thornton – A Brief History* (Unpub., 1991)

HALLIDAY, PEARSON & CO (Hallidays)

11 Spring Gardens, Manchester

History: Founded by James Halliday, in Manchester, Greater Manchester, in 1877 following the dissolution of his partnership with William Welch Deloitte, founder of the London firm Deloitte, Dever, Griffiths & Co, which became part of Deloitte Haskins & Sells (*qv*). By 1880, Halliday's firm, Halliday, Pearson & Co, was in practice at 20 Booth Street, Manchester, and subsequently moved to District Bank Chambers, 13 Spring Gardens, in 1893, and 11 Spring Gardens in 1920. In 1970 the firm amalgamated with Lysons, Haworth & Sankey (*qv*), although both firms continued to practise under their separate names. The combined firm amalgamated with Crofts & Naylor, 30 Spring Gardens, Manchester, in 1972, to form Hallidays.

Records: Hallidays, Harvester House, 37 Peter Street, Manchester M2 5QD

Partnership dissolution agreement (James Halliday and William Welch Deloitte) 1877; time ledger 1944–49; fees ledgers 1940–72; fees journal 1963–69; clients' disbursements books 1952–80; nominal ledger 1957–73; cash book 1966–77; trust cash book 1958–76; weekly wages books 1960–69.

Clients: Thomas Porter Trust: minutes 1893; **British Constructional Steelwork Association Ltd**: minutes 1906–date.

HARDCASTLE BURTON

Amwell House, 19 Amwell Street, Hoddesdon EN11 8TS

Also at Newmarket, Northwood, Redbourn and Royston

History: Founded by Beevor de Vic Hardcastle and Frederick William Burton who set up in practice in 1921, under the style B de V Hardcastle Burton & Co, at 15 New Broad Street, London. The London office occupied 15 New Broad Street 1921–23; Coventry House, South Place, 1923–79; Compter House, 4/9 Wood Street, 1979–80; and Beaver House, 5 Plough Place, New Fetter Place, 1980–82. In 1982 the firm's head office was moved to Amwell House, Hoddesdon, Hertfordshire. Offices were opened in Northwood, London, in 1921; Birchington, Kent, in 1955; Royston, Hertfordshire, in 1965; and, to meet the increase in the firm's farming and horse-connected clientele, in Newmarket, Suffolk, in 1988. The firm's name was changed to Hardcastle Burton in 1973.

Records: Hardcastle Burton, Amwell House, 19 Amwell Street, Hoddesdon EN11 8TS

Partnership agreements 1908–date; accounts: 1958–91, Royston 1965–73, Northwood 1958–78; private ledger 1921–57; staff register and wages book 1921–57; wages records, Northwood 1958–78; office leases 1923–52.

HARPER BROOM & CO (Harper Broom Roberts)

Beacon House, 113 Kingsway, London

Also at Maidenhead

History: Founded in March 1895 by J Payne and F C Harper, incorporated accountants, at 27 Chancery Lane, London, and renamed Harper & Broom in 1904 and Harper Broom & Co in 1948. The firm moved to 3/4 Clements Inn in 1928 and to Beacon House, Kingsway, in 1972. The first office in Maidenhead, Berkshire, opened at 2 York Road in 1977. In 1978 the firm merged with Fincham, Roberts & Co (est. *c.*1900), London, to form Harper Broom Roberts.

Records: Harper Broom Roberts, Data House, St Ives Road, Maidenhead SL6 1QS

Private ledgers 1952–79; photographs: partners *c.*1916, *c.*1940, Clements Inn *c.*1900.

HASWELL BROTHERS & CO

St John's Chambers, Love Street, Chester CH1 1QN

Also at Wrexham

History: Founded by George Haswell at 84 Foregate Street, Chester, Cheshire, in 1857 and subsequently renamed George Haswell & Sons in 1878; Haswell Brothers in 1890; and Haswell Brothers & Co in 1960. The practice moved to its present address in 1888. In 1902 an office was opened at 51 King Street, Wrexham, Clwyd, which acted for a number of coalmines and steelworks in the area.

Records (1): Haswell Brothers & Co, St John's Chambers, Love Street, Chester CH1 1QN

Time ledger 1947–61; fees ledgers 1942–68; clients' disbursements book 1961–67; ledgers: 1888–1924, nominal 1924–36, private 1919–40; journals 1912–53; cash books 1898–1960; copy reports on companies' accounts 1857–1926.

Records (2): National Library of Wales, Department of Manuscripts and Records, Aberystwyth SY23 3BU

In-letter books 1906–12, 1915–19; copy letters, North Wales Employers' Mutual Indemnity Co Ltd 1914–20.

HAWSONS

Pegasus House, 463a Glossop Road, Sheffield S10 2QD

Also at Doncaster and Northampton

History: Formed in 1963 as Hawson, Wing and Hubert Smith following the merger of W G Hawson, Wing & Co (*qv*) and Hubert Smith & Co (*qv*). The firm was renamed Hawson & Co in 1970 and Hawsons in 1988. It occupied Hartshead Chambers, Sheffield, South Yorkshire, before moving to its present address in 1971. Offices were established by merger in Northampton, Northamptonshire, in 1986 and Doncaster, South Yorkshire, in 1990.

Records: Hawsons, Pegasus House, 463a Glossop Road, Sheffield S10 2QD

Partnership accounts 1964–66; tax files 1964–65; bills and costings summaries 1969–81; cash books: 1963–71, private 1963–79.

HAYHOW & CO

19 King Street, King's Lynn PE30 1HB

History: Originated as the King's Lynn office of the Norwich, Norfolk, firm Harper-Smith, Hayhow & Co, incorporated accountants, founded by Harry Harper Smith and Harold Ernest Smith as Harper Smiths in 1915. Geoffrey Hayhow became a clerk to the firm, when it was at 23 Tuesday Market Place, King's Lynn, Norfolk, in 1921. He was admitted as a partner in 1928, when the King's Lynn office was at Purdy's Court, 84a High Street, and the name of the firm was changed to Harper, Smith, Hayhow & Co. In *c.*1945, Hayhow broke away from the firm and continued the practice in King's Lynn as Hayhow & Co. The firm moved to 19 King Street in 1951.

Records: Hayhow & Co, 19 King Street, King's Lynn PE30 1HB

Partnership accounts 1950s–date; cash books 1949–date; list of debtors 1957; copy letters to bank 1926–69

Clients: Hunstanton Pier Co: register of shareholders and transfers 1895–1942, share certificates 1899 on, ledgers 1908–62; **Roland Dennis Ltd**, farmers: minutes 1932–date.

HILL VELLACOTT (Chantrey Vellacott)
21 Whitefriars Street, London

Also at Birmingham, Canterbury, Croydon, Deal, Leicester and Northampton

History: The origin of the firm can be traced back to Edward Thomas Jones, author of *English System of Book-keeping* (1796). Jones completed his training as an accountant with a Bristol, Avon, merchant in 1788, but then abandoned his accounting ambitions in favour of a coal-mining venture in Monmouth, Gwent, financed by the publication of his book. The mining scheme subsequently ran into serious difficulties and Jones returned to Bristol in 1810 to set up as a coalmerchant. In 1821 he resumed his original profession, moving to London where he remained until his death in 1833. The practice was then continued by his son, Theodore. In 1846 Theodore took into partnership his nephew, Theodore Brooke Jones, and, in 1867, Arthur James Hill. Theodore Brooke Jones moved to Harrogate, North Yorkshire, in 1870 and opened offices in Leeds, West Yorkshire, known as Theodore B Jones & Co, and in Manchester, Greater Manchester, known as Jones Crewdson & Co. Both of these eventually became part of Spicer & Pegler, a predecessor firm of Touche Ross & Co. In 1878 the three offices split into separate partnerships, the London firm adopting the style Theodore Jones, Hill & Co of which William Edward Vellacott, articled to the firm since 1869, became a partner. The firm's name was changed to Theodore Jones, Hill, Vellacott & Co in 1884 and to Arthur J Hill, Vellacott & Co in 1888. By the beginning of the First World War, other offices had been opened in Belfast, Northern Ireland (1877), Cambridge, Cambridgeshire, and Northampton, Northamptonshire. The name of the firm was shortened to Hill, Vellacott & Co in 1927. In 1923 there were mergers with Hillyer & Hillyer in London and the Deal, Kent, practice of Powell, Hillyer & Co. A further merger, with Rabbidge, Sons and Hillyer, London, took place in 1935. One of the partners, Lancelot Hill, was twice president of the ICAEW, in 1931 and 1933. The firm underwent further mergers: with Gowar, Ashby & Barnsdale (London and Maidenhead, Berkshire), Goddard, Mellersh & Lepine (London and Guildford, Surrey) and Greenslade & Co (London and Northampton) in 1967; Allen, Baldry, Holman & Best (London and Guildford) in 1975; H H Sherwood & Co (Birmingham, West Midlands) in 1985; and Chantrey Wood King (formed by the 1984 merger of Chantrey, Button & Co (*qv*) and Wood, King & Co) in 1988. After this merger the name Chantrey Vellacott was adopted. The London office occupied 3 Chapel Place, Poultry (1821–23); 8 Old Jewry

(1824); 8 Coleman Street (1825–39); 24 City Road (1839–44); 34 Nicholas Lane (1845); 17 Clements Lane (1846–61); 8 Moorgate (1861–71); 1 Finsbury Circus (1871–1914); 2 Broad Street Place (1914–26); Finsbury Circus House, Blomfield Street (1926–46); 33 & 34 Chancery Lane (1946–66); and 6 Salisbury Square (1967–69). The firm's offices in Finsbury Circus House were damaged by floods following bomb damage in May 1941, at which time many of the firm's early records were destroyed. Offices were acquired in Croydon, Surrey, and Leicester, Leicestershire, in 1975.

Records: Chantrey Vellacott, Russell Square House, 10–12 Russell Square, London WC1B 5LF

Partnership agreements 1878–1988; partners' meeting minutes 1923, 1955–88; accounts 1931–88; bills book 1896–98; private ledgers 1879–87, 1914–19; journal 1898–1911; correspondence: clients 1881–93, associated firms 1908–64, clients' accounts 1940–47, Belfast office 1942–44, partnership 1944–45; office rules 1920, 1948; salary sheets 1925–29; office leases, tenancy agreements, plans, Broad Street Place and Finsbury Circus House 1925–41; speeches: Arthur J Hill 1889, Lancelot Hill 1934; photographs: partners 1800s–1988, staff dinner 1902; firewatching log book 1940–45.

Clients: Correspondence, audit reports, accounts, prospectuses, etc., incl. **Belfast Steam Ship Co Ltd** 1893–94; **Belgravia Estates Co** 1926; **British Shoe Co Ltd** 1926; **Cardiff & Penarth Steam Ferry Co Ltd** 1887 incl. audit programme n.d.; **Imperial Sugar Refining Co Ltd** 1863–64; **Jinman's Steam Navigation Co Ltd** 1877–79; **Longton and Fenton Permanent Benefit Building Society** 1850–74; **Mile End Distillery Co** 1882–95 incl. ledger of loans to publicans 1890; **Neptune Steam Shipping Co Ltd** 1879–87; **South Wales (Sieman's Patent) Glass Manufacturing Co Ltd**, Cardiff 1885; **UK Electric Telegraph Co Ltd** 1862; **Uskside Engineering & Rivet Co Ltd**, Newport 1883–1903 incl. audit programme *c*.1890–95; **Woolston & Belton**, stockbrokers, London 1876–78. Liquidation papers, **London Colonial Co Ltd** incl. accounts, liquidators' draft report, registers of shareholders and debentures, cash book 1867–75.

Anon., *Hill Vellacott: An Historical Account of their Development since 1788* (London, the firm, 1988)

Peter Boys, 'Two Toasts to Hill Vellacott', *Accountancy*, Vol. 102, No. 1139 (1988), p. 67

HILLIER HOPKINS

77/79 Marlowes, Hemel Hempstead HP1 1LW

Also at Watford

History: Started by John Hillier who established the firm Lewis, Hillier &

Co in Luton, Bedfordshire, in 1936. An office opened at 68 Marlowes, Hemel Hempstead, Hertfordshire, in *c*.1945, becoming Hillier Hopkins & Co in 1950, Leonard Carlyle Hopkins having joined the firm in 1945. The Luton practice was continued as Hillier, Hills, Frary & Co. Hillier, Hopkins & Co moved to 79 Marlowes, Hemel Hempstead, in 1950 and opened an office at 28 Station Road, Watford, Hertfordshire, in 1954. The Watford office moved to St Martin's House, 31–35 Clarendon Road, in 1985. The firm's name was shortened to Hillier Hopkins in 1985.

Records: Hillier Hopkins, St Martin's House, 31–35 Clarendon Road, Watford WD1 1JA

Partnership agreements 1952–date; partners' meeting minutes 1960s–date; private ledgers 1952–85; cash book 1945 on; articles of clerkship 1948, 1950; salaries books 1954 on; lease, 28 Station Road, Watford 1954.

HINES & CLOWES (Pannell Kerr Forster)
Sun Buildings, 35 Princes Street, Ipswich

Also at Brightlingsea and Hadleigh

History: Started by Charles George Hines who set up in practice in Ipswich, Suffolk, just after the First World War. In 1931 he went into partnership with Edward Norris Thyne Clowes and practised at Atlas Chambers, Lloyds Avenue, under the style Hines & Clowes until 1964 when the firm moved to 35 Princes Street. In 1974 the firm merged with the London firm Rowley, Pemberton, Roberts & Co, now part of Pannell Kerr Forster.

Records: Pannell Kerr Forster, Princes House, 31 Princes Street, Ipswich IP1 1PU

Fees ledger 1927–44.

HOWARD SMITH, THOMPSON & CO (Price Waterhouse)
Beaufort House, 96 Newhall Street, Birmingham

History: Founded by Howard Samuel Smith who set up in practice at Argyle Chambers, Colmore Row, Birmingham, West Midlands in 1867, after serving articles with Edward Carter of Kettle, Daniel & Carter, Birmingham. The firm was initially called Howard Smith & Co and later Howard Smith & Slocombe (1876), Howard Smith, Slocombe & Co (1888), Howard Smith, Brettell & Co (1919), and Howard Smith, Thompson & Co (1923). By the 1880s the firm was acting for many leading public and private companies in Birmingham and the West Midlands. The firm moved to 37 Bennetts Hill in 1879; 14 Waterloo Street in 1890; 11 Waterloo Street in 1901; and 96 Newhall Street in 1956. In 1963 it merged with Price Waterhouse & Co, now Price Waterhouse (*qv*).

Records: Price Waterhouse, Southwark Towers, 32 London Bridge Street, London SE1 9SY

Partnership agreements 1876–1945; partners' meeting minutes 1953–67; papers, partnership matters incl. merger with Price Waterhouse & Co *c*.1963; accounts 1947–53; draft accounts 1924–43; income tax computations 1914–64; private ledger 1940–50; Howard Smith's family Bible 1887.

Anon., *Howard Smith Thompson & Co, 1867–1967: The First 100 Years* (Birmingham, the firm, 1967)

HUBERT SMITH & CO (Hawsons)

2 Campo Lane, Sheffield, South Yorkshire

History: Founded in the 1870s by William Hubert Smith who by 1880 was practising under his own name at 10 Figtree Lane, Sheffield, South Yorkshire. The practice became Hubert Smith & Co in 1902. It moved to Hoole's Chambers, 45 Bank Street, in *c*.1890; Midland Chambers, High Street, in 1895; 7 York Street in 1912; and 2 Campo Lane in 1924. In 1963 the firm merged with W G Hawson, Wing & Co (*qv*) to form Hawson, Wing & Hubert Smith, now Hawsons (*qv*).

Records: Hawsons, Pegasus House, 463a Glossop Road, Sheffield S10 2QD

Clients' ledgers 1903–31, 1949–63; ledgers: incl. journal 1877–92, private 1902–14; cash books 1877–89, 1908–22; bank passbooks 1884–92, 1915–30.

HUDSON SMITH, BRIGGS & CO (Price Waterhouse)

St Giles House, 11 Quay Street, Bristol, Avon

Also at London

History: Formed in 1888 through the merger of Hudson, Smith, Williams & Co, Exchange, Bristol, Avon (est. 1846 as W H Williams & Co) and Geo. Edwin Swithinbank, Briggs & Co, of 7 St Stephen's Street, Bristol. The firm was renamed Hudson Smith, Briggs, Smith & Taylor in 1907, and Hudson Smith, Briggs & Co in *c*.1918. Until 1963 it occupied Exchange, Bristol, and then moved to St Giles House, 11 Quay Street, before merging with Price Waterhouse & Co, now Price Waterhouse (*qv*), in the same year. The firm had a London office, opened in 1893, at 70 Bishopsgate Street, which moved to 90 Cannon Street in 1894, and to 23 College Hill, Cannon Street, in 1907. Clare Smith was president of the ICAEW 1932–33.

Records: Price Waterhouse, Southwark Towers, 32 London Bridge Street, London SE1 9SY

Partnership agreements 1925–63 (w); Clare Smith's diaries 1892, 1899, 1909 incl. record of time spent 1892–98; analysis of fees journal 1947–57;

ledgers: 1888–1900, 1909–18, nominal 1959–69, private *c.*1880s on; journals 1895–1908, 1938–55; cash books 1888–91, 1940–63; register of clerks 1900–*c.*1950; photographs, partners *c.*1890–1957; historical notes 1960s.

Clients: William family estate: deeds, probate documents, accounts 1859, 1870–1919; **Plenty & Son Ltd**: printed accounts 1897, 1899–1903.

J & A W SULLY

8 Unity Street, College Green, Bristol BS1 5HH

Also at Barnstaple, Bideford, Bridgwater, Clevedon, Hatherleigh, South Molton, Torrington, Tiverton and Weston-super-Mare

History: Founded by James Wood Sully who entered into partnership with Alfred Allott in Sheffield, South Yorkshire, in 1865. By *c.* 1871 Sully had set up in practice at 23 Gresham House, Old Broad Street, London. He was joined by Maurice Nelson Girdlestone and, in 1873, by Alfred Willie Sully who became a partner in 1885. The firm was restyled J W & A W Sully, later shortened to J & A W Sully & Co. It moved to 78 Queen Victoria Street in 1880; 70 Queen Victoria Street in 1887; and 19/21 Queen Victoria in 1896. This office was destroyed during the blitz of 1941. An office opened in Bristol, Avon, in 1880, was closed after a few years but was reopened at 44 Corn Street in 1917. This practice amalgamated with the Bristol firms Charles Bartlett & Co, in 1941, and E J Tallack & Co in 1944. The Bristol office moved to the Norman Gatehouse, College Green, in 1951 and to 8 Unity Street in 1991. The firm had offices in Wells, Somerset (1953–72); Bath, Avon (1961–77); and Yeovil, Somerset (1923–86). Other offices were opened in Bridgwater (Bank Chambers, Cornhill), Somerset, in 1900; Weston-super-Mare (28 High Street), Avon, in 1907; South Molton (141 East Street), Devon, in 1941; Barnstaple (10 High Street), Devon, in 1947; Burnham-on-Sea (College Street), Somerset (now closed), in 1950; and Clevedon, Avon, in 1983. In 1965 the London office amalgamated with Griffiths & Miles, forming Griffiths, Miles, Sully & Co in 1967. In 1988 the partnership between J & A W Sully's offices was dissolved although they continue to practise as associated offices under the names J & A W Sully & Co (Bristol, Clevedon and Weston-super-Mare) and also Sully & Co (Barnstaple, Bideford, Bridgwater and South Molton).

Records (1): Sully & Co, 18–22 Angel Crescent, Bridgwater TA6 3AL

Partners' conference minutes 1949–date; fees: ledgers 1875–93, 1918–23, 1939–49, day books 1950 on, copy accounts 1891–1920, 1932–33; accounts 1945–date; private ledgers 1955 on; cash books: office 1937–60, clients' account 1947 on; letter books 1928–35; correspondence: tax 1928–29, private 1945–date; photographs: partners 1900, 1950, staff *c.* 1900, 1950; historical notes 1949.

Clients: Working papers, correspondence, accounts *c.* 1950–date; **Bridgwater Steam Laundry Ltd**: minutes 1902; **Combwitch & District Farmers Association Ltd**: certificate of incorporation 1893, register of members 1893–1902, minutes 1893–1943; **Enmore Park Golf Club**: accounts 1933–47; **Thompson Brothers Ltd**: minutes 1909–date, accounts 1923–date, private ledger 1909–40.

Records (2): J & A W Sully & Co, 8 Unity Street, College Green, Bristol BS1 5HH

Partners' meeting minutes 1949–87; partnership papers 1940–date; accounts 1940–date; photographs, partners 1940–date.

Records (3): Griffiths, Miles, Sully & Co, 95 High Street, Slough Sl1 1DH

Fees ledger 1941–65; accounts 1940–42; private ledger 1940–53; copy letters 1872, 1878.

A V Sully, *Towards the Centenary, 1865–1951: Notes on the Origin and History of an Accountancy Practice* (London, the firm, 1951)

J H CHAMPNESS, CORDEROY, BEESLY & CO (Saffery Champness)

10 St Swithin's Lane, London

History: Founded by John Henry Champness in London in 1868 as Champness & Maclerie and subsequently renamed J H Champness & Co in *c.*1880; J H Champness, Corderoy & Co in 1882; and J H Champness, Corderoy, Beesly & Co in *c.*1945. In 1880 the firm occupied 10 Basinghall Street, moving to 57 Moorgate Street in 1882; 103 Cannon Street in *c.*1892; and 10 St Swithin's Lane in 1926. In 1973 the firm merged with Somerset, Cowper & Co (*qv*), to form Champness, Cowper & Co (*qv*), now part of Saffery Champness.

Records: Saffery Champness, Fairfax House, Fulwood Place, Gray's Inn, London WC1V 6UB

Partnership agreements 1935–70; partner's diary 1871; private ledgers 1886–1971 incl. analyses of fees 1886–1926; cash receipts book 1870–71; petty cash book 1876–81; papers, partnership agreement incl. calculations of goodwill 1945–48; out-letter books 1891–1902; circulars 1868–1970s; leases, 10 St Swithin's Lane 1926, 1954.

JACKSON, TAYLOR, ABERNETHY & CO (Hays Allan)

24 St Mary Axe, London

History: Originated as the London office of Thomson, Jackson, Gourlay & Taylor (est. 1847), Glasgow, Strathclyde, opened in 1887. In 1923 the firm was practising at 20 Bucklersbury where it remained until *c.* 1941, when it moved to 24 St Mary Axe. In 1977 the firm amalgamated with Hays Allan, London, Bristol, Avon, Cambridge, Cambridgeshire, and Exeter, Devon.

Records: Hays Allan, Southampton House, 317 High Holborn, London WC1V 7NL

Bill book 1918–22; scrapbook incl. circulars, press cuttings, historical notes 1923–77.

JAMES & COWPER

Wesley Gate, 68/82 Queens Road, Reading RG1 4BP

Also at Henley-on-Thames, Newbury and Wantage

History: Originated in London as John James, Denton-Clarke & Co, in 1914, and by 1919 was practising at 4 Walbrook, London, as James & Cowper, Charles Somerset Swiney Cowper having been admitted as a partner in the firm. An office was opened in Newbury (Old Rectory, 2 & 3 Northbrook Street), Berkshire, in 1922. By 1931 James had left the firm; Cowper carried on the London office, first as C S S Cowper (1931–33) and then as Somerset, Cowper & Co (*qv*), which became part of Saffery Champness in 1982. The Newbury office retained the name of James & Cowper. This office moved to 14A Northbrook Street, Newbury, in 1924; to Whitehart House, Market Place in 1953; and to Phoenix House, 50 Bartholomew Street, in 1984. Offices were opened in Reading (5 Station Road), Berkshire, in 1959; and Wantage (9 Market Place), Berkshire, in 1976. The Reading office moved to 68/82 Queens Road in 1991. In 1991 the firm merged with Cook Sutton & Co (*qv*), Reading and Henley-on-Thames, Berkshire.

Records (1): James & Cowper, Phoenix House, Bartholomew Street, Newbury RG14 5QA

Nominal ledger 1930–44; cash books 1928–33 incl. job analysis 1930–42.

Records (2): Berkshire Record Office, Shire Hall, Shinfield Park, Reading RG2 9XD

Partnership agreements 1976–date.

JAMES M MCINTOSH & SON (Neville Russell)

Lancaster House, 67 Newhall Street, Birmingham, West Midlands

Also at West Bromwich

History: In 1926 James M McIntosh & Son was in practice at 6 Cherry Street, Birmingham, West Midlands. The firm subsequently moved to 11 & 12 Bennetts Hill in 1934; 13 Bennetts Hill in 1939; 15A Steelhouse Lane in 1949; and 67 Newhall Street in 1957. The firm had offices in London (*c*.1945–49) and West Bromwich, West Midlands (opened 1950). In *c*.1945 James M McIntosh & Son amalgamated with the local firm Dixon, Hopkinson & Co, although both firms continued to practise under separate names. In 1971 the combined firm merged with Neville Russell & Co, now part of Neville Russell.

Records: Neville Russell, Britannia House, 50 Great Charles Street, Queensway, Birmingham B3 2LY

Private ledger 1942–65; day book 1964–70; cash book summary 1964–76.

JARVIS BARBER & SONS (Barber, Harrison & Platt)
17 North Church Street, Sheffield, South Yorkshire

History: Founded by Jarvis William Barber, president of the Sheffield Institute of Accountants 1879–80, petitioner for the royal charter of the ICAEW in 1880 and president 1912–13. Barber set up in practice in George Street, Sheffield, South Yorkshire, in 1867. In 1880 he was practising at Alliance Chambers, George Street, under the style Barber Brothers & Wortley which was changed to Jarvis Barber & Sons in 1902. The firm moved to Chantrey Chambers, 27A High Street in 1912, to Telegraph Building, High Street, in 1914, and to 17 North Church Street in 1952. In 1970 the firm merged with Ransom Harrison & Lewis (*qv*) and Sissons, Platt & Co, 9 Broomhall Road, Sheffield, to form Barber, Harrison & Platt (*qv*).

Records: Barber, Harrison & Platt, 2 Rutland Park, Sheffield S10 2PD

Partnership agreement 1970; ledger balances: 1913, private 1913; out-letter books 1876–78; cash book, liquidation of Alfred Allott 1879–83; auditors' appointments 1884; photographs: Joseph William Barber *c.* 1900, meeting at Lindrick, North Yorkshire *c.* 1920; Barber family papers: autobiographical notes 1827–90s, correspondence 1840–70s.

JOHN ADAMSON, SON & CO (Cooper Lancaster)
1 Chancery Place, Booth Street, Manchester, Greater Manchester

History: Founded by John Adamson who left Chadwick, Adamson & Co, Manchester, Greater Manchester, and Chadwick, Adamson, McKenna & Co, London, in 1867 to set up his own practice at 29 Brazennose Street, Manchester. Adamson was an early member of the ICAEW and by 1880 was practising under the style John Adamson, Son & Co at 5 Norfolk Street. The firm moved to Tower Chambers, 30 Spring Gardens, in 1907 and to 1 Chancery Place, Booth Street, in 1932. In its early days the firm became associated with the quarrying and wallpaper manufacturing industries and for many years were the auditors of the borough of Darwen, Lancashire. In 1968 John Adamson, Son & Co merged with Cooper & Cooper, Bolton, Greater Manchester, to form Cooper, Adamson & Co, now part of Cooper Lancaster.

Records: Cooper Lancaster, Century House, 11 St Peter's Square, Manchester M2 3DN

Partnership agreements 1885–1947; draft heads of agreement 1892; accounts 1864–75, 1939; private ledgers 1864–98, 1939–72; photographs, centenary luncheon 1967.

Clients: Col Sir John Rutherford, dec'd: accounts 1966, balance sheets book 1953–66, ledger 1932–52, cash book 1932–66; **Steetley Lime Co Ltd**: accounts 1894; **Sutcliffe Ventilating & Drying Co Ltd**: directors' meeting minutes 1903–68.

JOHN GORDON, WALTON & CO

Yorkshire House, Greek Street, Leeds LS1 5ST

History: Founded by John Gordon who started practising *c.* 1870 at 23 Albion Street, Leeds, West Yorkshire, and by 1875 was practising under the name John Gordon & Co. In 1881 John Gordon, junior, was listed in practice at 1 Bond Street under the name J & J Gordon. The firm had an office in London (27 King Street) between 1899 and 1902. John Gordon became Lord Mayor of Leeds in 1899. In 1901 the firm moved to 19 Bond Street and 7 Bond Place. The firm was restyled John Gordon & Co in 1906. In 1920 John Gordon became president of the ICAEW. In 1934 the partnership between Alfred Walton, John Harrison and E Duncan Taylor was dissolved. Walton carried on the practice of John Gordon & Co under the name John Gordon, Walton & Co, at 7 South Parade, Leeds, and Harrison and Taylor continued in practice at 7 Bond Place as John Gordon, Harrison, Taylor & Co (now part of Touche Ross & Co). In 1965 John Gordon, Walton & Co moved to Aquis House, 12 Greek Street. The firm merged with George Osmond Winfield Pickard & Co, 14 East Parade, in 1969; E Warwick Broadbent & Co, 30 Albion Place, in 1973; and Atkinson, Smith & Atkinson, Permanent House, The Headrow, in 1975.

Records: John Gordon, Walton & Co, Yorkshire House, Greek Street, Leeds LS1 5ST

Partnership agreements: 1925, 1936, 1988, dissolution 1934; papers, dissolution of partnership incl. accounts, time and fees analysis, journal summaries, trial balances, time ledger sheets, lists of clients, schedules of debtors, valuation of work-in-progress, notes re matters in dispute, inventories of office furniture 1934–36; private ledger 1934–56; audit summary 1906–40; correspondence: partnership agreement and partnership matters 1934, dissolution 1935–37, mergers, G W Pickard & Co 1969–77, E Warwick Broadbent & Co 1972–85, Atkinson, Smith & Atkinson 1975; monthly salaries book 1934–56; lease, office premises 1926.

Clients: Claughton Bros Ltd, lead founders: balance sheet and trading account 1896; **Harrogate Club**: balance sheet and revenue account 1912; **Society for Promoting Christian Knowledge**: balance sheet and trading account 1902.

JORDAN, BROOKES & CO

Parmenter House, Tower Road, Winchester SO23 8TD

Also at Fareham and Romsey

History: Founded *c.*1870 by Charles Johnson who set up in practice at 1 Station Hill, Winchester, Hampshire, after returning from a tour of duty in County Cork, Ireland, with the Royal Hampshire Regiment. By 1884 Johnson had an office at 15 Jewry Street. He was joined in 1897 by his son, Alfred, and the practice became C Johnson & Son, incorporated accountants. In 1904 the firm moved to 41 & 44 Jewry Street, followed by moves to 2 Jewry Street in 1912; 35 Southgate Street (purchased by Alfred Johnson and renamed Southgate Chambers) in 1920; and 57 Tower Street in 1965. 55 Tower Street was acquired in 1977. The firm's name changed to Johnson, Son & Gledhill when Alfred Johnson was joined by Norman Gledhill, a chartered accountant from the Leeds, West Yorkshire, firm, Morgan & Gallant, in 1933. After Johnson's death in 1951, Gledhill continued in practice on his own, with a small staff, until 1961 when he took John Jordan into partnership. The firm was styled Gledhill & Jordan until Colin Brookes became a partner in 1970, Norman Gledhill having died in 1964. It acquired offices at 24 Bell Street, Romsey, Hampshire, in 1974 and at 1A Osborn Road, Fareham, Hampshire, in 1982. The Winchester office was extended in 1989, when its main entrance was moved from Tower Street to Tower Road.

Records: Jordan, Brookes & Co, Parmenter House, Tower Road, Winchester SO23 8TD

Private ledger 1933–61; cash book 1933–57; copy returns of audits on Friendly Society accounts 1923–27; press cuttings, history of firm 1950–date; photographs: Alfred Johnson 1928, 57 Tower Street 1965.

Clients: John M Carter Ltd, rope manufacturers: trading and profit and loss accounts 1917–47, correspondence 1917–47; **Hampshire & General Friendly Society**: cash book 1961–66; **C Watts**: working papers 1928–64, bankruptcy certificates 1884.

JOSEPH CROSSLEY & SONS

Barton House, 227 Upper Brook Street, Manchester M13 0HA

Also at Wilmslow.

History: Established in 1876 by Joseph Crossley and his brother, William, in Manchester, Greater Manchester. In 1880 the brothers were practising as W & J Crossley at 20 Thomas Street. The firm moved to 72 Market Street in *c*.1888, 23 Cross Street in *c*.1893, 55 Cross Street in 1899 and the present address in 1961. Over the years the firm has acted for many clients in Smithfield Market, Manchester. During the 1870s and the 1880s the firm acted as auditors to Gladstone Spinning Co Ltd, Failsworth, Greater Manchester, and Alma Spinning Co Ltd, Lansdowne Spinning Co Ltd and Borough Spinning Co Ltd, Oldham, Greater Manchester.

Records: Joseph Crossley & Sons, Barton House, 227 Upper Brook Street, Manchester M13 0HA

Partnership agreements 1958–date; accounts 1949, 1965–date; fees ledgers 1943 on, nominal ledger 1946–*c*.1955; photograph, anniversary dinner 1956.

KIMBERLEY, MORRISON, MOORE & CO (Moore Stephens)
St Philips House, St Philips Place, Birmingham, West Midlands

Also at Dudley

History: Thomas Edwin Kimberley started practising at 12 Cannon Street, Birmingham, West Midlands, after qualifying as a chartered accountant in 1888. Shortly afterwards he moved to Temple Courts, 55 Temple Row, and in 1897 was joined by Percy Archibald Morrison. The partnership became Kimberley, Morrison & Co in 1899. In 1924 Alfred Norman Moore joined the firm. The present style was adopted in 1948 and in the same year the firm moved to 47 Temple Row. During the 1970s and 1980s the firm absorbed a number of local practices, including: Clarke & Co, Edgbaston, in 1978; Griffin & Co, Edgbaston, in 1981; Harold Brown & Co, Birmingham, in 1987 and Malcolm Wood, Birmingham, in 1989. The firm acquired an office in Dudley, West Midlands, through its merger with William Lloyd & Co in 1986. During the 1940s the firm also had an office at 27 Rodney Road, Cheltenham, Gloucestershire. In 1987 the firm moved to St Philips Place. In March 1991 it began to practise as Moore Stephens (Birmingham firm).

Records: Moore Stephens, Charterhouse, 165 Newhall Street, Birmingham B3 1SW

Partnership agreements: 1941, 1946, dissolution 1954; time record books 1929–31, 1946–71; accounts 1920–91; ledgers: 1929–42, general 1930–56, private 1920–71; journals: 1920–39, private 1934–48; cash books 1899–47; staff record book *c*.1915–59; lease, Temple Courts 1909; tenancy agreement, 47 Temple Row 1948; photograph, partners *c*.1900–60.

KNOWLES, NORRIS & CO (Brooking, Knowles & Lawrence)
51 Southgate Street, Winchester, Hampshire

History: Established by Eric Nelson Knowles in 1926 as the Winchester, Hampshire, office of the Oxford, Oxfordshire, based firm Critchley, Wood & Pigott. The office opened at 117 High Street, Winchester, under the style Critchley, Pigott & Knowles. The practice subsequently moved to 96 High Street in 1932; 109a High Street in 1951; and 51 Southgate Street in 1961. It was restyled Knowles Barron in 1955 and Knowles, Norris & Co in 1965. In 1971 the firm merged with Brooking, Lawrence & Co, which was formed by the merger in 1968 of Lawrence, Mayes & Co (*qv*), Basingstoke, Hampshire, Brooking, Holmes & Co (*qv*), Basingstoke, and Berry, Weeks & Brooking (*qv*), Winchester. The firm which resulted from the merger of Knowles, Norris & Co and Brooking, Lawrence & Co, became Brooking, Knowles & Lawrence.

Records: Brooking, Knowles & Lawrence, Clifton House, Bunnian Place, Basingstoke RG21 1JE

Partnership agreement 1968; private ledger 1950–71; correspondence, valuation of goodwill 1950s–60s.

L MILBURN & CO (Torgersen, Nicholson & Co)
Somerford Buildings, Norfolk Street, Sunderland, Tyne and Wear

History: Founded by Leonard Milburn who set up in practice under his own name at Central Buildings, West Sunniside, Sunderland, Tyne and Wear, in 1922. On the death of Milburn in 1940, the firm of L Milburn & Co continued as a separate entity with J H Pigg and R E Bolton as partners. They were later joined by S J Cowey who had been an employee since 1927. In 1971 the firm was restyled Milburn Torgersen & Co following a merger with the sole practitioner P F Torgersen, 12 Frederick Street, Sunderland. In 1980 the firm merged with Nicholas, Forsythe & Co, 19 John Street, Sunderland, to become Torgersen, Nicholson & Co. The firm moved to 48 West Sunniside in 1956 and to Somerford Buildings, Norfolk Street, in 1971.

Records: Tyne and Wear Archives Service, Blandford House, Blandford Square, Newcastle upon Tyne NE1 4JA

Private ledger 1927–52; cash book, incl. costs journal, income tax account, balance sheets 1931–35; correspondence, S J Cowey's employment 1927; Leonard Milburn's articles of clerkship 1915; photograph, Milburn 1933.

Clients: Sunderland Housing Association Ltd: management committee minutes 1933–69.

LAWRENCE, MAYES & CO (Brooking, Knowles & Lawrence)
35 Winchester Street, Basingstoke, Hampshire

Also at Andover

History: Started by William John Lawrence as W John Lawrence & Co at 11a New Street, Basingstoke, Hampshire, in 1947. The practice subsequently moved to New Street in 1950, 36a Sarum Street in 1959 and 35 Winchester Street in 1963. The firm was restyled Lawrence, Mayes & Co in 1963. An office was opened at 80 High Street, Andover, Hampshire, in 1967. In 1968 the firm merged with Brooking, Holmes & Co (*qv*), Basingstoke, and Berry, Weeks & Brooking (*qv*), Winchester, Hampshire, to become Brooking, Lawrence & Co, now Brooking, Knowles & Lawrence.

Records: Brooking, Knowles & Lawrence, Clifton House, Bunnian Place, Basingstoke RG21 1JE

Partnership agreement 1963; papers, merger with Brooking, Holmes & Co 1968; accounts 1964; fees day book 1963–67; private ledger 1963–68.

LEAROYD & LONGBOTTOM

4 North Park Road, Harrogate HG1 5PA

History: Founded by Jonathan Ingham Learoyd who started practising under the style Learoyd & Co at 18 Cheapside, Halifax, West Yorkshire, in 1888, moving to Bank Chambers, Commercial Street, in *c.*1892. The firm was restyled Learoyd & Son in 1896 and Learoyd & Sons in 1902. In 1915 Learoyd went into partnership with John Singleton Longbottom, under the style Learoyd & Longbottom, at 2 Princess Square, Harrogate, North Yorkshire. From 1921 the Halifax office continued to practise as a separate firm under the style Learoyd & Sons. Learoyd & Longbottom moved to the present address in 1972.

Records: Learoyd & Longbottom, 4 North Park Road, Harrogate HG1 5PA

Nominal ledger 1942–88; cash books 1970–date; list of clients 1920s; wages books 1920–73; lease, 2 Princess Square 1939; audit appointment, Harrogate Corporation 1934.

Clients: J F Longbottom, dec'd: ledgers 1942–49; **Edward Standing Ltd**, cafe proprietors: register of members 1894–1966, share transfer register 1894–1980, share ledger 1941–78, share certificates 1898–1974, register of directors 1905–66, ledgers 1940–69, cash books 1957–74.

LEMAN, HILL & HILTON

29 Arboretum Street, Nottingham NG1 4JA

History: Founded by Thomas Leman who was practising at Exchange Chambers, 1 Greyhound Street, 21 Long Row, Nottingham, Nottinghamshire, in 1880. By 1890 he had moved to 1 St Peter's Church Walk and had acquired an office in London which was retained until 1919. The practice became Leman, Son and Sands in *c.*1892 and was subsequently renamed Leman & Sons in 1898 and Leman, Hill & Hilton in 1919, when Sydney Hill and Harold Hilton were admitted as partners. Leman, Hill & Hilton moved to 7 College Street in 1952 and to the present address in 1980.

Records: Leman, Hill & Hilton, 29 Arboretum Street, Nottingham NG1 4JA

Partnership agreements 1919, 1958; profit and loss account and balance sheet 1940; accounts book 1920–50; private ledger *c.*1919–58; cash books: 1955–71, private 1947–64; articles of clerkship 1914–63.

Clients: Beeston Embroidery Co Ltd: statement of accounts 1914.

LEVY GEE

100 Chalk Farm Road, London NW1 8EH

Also at Worthing

History: Started by Gerald Levy who set up in practice at 31 Elers Road, West Ealing, London, in 1953 under the style G A Levy & Co. He moved to 10 Dyers Buildings, Holborn, in 1954 and 120/121 Newgate Street, Holborn, in 1958. In 1963 he took M J Gee into partnership and the firm was restyled Levy Gee & Co, later Levy Gee. The firm moved to its present address in 1974. An office was opened in Worthing, West Sussex, in 1978.

Records: Levy Gee, 100 Chalk Farm Road, London NW1 8EH

Partnership agreements: 1978, draft 1986; files, partnership matters 1980–83; accounts and working papers 1954–81; tax papers 1981–86; fees day books 1966–72; bill books 1963–81; bills delivered book 1964–65; nominal ledgers 1964–82; cash books: office account 1962–76, clients' account 1964–72; work-in-progress summaries 1976.

LITHGOW, NELSON & CO

Gray's Inn House, 127 Clerkenwell Road, London EC1R 5DB

History: Established by W Bertram Nelson and William Gilbert Lithgow of W E Nelson & Co (est. 1856), Liverpool, Merseyside, and W G Lithgow & Co (est. 1926), Southport, Merseyside, respectively, who opened an office at Hastings House, 10 Norfolk Street, Strand, London, in 1934. The office practised under the style Hannah, Dolby, Lithgow, Nelson & Co, Alexander Hannah and Charles Dolby, two Liverpool accountants, having become partners in the firm. The London office changed its name to Lithgow, Nelson & Co in 1939 followed by the Liverpool and Southport offices in 1946, although at all times they practised independently of one another. The London firm moved to 39 Broad Street in 1939; Imperial House, Kingsway, in 1969; and the present address in 1991. The Southport firm also practises as Lithgow, Nelson & Co (*qv*).

Records: Lithgow, Nelson & Co, Gray's Inn House, 127 Clerkenwell Road, London EC1R 5DB

Partners' diaries 1939; time record sheets 1946–58; fees day book 1954–59; clients' ledger balances 1940–46; cash book 1934–40; general office instructions 1943.

LITHGOW, NELSON & CO

399 Lord Street, Southport PR9 0AS

History: Founded by William Gilbert Lithgow, an incorporated accountant, who opened an office at 429A Lord Street, Southport, Merseyside, in 1926 under the style W G Lithgow & Co. In 1934 Lithgow joined forces with W Bertram Nelson, senior partner of W E Nelson & Co (est. 1856), Liverpool, Merseyside, and opened an office in London at 10 Norfolk Street, Strand. This office practised under the style Hannah, Dolby, Lithgow, Nelson & Co. In 1946 the Liverpool and Southport offices changed their name to Lithgow, Nelson & Co (the London office having done so in 1939), although they continued to practise independently of one another. The Southport firm moved to 399 Lord Street in 1969. The Liverpool office amalgamated with Pannell Kerr Forster in 1972. Bertram Nelson was president of the Society of Incorporated Accountants 1951–54 and was one of the leading figures in negotiations for the Society's amalgamation with the ICAEW in 1957. The London firm also practises under the name Lithgow, Nelson & Co (*qv*).

Records: Lithgow, Nelson & Co, 399 Lord Street, Southport PR9 0AS

Partnership accounts 1964–69; fees journal 1934–38; nominal ledgers 1934–65; cash books 1941–76; salary books 1937–68; articles of clerkship 1952–70s.

LITTLEJOHN, WILSON, MCKNIGHT & CO (Littlejohn Frazer)

15 Cullum Street, Fenchurch Street, London

History: Started by Ernest Littlejohn who set up in practice in 1875 and was admitted to the ICAEW in 1884. In 1888 he was practising under the style E Littlejohn & Co at 20 Bucklersbury, London. The firm was subsequently renamed E Littlejohn, Robertson & Co in 1893; E Littlejohn, Robertson, Wilson & Co in 1898; E Littlejohn Wilson & Co in 1902; Littlejohn, Wilson, McKnight & Co in 1920; Littlejohn, Wilson, McKnight & Hill in 1926; and Littlejohn, Wilson, McKnight & Co in 1929. The firm moved from 20 Bucklersbury to 85 Gracechurch Street in 1904 and to Egypt House, New Broad Street, in 1910; Bilbao House, 36 & 38 New Broad Street, in 1923; 4 Union Court, Old Broad Street, in 1924;

122 London Wall in 1928; and 15 Cullum Street, Fenchurch Street, in 1929. In 1963 Littlejohn, Wilson, McKnight & Co merged with R J Jeffreys (est. 1908), 22 Billiter Street, London, to form Jeffreys, Littlejohn & Co. In 1984 this firm, through amalgamation, became part of Littlejohn de Paula which merged with Frazer, Whiting & Co (*qv*) in 1986 to form Littlejohn Frazer.

Records: Littlejohn Frazer, 1 Park Place, Canary Wharf, London E14 4HJ

Partnership agreements: 1893–1900, dissolution 1902, 1920, 1962; fees journal 1894–1908; profits ledger 1894–1902; journal 1883–1893; cash books 1883–1902; analysis of firm's profits 1894–1905; private letter books 1894–22; salaries book 1925; leases 1925, 1945; sale of leasehold 1931; articles of clerkship, C H McKnight 1909.

LOVELOCK, WHIFFIN & DICKINSON (Price Waterhouse)

19 Coleman Street, London

History: Founded by Samuel Lovelock and Henry William Sharp Whiffin who were admitted to the ICAEW in 1880. The first office was opened at 19 Coleman Street, London, under the name Lovelock & H W S Whiffin and was renamed Lovelock, Whiffin & Dickinson in *c.* 1887 when Arthur Lowes Dickinson was admitted as a partner. In 1900 the firm merged with Price, Waterhouse & Co, now Price Waterhouse (*qv*). Dickinson then went to the USA where he became senior partner of the American firm of Price Waterhouse & Co.

Records: Price Waterhouse, Southwark Towers, 32 London Bridge Street, London SE1 9SY

Time record book 1900.

J R Edwards, 'Arthur Lowes Dickinson', in David J Jeremy (ed.), *Dictionary of Business Biography*, Vol. 2 (London, Butterworth, 1984)

LOVEWELL BLAKE

Havenbridge House, North Quay, Great Yarmouth NR30 1HE

Also at Aylsham, Beccles, Halesworth, Lowestoft, North Walsham, Norwich, Thetford and Wymondham

History: Believed to be the oldest accounting firm in East Anglia, it was founded in Great Yarmouth, Norfolk, by Lovewell Blake *c.*1858 at the time he was taken into partnership by his father, a shipowner, broker and merchant. During the 1860s he became involved with insolvency and the promotion of companies and businesses and in 1866 successfully petitioned Parliament to form a building society. In 1867 he became the first secretary of the Norfolk & Suffolk Permanent Benefit Building Society. He was one of the original associate members of the Society of Accountants in England when it was formed in 1872 and was a founder member of the new ICAEW in 1880. By 1900 the firm, known as Lovewell Blake & Co, had offices in Beccles (Blyburgate Street) and Lowestoft (148 High Street), Suffolk, as well as Great Yarmouth. The Great Yarmouth office moved *c.*1889 from Hall Quay Chambers to an office on South Quay (also known as Hall Quay Chambers) where it remained until 1983 when it moved to its present address. An office was established in Norwich (at Old Bank of England Court, Queen Street), Norfolk, in 1927 by A E Lark and Arthur Dicker. Both partners became active in the promotion of the East Anglian Society of Chartered Accountants and Arthur Dicker eventually became president of the ICAEW in 1956. In 1964 the firm formed an association with Cooper Brothers & Co, later Coopers & Lybrand (*qv*), which lasted until 1980. The firm merged with the Norwich practice of Bullimore & Co (71 The Close) in 1965, with Carter Edmunds & Co (60 St Faith's Lane) in 1987 and with E J Riches & Son (4, 6 & 8 Cathedral Street) in 1988. The firm's name was shortened to Lovewell Blake in 1988.

Records (1): Lovewell Blake, Havenbridge House, North Quay, Great Yarmouth NR30 1HE

Partnership agreements 1950–date; partners' meeting minutes 1964–date; accounts 1917–date; clients' ledger 1934–53; ledgers: 1918–34, private 1951–53; staff rules 1919; employee records incl. weekly salaries 1915–57; clerks' salaries 1918–51; office manual 1964; photographs, senior partners *c.*1900–65.

Clients: Great Yarmouth Investment Co Ltd: memorandum and articles of association and prospectus 1877, minutes 1877–1922, register of members and share ledger 1877–1921, private ledger 1941–50, cash book 1913–49, property ledger 1877–1921; **Great Yarmouth Sale & Purchase Co Ltd**: memorandum and articles of association 1911; **Great Yarmouth Traders' Association**: memorandum and articles of association 1915; **Grout & Co Ltd**: memorandum and articles of association 1924; **Norfolk & Suffolk Permanent Benefit Building Society**: minutes 1906–50, registers of members 1900–33, share register 1888–1929, subscription register 1903–31, premium books 1893–1943, payments book 1907–39, investments ledger 1909–41, receipts cash book 1923–40, list of securities 1874–1939, rules 1890; **Norfolk Finance & Property Co Ltd**: register of members 1901–47.

Records (2): Suffolk Record Office, Central Library, Clapham Road South, Lowestoft NR32 1DR

Clients: Lowestoft Steam Herring Drifters Co Ltd: title deeds and papers, property in Pakefield and Kirkley 1897–1914.

'Lovewell Blake – a short history?', *EASCA News*, Vol. 3, No. 2, 1991, p. 7

LUND & FUREY (Halpern and Woolf)
34 Avenue Parade, Accrington, Lancashire

History: Started by Harry B Britcliffe who set up in practice under the style H B Britcliffe & Co at 15 Avenue Parade, Accrington, Lancashire, in 1925. The firm was restyled Hodgkinson, Lund & Monk in 1966 and Lund & Furey in 1979. The office was moved to 34 Avenue Parade in 1979. In 1989 Lund & Furey merged with Halpern and Woolf, London, Chichester, West Sussex, Cowes and Newport, Isle of Wight, Manchester, Greater Manchester, Portsmouth, Hampshire, and Skelmersdale, Lancashire.

Records: Halpern and Woolf, Halpern House, 34 Avenue Parade, Accrington BB5 6PP

Private ledger 1925–67.

LYSONS, HAWORTH & SANKEY (Hallidays)
11 Spring Gardens, Manchester

History: Founded by Herbert Stewart Lysons who, in 1899, was practising at Exchange Buildings, 6 St Mary's Gate, Manchester, Greater Manchester. The firm became Lysons, Holt & Co in 1902 and was subsequently renamed Herbert S Lysons & Co in 1906; Lysons & Talbot in 1926; and Lysons, Haworth & Sankey *c.*1945. The firm opened an office in Rochdale, Greater Manchester, in 1902. The Manchester office moved from Deansgate, to 3 St Ann's Place, St Ann Street, in 1906, and then to 16 Albert Square in 1921; 9 St Peter's Square in 1924; 71 King Street in 1930; Midland Bank Building, Spring Gardens, in 1953; Canada House, 3 Chepstow Street, in 1959, and 11 Spring Gardens in 1969. In 1970 the firm merged with Halliday, Pearson & Co (*qv*), although the firms continued to practise under separate names. In 1972 the combined firm amalgamated with Crofts & Naylor, 30 Spring Gardens, Manchester, to form Hallidays. Arthur Walton, a partner in Lysons, Haworth & Sankey, was president of the ICAEW 1971–72.

Records: Hallidays, Harvester House, 37 Peter Street, Manchester M2 5QD

Private ledgers 1926–35, 1943–76; photograph, H S Lysons *c.*1930.

MACINTYRE HUDSON
Moorgate House, 201 Silbury Boulevard, Central Milton Keynes MK9 1LZ

Also at Bedford, High Wycombe, Leicester, London, Northampton, Peterborough, Richmond and Whetstone

History: The practice was started by Harry Gouldie Wilson and John Farrer Hudson in 1918 as H Gouldie Wilson & Co. Wilson had previously been in partnership with William Orton Attree whose London practice, Barnes & Attree, originated some time before 1880. In 1900 Wilson left the firm, which he had carried on in his own name since the death of Attree in 1898, to join Dixon, Wilson, Tubbs & Co of London, a predecessor of Dixon Wilson, but he left there during the First World War to practise on his own. It was whilst he was carrying out administrative work for the Admiralty that he met John Hudson. When Wilson died in 1924 Hudson joined in partnership with Robert Hamilton MacIntyre who had started practising in London (Victoria Street) and Bristol, Avon, in 1922. The new practice, MacIntyre Hudson, Gouldie, Wilson & Co, moved to Dacre House in Arundel Street, Strand, London. The name of the firm was changed in 1928 to MacIntyre Hudson & Co. During the next sixty years the London offices were moved successively to 118 Chancery Lane (1939); 25 Whitehall (1946); 22 Chancery Lane (1975); and 28 Ely Place (1982). The firm opened offices in Slough, Buckinghamshire, and Bedford, Bedfordshire, in 1935 and 1959 respectively. These were followed by the establishment of further new offices during the 1970s and a number of mergers which extended the practice to other provincial areas, including: Howard, Jolly, Rowe & Co, Bedford, in 1976; Mold, Reffin & Winter, Leicester, Leicestershire, Peterborough, Cambridgeshire, and Bedford in 1977; and the Northampton, Northamptonshire, office of the London firm, Greshams, in 1977. Mergers with the old firms of Norman & Whitehead (est. as Cape & Harris *c.*1865) and Sprague, Nicholson, Morgan & Co (*qv*), in 1968 and 1971 respectively, helped to increase the firm's operations in London, Richmond, Surrey, and High Wycombe, Buckinghamshire. In 1973 the firm acquired an office in Whetstone, London, through an amalgamation with the practice of Townsend, Watson & Stone. This office took in the practice of Tubbs, Clarke & Co in 1980. A merger with Meeson Makinson in 1987 substantially enlarged the Richmond office. Following the demerger of the central London office in 1991, the Milton Keynes, Buckinghamshire, office became the administrative centre of the firm, although a central London presence has been maintained in High Holborn.

Records: MacIntyre Hudson, Equipoise House, Grove Place, Bedford MK40 3LE

Partners' meeting minutes 1971–76; papers, merger with Turquand, Terry & Co, Dunstable 1981–86; accounts 1960–66; fees day book 1959–67; private ledger 1959–71; client record book 1959–68.

Stanford Letts, *MacIntyre Hudson, May 1880 – May 1980* (The firm, 1980)

MACNAIR MASON
St Clare House, 30–33 Minories, London EC3N 1DU

History: Founded by J A H Macnair, a Scottish chartered accountant who, after qualifying in Edinburgh, Lothian, in 1884, moved to London. By 1898 he had set up a practice at 206 Gresham Street under the name of Macnair, Rorie, although he was probably in practice earlier under his own name. By 1914 Macnair had been joined in partnership first by Henry Mason and then by Eric Evans and the firm became known as Macnair, Mason, Evans & Co. This name was retained until 1975 when the present style was adopted. The practice has always been in the City, having occupied 3 London Wall Buildings (from 1912); 4 London Wall Buildings (*c.*1945); 62 New Broad Street (1952); 58 Houndsditch (1974) and since 1986 the present address. The offices in London Wall Buildings were destroyed by enemy action during the blitz and many of the firm's early records were lost. Clients range from one-person firms to small public companies, the majority now being medium-sized private family businesses. The firm also deals with large private estates and trusts.

Records: Macnair Mason, St Clare House, 30–33 Minories, London EC3N 1DU

Partnership agreements 1914–88; partners' meeting minutes 1988–date; memoranda, partnership changes 1963–date; private ledgers 1934–date; cash books 1969–date; staff registers 1919–69; salaries book 1963–78; office leases, 62 New Broad Street and St Clare House 1966–86.

Clients: Messrs James Lock & Co, hatters: accounts 1925.

MAJOR & CO (Wenham Major)
89 Cornwall Street, Birmingham, West Midlands

Also at Walsall

History: Started by Everard P Major who carried on a practice under his own name at 47 Temple Row, Birmingham, West Midlands, between 1907 and 1935. In 1935 the practice was restyled Major & Co and moved to 89 Cornwall Street. From 1958 the firm had an office in Walsall (44 Bradford Street), West Midlands, and for a short time in Hinckley (35 Castle Street), Leicestershire. In 1962 the firm amalgamated with Wenham Brothers & Co (*qv*), also of Birmingham, to become Wenham, Major & Clarke, now Wenham Major (*qv*).

Records: Wenham Major, 89 Cornwall Street, Birmingham B3 3BY

Private ledger 1925–62; wages book 1925–40; plans, 89 Cornwall Street 1904.

MARTIN, FARLOW & CO (KPMG Peat Marwick)
27/28 Finsbury Square, London

History: Founded *c.*1882 by James Martin and Arthur King Farlow as

Martin & Farlow, of 3 Newgate Street, London. James Martin was involved in the formation of the Society of Incorporated Accountants and Auditors (est. 1885) and became its first secretary (1886–1919) and its thirteenth president (1922–23). The firm was restyled Martin, Farlow, Eldridge & Co in 1892, and Martin, Farlow & Co in 1900. It moved from Newgate Street to 4 King Street, Cheapside, in 1844, 50 Gresham Street in 1908, and 34/36 Gresham Street in 1928. When the firm's offices were bombed, in 1941, it moved into the Kingsley Hotel, Bloomsbury Way, remaining there until 1960, when it moved to 27/28 Finsbury Square. In 1968 the firm merged with Thomson McLintock & Co (*qv*), now part of KPMG Peat Marwick.

Records: KPMG Peat Marwick, 1 Puddle Dock, Blackfriars, London EC4V 3PD (enquiries to P D Bailey, FCA)

Partnership agreements 1938–65; partners' meeting minutes, papers re partnership agreements and merger discussions, correspondence, memos, periodical accounts 1962–69.

A A Garrett, *The History of the Society of Incorporated Accountants, 1885–1957* (Oxford, Oxford University Press, 1961)

MERRETT, SON & STREET (BDO Binder Hamlyn)

120 Moorgate, London

History: Founded by John Henry Merrett who set up in practice in Coleman Street, London, in 1888. In 1904 he was succeeded by his son H C Merrett who formed a partnership which became known as Merrett, Son & Street in 1910. The firm moved to 41 Finsbury Square in 1908; 32 Finsbury Square in 1928; 1–5 Queen Street in 1941; Copthall Avenue in 1951; and 120 Moorgate in 1957. From 1931 the firm was a pioneer in the field of 'running down' investigations, now known as 'forensic' work. By the Second World War, clients included leading firms on the Stock Exchange, the Rubber Market, the Baltic Exchange and the legal profession. In 1969 the firm amalgamated with Viney, Price & Goodyear (*qv*) to form Viney Merretts (*qv*), now part of BDO Binder Hamlyn.

Records: BDO Binder Hamlyn, 20 Old Bailey, London EC4M 7BH

Partnership agreements 1934–68; partners' meeting minutes 1963–69; accounts 1905–68.

MICHAEL LYON & CO

19 Castle Street, Liverpool L2 4SY

History: Founded by Louis Nicholas who started practising at 19 Castle Street, Liverpool, Merseyside, in 1901. The firm was restyled Louis Nicholas & Co in 1925. This name was retained until 1983 when the firm became Michael Lyon & Co. The firm amalgamated with the practice of

Geoffrey Boocock Baxter, 6 Egypt Street, Warrington, Cheshire, in 1964; Hugh Jones & Lewis, Victoria Street, Liverpool, in 1965; and Simon Jude & West, Victoria Street, Liverpool, in 1975.

Records: Michael Lyon & Co, 19 Castle Street, Liverpool L2 4SY

Partnership agreements 1946, 1961–date; agreement, amalgamation with Hugh Jones & Lewis 1965; accounts 1902–15, 1926–48, 1957–date; ledgers: private 1924–58, nominal 1925–69; weekly wages books 1907–12, 1937–65.

MONKHOUSE, STONEHAM & CO (Morison Stoneham & Co)

5 Queen Street, London

History: Originated as the London office of the Newcastle upon Tyne, Tyne and Wear, firm Monkhouse, Goddard & Co (est. 1868) which amalgamated with Price, Waterhouse & Co, now Price Waterhouse (*qv*), in 1920. George Benson Monkhouse moved to London in 1882 and set up an office with Allen H P Stoneham at 28 & 29 St Swithin's Lane which became a separate firm, styled Monkhouse, Stoneham & Co, in 1894. In 1902 the firm moved to Salisbury House, London Wall, where it remained until 1970 when it moved to 5 Queen Street. The firm amalgamated with Wm Arthur Smith & Co, 93 Cannon St, London, in 1896; the Scottish firm McAllister, Hankins & Co in 1932; W Rowland Waller & Co, Temple Chambers, Temple Avenue, London, in 1967; and Downes, Munns & Co (with whom an association had been formed in 1920), Salisbury House, London Wall, in 1968. In 1971 Monkhouse, Stoneham & Co merged with Morison, Rutherford, Osborne & Co to form Morison Stoneham & Co.

Records: Morison Stoneham & Co, 805 Salisbury House, 31 Finsbury Circus, London EC2M 5SQ

Partnership agreement 1958; partners' meeting minutes 1966–70; heads of agreement, merger with Morison, Rutherford, Osborne & Co 1971; accounts 1972; staff record book 1892–1970; leases, Salisbury House 1902–62; articles of clerkship 1939; staff reminiscences 1954.

MOORE FLETCHER & CO

26 Paradise Square, Sheffield S1 1TU

History: Founded by Walter Edward Moore who set up in practice under his own name at King's Chambers, 19 Angel Street, Sheffield, South Yorkshire, in 1931. The firm was subsequently restyled Walter Moore, Atkin & Co in 1946; Walter Moore & Co in 1949; Moore, Fletcher, Forsdyke & Shaw in 1968; and Moore Fletcher & Co in 1975. The firm moved from Angel Street to 95 Queen Street in 1935; to 19 Paradise Square in 1946; and to the present address in 1966.

Records: Moore Fletcher & Co, 26 Paradise Square, Sheffield S1 1TU

Partnership agreement 1947; accounts and working papers 1931–date; bill books 1931–date; private ledgers 1931–date; cash books 1931–date.

MORRIS GREGORY

368 Lees Road, Oldham OL4 5ER

History: The founder of the firm, Alexander Morris, was born *c.*1800 near Aberdeen, Grampian, and moved to Manchester, Greater Manchester, where he set up a linen drapery business at 22 St Ann's Square, some time before 1848. After a short period as a partner in a manufacturing firm, around 1850 he became employed by the leading drapery houses, representing them in insolvency cases in which they were creditors. To this he added some insurance business and moved to premises at 59 King Street, Manchester. By 1852 he was working as an accountant with his son, William, as Alexander Morris & Son. A second son, Walter, who had previously been a schoolteacher, joined the firm in 1865. Shortly thereafter William left and the style Alexander & Walter Morris was adopted. Soon after a move to 68 Fountain Street, Manchester, in 1870, Theodore Gregory was engaged as a clerk. Later, after a brief absence, he was made a partner. The Manchester office then moved, successively, to 5 Mosley Street (*c.*1878), 26 Mosley Street (1884), 32 York Street (1895) and 3 York Street (1976). During the same period the firm was renamed A & W Morris & Gregory (1880); Morris, Gregory & Holmes (1883); Morris, Gregory, Holmes & Hansford (1901); and Morris, Gregory & Co (1947). A permanent office in Jordangate, Macclesfield, Cheshire, was established in 1915; a Widnes, Cheshire, office was associated with the firm in 1935, by an agreement with a local accountant, and an Oldham, Lancashire, office, at 3 Clegg Street, was added in 1950 on the purchase of the business of Berry & Fullen. This office moved to 368 Lees Road, Oldham, in 1967. A turning point in the history of the firm came in 1978 when Morris Gregory & Co merged with Josolyne Layton-Bennett which, with the exception of the Macclesfield office, merged, in 1981, with Arthur Young. In 1986, the Oldham office of Arthur Young was bought out and the name Morris Gregory was adopted.

Records: Morris Gregory, 368 Lees Road, Oldham OL4 5ER

Partnership agreements: 1949, draft 1969; photographs, centenary dinner 1952.

Anon., *A History of One Hundred Years of Accountancy Practice, 1852–1952* (Manchester, the firm, 1952)

Sir Harold Howitt (ed.), *The History of the Institute of Chartered Accountants in England and Wales, 1880–1965, and of its Founder Accountancy Bodies, 1870–1880* (London, Heinemann, 1966)

MOSS & WILLIAMSON
Booth Street Chambers, Ashton-under-Lyne OL6 7LQ

Also at Stalybridge and Cheadle Hulme

History: Founded by William Moss who set up in practice in Market Place, Ashton-under-Lyne, Greater Manchester, in 1871. A prominent local figure and author of *Cotton Spinners' Accounts* (1905), he took into partnership William Henry Barker in 1893 and James Harry Williamson in 1901. The firm was restyled Moss & Barker in 1893 and Moss & Williamson in 1927. Moss's son and grandson subsequently became senior partners of the firm. Moss & Williamson moved to Booth Street Chambers in 1933.

Records: Moss & Williamson, Booth Street Chambers, Ashton-under-Lyne OL6 7LQ

Partners' photographs *c.* 1900–date; articles of clerkship 1922; historical notes 1913, 1933.

MUNDY, BREWER & JOHNSON
37 Great Pulteney Street, Bath BA2 4BZ

History: Founded by H B Mundy who established a stockbroking and accountancy business in *c.* 1841 at 7 Trim Street, Bath, Avon. Mundy was also secretary of the Bath Equitable Property & Investment Society and of the Bath Chamber of Commerce. By 1902 the firm was practising as incorporated accountants at 41 Milsom Street under the style Mundy, Brewer & Mundy, the partners being H Brice Mundy, Charles Mundy and Andrew Herbert Brewer. The firm was subsequently restyled Mundy, Brewer & Co in 1922 and Mundy, Brewer & Johnson in 1929. The firm moved to 22 Milsom Street in 1913; 3 Wood Street, Queen Square, in 1923; and 37 Great Pulteney Street in 1956. It also had a second office, at 100 Sydney Place, Bath, between *c.* 1945 and 1955. The firm undertook stock and share broking until 1957. In 1974 the firm amalgamated with Pearson May & Co, Bath, Avon, and Trowbridge, Wiltshire. It continues to practise under the name Mundy, Brewer & Johnson.

Records: Mundy, Brewer & Johnson, 37 Great Pulteney Street, Bath BA2 4BZ

Time records 1940s–60s; ledgers: 1840s–*c.* 1950, estates (rents and insurance) 1852–1905 (w); journals 1840s–*c.* 1950; cash books 1840s–*c.* 1950; share transfer register 1949–55; salary books 1940s–60s; press cuttings 1908, 1936.

NEVILL, HOVEY, GARDNER & CO (Moores Rowland)
94 Old Broad Street, London

Also at Hove

History: Founded in 1875 by Charles Henry Nevill who by 1880 was practising under his own name at 11 Queen Victoria Street, London. The practice became C H Nevill, Biddell & Co in 1895 and was restyled C H Nevill & Co in 1897, Nevill, Hovey & Co in 1901 and Nevill, Hovey, Gardner & Co in 1921. The firm moved to 1 & 2 Great Winchester Street in 1901; 65 New Broad Street in 1914; and 94 Old Broad Street in 1925. Offices were opened in Plymouth, Devon, in 1914 (this partnership was dissolved in 1943) and Hove, East Sussex, in 1921. It also had offices in Antwerp and Brussels, Belgium, and Amsterdam, Netherlands, in the 1920s and 1930s. Robert McNeil, a partner in the firm, was president of the ICAEW 1965–66. In 1976 the firm merged with the London firm Rowland & Co to form Rowland, Nevill & Co. This firm, restyled Rowland Nevill in 1983, amalgamated with Edward Moore & Sons (*qv*) in 1985 to become Moores & Rowland, now Moores Rowland.

Records: Moores Rowland, Nile House, PO Box 1034, Nile Street, Brighton BN1 1JB

Partnership agreements 1919–75; partners' meeting minutes 1927–40, 1944–76; accounts 1925, 1929, 1940–70 (w); ledger 1879–86; journals 1887–1900; cash books 1896–1911; revenue account and balance sheet book 1927–33; notes, goodwill and profit shares 1939–45; correspondence, dissolution of Plymouth office *c*.1943; articles of clerkship 1930; draft service agreement 1929; agreement, management of Hove office 1920; planning application 1954; lease, Plymouth office 1937; photograph, centenary dinner 1975.

NOTLEY PEARSON SHEWRING
38 Chepstow Road, Newport NP9 1PT

History: Founded by S T Harse and L Brown who set up in practice at 6 Dock Street, Newport, Gwent, in 1862. The firm was carried on by Brown's son, Lucian, who was joined by Frederick J Notley in 1930 when the style was changed to Lucian J Brown, Henney & Notley. The firm was renamed Lucian J Brown & Notley in 1958; Notley & Pearson in 1962; and Notley Pearson Shewring in 1979. The firm remained in Dock Street until 1962 when it moved to 8 Friars Street. It moved to its present address in 1969. The firm has had a long connection with the Archdiocese of Cardiff and for many years administered the affairs of the Monmouthshire Building Society.

Records: Notley Pearson Shewring, 38 Chepstow Road, Newport NP9 1PT

Partnership agreement: 1930, dissolution 1932; private ledger 1968–75.

Clients: Baker & Manhire Ltd, drapers: register of members and share ledger 1911, directors' minutes 1911–70, share certificates 1911–date; **Davies Bros Ltd**, builders' merchants: memoranda and articles of association 1937, register of members and share ledger 1900; **Monmouthshire & South Wales Permanent Benefit Building Society**: prospectus 1881, actuary's report 1896.

PARKER GRADWELL & CO
17 Chapel Street, Hyde SK14 1LF

Also at Stretford

History: Formed in 1931 as a result of the merger between Percy Parker and Sydney Gradwell, Manchester, Greater Manchester. The firm was styled Parker, Gradwell & Co and moved to Hollins Chambers, 64A Bridge Street, in 1931 and to 17 Chapel Street, Hyde, Greater Manchester, in 1984, following a merger with Smith, Lockett & Gowlar, certified accountants, Hyde.

Records: Parker Gradwell & Co, 17 Chapel Street, Hyde SK14 1LF

Fees ledger 1931–59; cash book 1959 on; insurance register 1931; historical notes n.d.

Clients: Denton Engineering Co Ltd: register of members and share ledger 1931; **J Titterton & Son Ltd**, butchers: register of members and share ledger 1901, share certificates 1896.

PARKIN S BOOTH & CO (Booth White)
5 Rumford Place, Chapel Street, Liverpool

Also at London

History: Founded by Parkin S Booth who set up an insolvency practice in Liverpool, Merseyside, in 1907. He also acted as proprietor of the Palatine Trade Protection Office. The firm opened an office in London, at Kimberley House, Holborn Viaduct, in 1949. In 1967 the firm amalgamated with the insolvency practice Francis Nicholls White & Co (*qv*) to form Booth White & Co, now Booth White (*qv*). The Liverpool office continues to practise under the name Parkin S Booth & Co.

Records: Guildhall Library, Aldermanbury, London EC2P 2EJ

Fees ledgers, Parkin S Booth and the Palatine Trade Protection Office Ltd 1929–68.

PEARCE, CLAYTON & MAUNDER
48 High Street West, Dorchester DT1 1UT

History: In 1894 Thomas Alfred Pearce was practising at 52A South Street,

Dorchester, Dorset, having set up as an accountant some time earlier, possibly in the 1870s. In 1900 he moved to 47 South Street. The practice was restyled Thos A Pearce & Clayton in 1914, when Arthur Essex Clayton became a partner, and Pearce, Clayton & Maunder in *c.*1942. Pearce's daughter joined the firm in 1925. The firm occupied Old School Buildings (formerly Dorchester Grammar School), South Street, from 1930, moving to National Provincial Bank Chambers in 1964 and to its present address in 1971.

Records: Pearce, Clayton & Maunder, 48 High Street West, Dorchester DT1 1UT

Partnership agreements 1951–date; private ledgers 1927–date; cash books 1970–date; lease, Old School Buildings 1930.

PEAT, MARWICK, MITCHELL & CO (KPMG Peat Marwick)
1 Puddle Dock, Blackfriars, London

Also at Aberdeen, Birmingham, Bradford, Brighton, Bristol, Cardiff, Carmarthen, Chepstow, Congleton, Darlington, Derby, Douglas, Edinburgh, Glasgow, Guernsey, Guildford, Ipswich, Jersey, Keighley, Leeds, Leek, Leicester, Liverpool, Maidstone, Manchester, Middlesbrough, Milton Keynes, Newcastle upon Tyne, Newport, Norwich, Nottingham, Plymouth, Poole, Preston, Reading, Sheffield, Southampton, St Austell, Stoke-on-Trent, Swansea, Truro and York

History: Founded by Robert Fletcher who set up an accountancy practice in Aberdeen, Grampian, in 1866 having started out as a clerk in an insurance company. In 1867 he moved to London where he opened an office at 2 Moorgate Street under the style Robert Fletcher & Co, moving to 3 Lothbury in 1876. Fletcher was a pioneer of the accountancy profession; he was one of the twelve original members of the Society of Accountants in Aberdeen (est. 1867) and was later elected president (1875–77). In 1877 he took William Barclay Peat into partnership. Peat had been taken on as a clerk in 1870 and had established the firm's first branch office in Middlesbrough, Cleveland, in 1876. In 1879 Roderick Mackay, a member of the first council of the ICAEW, became senior partner, following the retirement of Fletcher, and the firm was restyled R Mackay & Co. On Mackay's death in 1891 Peat returned to London from Middlesbrough; he became senior partner and the firm was renamed W B Peat & Co. Peat (later to become Sir William Barclay Peat) remained senior partner until 1923. By 1925 the firm had built up a large practice with connections in railway, insurance and industrial undertakings. It had expanded within the UK and abroad and had fourteen branch offices, established between 1876 and 1928: Middlesbrough, Cleveland (1876); Barrow-in-Furness, Cumbria (1891); York, North Yorkshire (1901); Cardiff, South Glamorgan (1910);

Darlington, County Durham (1910); Leeds, West Yorkshire (1910); Glasgow, Strathclyde (1912); Swansea, West Glamorgan (1913); Birmingham, West Midlands (1917); Sheffield, South Yorkshire (1919); Nottingham, Nottinghamshire (1920); Camborne, Cornwall (1921); Newcastle upon Tyne, Tyne and Wear (1924); and Manchester, Greater Manchester (1928). In 1911 the firm became associated with Marwick, Mitchell & Co in the USA (est. 1895), an arrangement intended to serve the mutual interests of both firms in the USA, Canada and Europe. Marwick, Mitchell & Co also had offices in London and Glasgow, the UK firm having been established by James Marwick in Glasgow in 1887. In 1925 a full merger took place and Peat, Marwick, Mitchell & Co came into being. The firm acquired or merged with a number of provincial practices, including: Leather & Veale, Leeds (est. 1899), in 1930; Wykes & Co, Leicester, Leicestershire (est. 1859), in 1954; Edwin Guthrie & Co (*qv*), Manchester (est. 1875), in 1955; Sharp, Parsons & Co (*qv*), Birmingham (est. 1870s), in 1961; Bourner, Bullock & Co (*qv*), Hanley, Leek and Stoke-on-Trent, Staffordshire, and Congleton, Cheshire (est. 1889), in 1964; Beevers & Adgie, Leeds (est. 1849), in 1967; Freeman, Bream & Co (*qv*), Leicester (est. *c*.1895), in 1967; and Bottomley & Smith, Keighley, West Yorkshire (est. 1889), in 1967. The firm produced six presidents of the ICAEW, namely: William Barclay Peat (1906–08); Sir Harold Gibson Howitt (1945–46); Charles Urie Peat (1959–60); Ronald George Leach (1969–70); John Peter Grenside (1975–76); and Alan John Hardcastle (1983–85). From 1906 to 1976, Peat, Marwick, Mitchell & Co occupied offices in Selborne Lane, formerly known as 11 Ironmonger Lane, in the City of London. In June 1944, the building sustained extensive bomb damage. Rebuilding work after the war led to the discovery of a Roman pavement and other Roman and medieval structures which were subsequently excavated. In 1976 the London office moved to 1 Puddle Dock, Blackfriars. The firm merged in 1987 with KMG Thomson McLintock, to form Peat Marwick McLintock, now called KPMG Peat Marwick.

Records (1): KPMG Peat Marwick, 1 Puddle Dock, Blackfriars, London EC4V 3PD

Partnership agreements: 1870–1932, dissolution 1878, 1885; international agreements 1911–67; report on organisation of the London office 1971; comparative statement of liquidations made under the Companies Acts 1866–87; notes on receivership and liquidation work and list of audits 1902, 1904; particulars of capital of public companies in which firm holds official positions 1927; papers, London & South Western Railway Co audit 1885–99; time summary (London) 1914–17; time accounts not transferred 1879; balance sheets, notes re cash income and division of fees (R Mackay & Co and W B Peat & Co) 1890–96; summary of annual expenditures, lists of profits (London and branches) 1905–18; bad debt charges 1912–14;

correspondence: publication of firm's history 1950, 1964, 1968, excavation of 11 Ironmonger Lane, incl. archaeologist's report 1951–60; Sir William Peat: speech to ICAEW council 1931, settlement and papers 1917–62; office rules (London) *c.*1920; list of offices and office regulations 1925; list of staff *c.*1915; abstract of salaries sheets 1882–96 and book 1886; holiday book (London) 1868–1917; clerks' late arrival lists 1879–87; draft examination for applicants for employment *c.*1867; audit instructions and notebook 1909–20; audit programme (London) *c.*1900; audit procedure manuals 1931, 1950; title deeds, leases, tenancy agreements, ground plans, papers, 11 Ironmonger Lane 1688–1953; photographs: Robert Fletcher, Roderick MacKay and Sir William Peat *c.*1870–1900, Middlesbrough office staff 1910; historical notes 1909–48.

Records (2): KPMG Peat Marwick, Marlborough House, Fitzalan Court, Fitzalan Road, Cardiff CF2 1TE

Partnership agreements 1913, 1925, 1954; London partners' meeting minutes 1922, 1954; draft annual reports 1913–25; accounts: 1913–26 incl. working papers, 1955, 1961–64; lists of fees rendered 1919, 1924; correspondence and memos: staff appointments 1910–14, merger of W B Peat & Co and Peat Marwick, Mitchell & Co 1924, partnership agreement 1954, between London and Cardiff offices 1923–48; salaries: analysis, UK practice, 1923; sheet, S Wales offices, 1943; articles of clerkship, Edward Granger 1900; photographs: London office dinner *c.*1925, South Wales office 1964.

Records (3): KPMG Peat Marwick, St Nicholas House, 31 Park Row, Nottingham NG1 6FQ

Clients' ledger 1947–52.

Records (4): KPMG Peat Marwick, 1 The Embankment, Neville Street, Leeds LS1 4DW

Fees rendered books 1929–41; correspondence, staff appointment 1927; list of clients 1966–87.

Clients: Ampleforth Abbey: statement of the Abbey's claim to exemption from income tax 1930; **Joseph William Craven**: executors' account book 1904–05, ledger balances 1905, accounts 1904–14, income tax assessments 1914–16; **M A Craven & Son**, confectioners: audit programmes 1906–17; **Hunter & Smallpage Ltd**, furnishers: balance sheets and profit and loss accounts 1904–11; **G T Ripley Ltd,** potato merchants: audit programme 1920–73; **York Race Course**: audit programme 1909–73, balance sheets and profit and loss accounts 1904, 1907.

Donovan Dawe, *11 Ironmonger Lane: The Story of a Site in the City of London* (London, Hutchinson, 1952)

R H Parker, 'Sir William Barclay Peat', in David J. Jeremy (ed.), *Dictionary of Business Biography*, Vol. 4 (London, Butterworth, 1985)

T A Wise, *Peat, Marwick, Mitchell & Co: 85 years* (New York, the firm, 1982)

PEPLOWS

Moorgate House, King Street, Newton Abbot TQ12 2LG

Also at Teignmouth

History: Charles Peplow, clerk to Harper, Kent & Wheeler of Shrewsbury, Shropshire, moved to Newton Abbot, Devon, in 1937 and set up in practice with Gerald Anderson as Anderson & Peplow, incorporated accountants, at 15 Courtenay Street. Anderson retired at the beginning of the Second World War and Peplow continued the practice under his own name until 1945 when he was joined by Arthur Hooker, who remained a partner until 1948. On his departure the practice, by this time at 6 Sherborne Road, was renamed Peplow & Co. In 1949 Arthur Warren, who had trained with the firm, was introduced as a partner and the practice was restyled Peplow, Warren & Co. In 1958 it joined forces with John Furler who had an office at 28a Courtenay Street. The style Peplow, Warren & Furler was retained until 1983 when the present name was adopted. The practice moved to offices in Barclays Bank Chambers in 1963 and to the present address in 1991. An office was opened in nearby Teignmouth, Devon, at 7 The Triangle in 1984. This moved to 10 Somerset Place in 1991.

Records: Peplows, Moorgate House, King Street, Newton Abbot TQ12 2LG

Partnership agreements: 1957–79, dissolution 1974; fees journal 1945–57; leases, tenancy agreements, Courtenay Street, Sherborne Road and Barclays Bank Chambers offices 1956–71; photograph, fiftieth anniversary dinner 1987.

PETERS, ELWORTHY & MOORE

Salisbury House, Station Road, Cambridge CB1 2LA

Also at Saffron Walden

History: In 1875 Robert Peters and his brother, Ebenezer, set up in practice as R & E Peters in a small house at 7 Downing Street, Cambridge, Cambridgeshire, a part of the site now known as January House. Robert was an accountant, becoming chartered in 1881, whilst Ebenezer was a property agent and a part-time collector of taxes. The accountancy side of the practice flourished and around the turn of the century the brothers were joined, first by William Elworthy in 1902, when the practice was restyled Peters, Peters & Elworthy, and then by Frank Moore in 1907. In 1911 the firm became Peters, Elworthy & Moore. In 1936 the firm moved to larger premises in the Norwich Union Buildings in Downing Street, opposite the original offices. The firm remained in Downing Street until 1971 when it moved to the present offices in Station Road. A branch was established at Saffron Walden (King Street), Essex, in 1932. The firm has, historically, served mainly the Cambridge business community but there has been a growing University connection and today the firm audits many of the Cambridge colleges.

Records: Peters, Elworthy & Moore, Salisbury House, Station Road, Cambridge CB1 2LA

Nominal ledgers incl. accounts and related papers 1913–72; cash books 1965–71; wages records 1953–71.

PRICE WATERHOUSE

Southwark Towers, 32 London Bridge Street, London SE1 9SY

Also at Aberdeen, Beverley, Birmingham, Bristol, Cardiff, Edinburgh, Glasgow, Hull, Leeds, Leicester, Liverpool, Manchester, Middlesbrough, Newcastle upon Tyne, Nottingham, Redhill, Southampton, St Albans, West Malling and Windsor

History: Founded in 1849 by Samuel Lowell Price, a founding member of the Institute of Accountants in London (*qv*) and a member of the first council of the ICAEW. An earlier partnership with William Edwards was dissolved in 1848 and both partners continued in practice under their own names at 5 Gresham Street, London. In 1865 Price, still practising at this address, was joined in partnership by William Hopkins Holyland and Edwin Waterhouse; the former was principal clerk at Coleman, Turquand, Youngs & Co, now Ernst & Young, the latter a sole practitioner since 1864 at Old Jewry Chambers, London. The firm became Price, Holyland & Waterhouse and moved to 13 Gresham Street. It continued in practice under this name until 1874, except for a brief period in 1868 when George Harvey Jay became a partner and the firm was renamed Price, Jay, Holyland & Waterhouse. In 1874 the style Price, Waterhouse & Co was adopted, becoming Price Waterhouse & Co from 1940. The principal business of the firms' early years consisted of accountancy work, auditing, arbitrations and some insolvency work. Work for railway companies started in 1867. Under Edwin Waterhouse, senior partner from 1887 to 1905, the firm's work in Britain and overseas increased. During the 1880s and 1890s he became closely associated with many financial and business concerns in the UK and undertook work for the War Office and the Admiralty. He was a member of the committee which framed the Companies Act 1900 and became involved in bank amalgamations and the conversion of private businesses into public companies. He was accountant and auditor of the

London & North Western Railway and joint auditor of the National Provincial Bank of England and of the London & Westminster Bank. Overseas, the first office was opened at 45 Broadway, New York, USA, in 1890 and an agency was opened in Australia, in 1896. By 1900 the London partners and staff totalled around sixty and the American firm twenty-seven. The first UK office outside London was opened in Liverpool, Merseyside, in 1904. In 1906 Edwin Waterhouse retired from the firm and was succeeded as senior partner by George Sneath. His son, Nicholas Edwin Waterhouse (later Sir Nicholas Waterhouse), who became president of the ICAEW in 1945, became a partner in the firm in 1906. The London office of the firm moved to 3 Frederick's Place in 1899. Offices were opened in Newcastle upon Tyne, Tyne and Wear (1912); Leeds, West Yorkshire (1928); Cardiff, South Glamorgan (1932); Manchester, Greater Manchester (1932); Birmingham, West Midlands (1939); Glasgow, Strathclyde (1950); Edinburgh, Lothian (1976); Aberdeen, Grampian (1981); Middlesbrough, Cleveland (1983); Windsor, Berkshire (1983); St Albans, Hertfordshire (1988); Redhill, Surrey (1988); and West Malling, Kent (1991). The firm also established a presence in other major cities through mergers with long-established provincial firms, including: Monkhouse, Goddard & Co, Newcastle upon Tyne, in 1920; Howard Smith, Thompson & Co (*qv*), Birmingham, in 1963; Hudson Smith, Briggs & Co (*qv*), Bristol, Avon, in 1963; Mellors, Basden & Mellors (est. 1854), Nottingham, Nottinghamshire, in 1966; Bolton, Bullivant & Co (est. 1908), Leicester, Leicestershire, in 1969; and Whittaker, Bailey & Co (est. 1863), Southampton, Hampshire, in 1975. The London office of the firm moved to Southwark Towers, 32 London Bridge Street, in 1975. In 1989 the firm acquired the Hull and Beverley, Humberside, practice of Hodgson Impey, now part of Kidsons Impey.

Records (1): Price Waterhouse, Southwark Towers, 32 London Bridge Street, London SE1 9SY

Partnership agreements: UK 1865 on, America 1898 on, other overseas firms 1875 on; partners' meeting minutes, agendas, papers: 1910, 1911, 1936–48, 1965 on, Continental firm 1935–40, European firm 1945–69, US firm 1923–40, international firm 1946 on, Birmingham (UK) office 1964–77; committee minutes: executive 1931–date (w), general 1967–72, standing 1966, technical *c.*1967 on; reports: international firm *c.*1970 on, London office 1950–54, UK firm 1948 on, US firm *c.*1966 on, European firm *c.*1955 on, regional offices: Birmingham 1965–78, Manchester 1939, Liverpool 1939; merger papers: Monkhouse, Goddard & Co 1920, Hudson, Smith, Briggs & Co 1957–63, Howard Smith, Thompson & Co 1963–66, Mellors, Basden & Mellors 1963–67, Bolton, Bullivant & Co 1968–69; papers, establishment of overseas offices: American agency/firm 1890–1900, other PW firms overseas *c.*1920 on; reports on and visits to PW offices overseas *c.*1920 on; legal papers: Rex v. Kylsant and Rex v. Morland (Royal Mail Steam Packet Co) 1931, McKesson & Robbins Inc. (USA) 1936, Hatrey 1930, Farrows Bank Ltd n.d.; time ledgers: 1940s–60s, balances 1887–88, 1894; time estimates, summaries, analyses 1887–1929 (w); accounts: 1932–47, 1954–56, drafts incl. trial balances 1932–43, working papers 1947–61, profit and loss accounts 1896–1900, 1913–19, balance sheets 1893, 1908–12, 1932–33, London, with working papers 1957–61, Leeds 1932–33, 1940–41, Manchester 1933, Newcastle 1928–34, 1939–48 and balance sheets and profit and loss accounts 1912–14, 1932–39, Plymouth 1941, Continental firm 1934–44 and profit distributions 1935–39, European firm 1944–64, international firm 1937–60, American firm 1930–39 and balance sheets, profit and loss accounts, trial balances, summaries of fees, time and cash accounts, journal entries 1890–1913, 1918–20, other PW firms overseas *c.*1925 on; income tax returns and computations 1888–1900, 1930–40; clients' ledgers 1865–1960s; clients' charges journals 1957–59; fee income 1849 to date; fee estimates 1889–1905; audit fees: summary 1897–1900, acquired and lost 1896–1902; audit record books pre-1900; time charged and fees 1891–97; analysis of difference in time and fees 1889, 1893–94; copies of clients' fee notes 1897; comparison of estimated and actual billings 1911–12; charging rates: UK firm 1934, European firm 1934, 1959, 1963–66, PW firms overseas 1920s–30s; ledgers: incl. details of annual fees 1932–57, general 1931–60s, private 1865–1962, American agency/firm 1893–94; journals: 1898–1956, 1967–70, private account 1906–17, 1957–62, American firm 1895–99; cash books: 1915–24 incl. accounts, 1948–62, 1969–71; ledger balances: 1887–96, general 1900; trial balances 1887–1905 (w) 1961; William Edwards's notes, amounts due to Holyland on his retirement 1871; salaries and profits 1887–95; bad debts account 1888; reserve for doubtful debts schedules 1890–1910; analysis of rent account 1900–06; lists of clients: UK firms 1946, Cardiff 1932 and summary of work 1945–46, Manchester 1941–53, European firm 1948–52, PW firms overseas *c.*1940 on; audits: list 1900, transferred from Lovelock & Co to PW 1900; out-letter books: Edwin Waterhouse 1864–86, George Sneath 1871–1905; correspondence: partnership agreements 1878 on, American agency/firm, partnership arrangements, merger with Jones, Caesar & Co, professional standards, goodwill 1890–1902, W B Peat & Co, proposed amalgamation with PW overseas 1915, 1921–22 and pooling agreement in north of England 1920–23, Western Australia agency 1897–1901, Continental firm 1933–47, formation of PW International 1972–73, overseas offices *c.*1920 on, UK offices, London, Newcastle, tax and profits 1938–41, Liverpool 1933–42, Manchester 1941–53, clients, payment of fees 1871–96, audits of particular clients 1871–72, clients and liquidations incl. Albert Life Assurance Co, Blakely Ordnance Co Ltd, Bucktrout Ltd, Chemical Co, Company of Proprietors of the Royal Coppermines of Cobre Ltd, Consolidated Land

Co of France, Enfield Ironworks, Flour Mill Colliery Co Ltd, Hampson & Fish Ltd, the Southern States Coal Iron & Land Co Ltd (USA), West Chiverton Mine, Cornwall, Western Life Society 1870–86, prospective clients *c.*1930 on, prospective employees 1871–1900, Samuel Lowell Price dec'd 1880s, estate of Sir Albert Wyon 1937–40; registers of professional staff 1959–61, 1964–66; clerks' address books 1891, 1909, 1920; staff lists 1902, 1935–54; holiday registers 1969 on; salaries: records 1860–1967 (w), comparison 1891, analysis 1900; clerks' monthly salaries lists 1894–96; Christmas bonus lists 1895–99; articled clerks' bonuses 1937–58; pension scheme: rules 1950, papers 1954 on; papers, staff figures, articled clerks, staff training, positions overseas *c.*1940 on; internal circulars 1950s on; manuals: office manager 1925, office (US firm) 1913, audit 1971; recruitment material *c.*1925 on; partners' personal papers: articles of clerkship 1887–1960s, appointments as auditors 1886 on; Edwin Waterhouse's papers: appointments as auditor 1905 and arbitrator in East London Railway Co v. London, Brighton & South Coast Railway Co 1885 and Richard G Casey v. Col. John T North 1895–96, memoirs 1845–1916 (p); notes, Edwin Waterhouse's retirement *c.*1906; Nicholas Edwin Waterhouse's papers: articles 1899, ledger 1900–63, journal 1900–63, cash books 1900–64; papers presented to conferences, seminars 1950s–date; mortgages, leases, tenancy agreements: London office *c.*1885 on, Cardiff 1947, Glasgow 1937–38, Liverpool 1934–35; fire policy, London office 1879; inventory, Newcastle office 1966; partners' reminiscences 1920s–date; scrapbook incl. press cuttings, opening of offices in America *c.*1899–1918; historical and biographical notes, PW partners, Price family, Waterhouse family, Monkhouse, Goddard & Co, Hudson, Briggs & Co *c.*1910–date; firm's publications: partners' and managers' newsletters 1967–88, staff newsletters 1914–18, 1968–date, technical by PW authors 1914 on, overseas bulletins 1969 on.

Clients: American Steel Foundries, New York: correspondence, papers, accounts 1902–03; **Chicago City Railway Co**: report on investigation into accounts 1907–09; **Cook's Court Improvement Co**: published accounts, directors' reports 1837–1917; **Devon & Somerset Railway Co**: accounts 1877, details of mortgage debenture stock issue n.d.; **Ebbw Vale Steel, Iron & Coal Co**: accounts 1890; **Gridley Miskin**: accounts 1920, 1923, tax 1919, 1930–32; **London & Collins Music Halls**: correspondence, papers, accounts 1901; **London & North Eastern Railway Co**: amalgamation assets and liabilities adjustments accounts 1923, audit programmes (Southern area) 1926, 1934, correspondence with PW on borrowing powers of railway companies and notes on audit 1923–28; **London & North Western Railway Co**: auditors' report 1867; **London & Westminster Bank Ltd**: papers and published accounts 1901–02; **London, Midland & Scot-**

tish Railway Co: balance sheets and working accounts 1928–36, audit memoranda books incl. details of expenditure and receipts, reserve, depreciation and suspense accounts 1926–30, extracts from private ledger n.d., statistics handbook 1913, 1922–26, correspondence, dividend policy 1936; **Mexican Coffee Syndicate Ltd**: correspondence, papers, accounts 1900; **Metropolitan Railway Co**: income tax accounts 1918–20, PW memo commenting on work of the company's audit office 1878, details of the company's bookkeeping system n.d., memo, provision for renewals of rolling stock 1930; **North Eastern Railway**, Darlington: locomotive statistics 1881–1913, memo, accounting methods 1910; **Edwin Waterhouse Will Trust**: copy will 1914, estate administration statements 1917–20; **Worshipful Company of Grocers**: recommendations, bookkeeping system 1892.

Records (2): Price Waterhouse, 89 Sandyford Road, Newcastle upon Tyne NE99 1PL (enquiries to John Barrett, London office)

Record book incl. profit and loss accounts, new work 1950–64, profits record 1921–59, list of principal audits 1950, correspondence, Monkhouse, Goddard & Co n.d., notes on staff changes 1920–50, staff in forces and war conditions 1939–45; historical notes n.d..

Peter Boys, 'What's in a Name – Firms' Simplified Family Trees: Price Waterhouse', *Accountancy*, Vol. 104, No. 1154 (October 1989), p. 160

C W DeMond, *Price Waterhouse & Co in America: A History of a Public Accounting Firm* (New York, the firm, 1951. Reprinted Arno Press, New York, 1980)

J R Edwards, 'Edwin Waterhouse', in David J Jeremy (ed.), *Dictionary of Business Biography* Vol. 5 (London, Butterworth, 1986)

J R Edwards, 'Sir Gilbert Garnsey' in David J Jeremy (ed.), *Dictionary of Business Biography* Vol. 2 (London, Butterworth, 1984)

Edgar Jones (ed.), *The Memoirs of Edwin Waterhouse: A Founder of Price Waterhouse* (London, Batsford, 1988)

G E Richards, *History of the Firm: The First Fifty Years, 1850–1900* (London, the firm, 1950)

PRITCHARD, READ & CO (Bevan & Buckland)

45 High Street, Haverfordwest, Dyfed

History: Founded by Oswald Neale Ellis who started practising with Sutcliffe & Rhodes, Fountain Chambers, Fountain Street, Halifax, West Yorkshire, in 1931, moving to Bell & Owen, 3 Castle Square, Haverfordwest, Dyfed, in 1933. The firm's name was changed to Ellis, Pritchard & Co in *c.* 1945; Pritchard & Co in 1953; and Pritchard, Read &

Co in 1959. The firm moved to 9 Victoria Place in 1958 and to 45 High Street in 1970. In 1988 two of the partners of Pritchard, Read & Co joined Bevan & Buckland, formerly Frank C Bevan & Co (*qv*); another partner continued in practice as Pritchard, Read & Co before amalgamating with Ashmole & Co in 1989 to form Ashmole, Pritchard, Read & Co.

Records: Dyfed Archives Service, The Castle, Haverfordwest SA61 2EF

Audit progress books: 1953–55, Haverfordwest 1955–56, St David's 1955–57, 1962–63; cash receipts day book 1941–46; correspondence: 1953–63, clients' 1930–60s; publications, farm accounts, accounting 1938–63.

Clients: Audit, correspondence files 1932–63; insurance agency records 1943–57; **Bridgend Bakeries**, Haverfordwest: share register 1948, minutes 1948–53, annual accounts 1952–53; **V T Brown**, innkeeper: accounts 1947, day book 1943–47; **H Dickenson & Sons Ltd**: memorandum of association 1943, register of members 1948, cash books 1954–64, correspondence 1957–63; **Don Trawling Co Ltd**: special ledger 1940–50, day books 1940–54, wages and poundage books 1950–55, voyage account book 1954–55; **Goodleigh Fisheries Ltd**: memoranda and articles of association 1948, minutes 1948–53, annual accounts 1948–51, ledgers: customers' 1951–53, general 1949–53, impersonal 1950–53, correspondence 1948–52, insurance claims 1950–53, liquidation papers 1953–57; **Hamilton Fishing Co Ltd**: memoranda and articles of association 1948, register of members 1946, minutes 1946–53; **Harford Builders' Supply Co Ltd**: memoranda and articles of association 1952, share register 1952, minutes 1952, annual accounts 1951–57, sales ledger 1952, 1954, day books 1951–56, cash books 1952–56, liquidation papers 1953–57; **C B Jenkins & Son (Builders) Ltd**, Saundersfoot: ledger 1961–63, purchases day book 1963–64, cash book 1963, correspondence 1961–64, time and wages books 1962–63; **Ocean Fisheries Ltd**: memoranda and articles of association 1941, share register 1941, share certificate book 1946, minutes 1941–53, balance sheets 1947–52; **South Pembrokeshire Grass Driers Association Ltd**: register of members 1950, share certificates book 1950, rules book n.d., minutes 1950–54, annual accounts 1950–54, general ledgers 1950–51, customers' ledgers 1952, purchases day book 1950, work record book n.d., baling record book 1951–54.

RABJOHNS

1, 2, 3 & 4 College Yard, Worcester WR1 2LB

History: Started by Phillip Rabjohns, an incorporated accountant, at 1 College Yard, Worcester, Worcestershire, in 1935. Initially Rabjohns practised under his own name. During the Second World War he absorbed the country practice of Stoy Hayward & Co, now Stoy Hayward, and carried on the local firm of Harry, Day & Co, one of the oldest accountancy firms in Worcester, on a caretaker basis. Part of this firm was retained by Rabjohns after the war, the remainder joining the firm of Bowen, Dawes, Wagstaff & Co. In 1945 Harold Leopard was admitted as a partner and the practice became Rabjohns, Leopard & Co. Following the war the firm flourished, attracting the majority of its clients from small businesses and farmers and also serving a few larger clients, such as Berrows Newspapers Ltd. The firm also commenced a specialisation in insolvency matters and has more recently developed a particular expertise in dealing with ecclesiastical matters and educational foundations. In 1970 the firm absorbed the Evesham, Worcestershire, practice of Charles Raymer & Son. This practice at 4 Avon Street was originally the Evesham office of Impey, Cudworth & Co, a predecessor of Kidsons Impey. This was followed in 1981 by a merger with Dauncey & Co (Lloyds Bank Chambers, The Cross), previously the Worcester office of the long-established local firm Hubert Leicester & Co. In 1983 the firm adopted the style of Rabjohns. In 1986 and 1990 there were further mergers, first with the Evesham practice of Kingscott, Dix & Co and then with the Birmingham, West Midlands, based firm of Clement, Keys & Co. The latter merger resulted in a demerger in 1991 of the Worcester office which then reverted to its former name of Rabjohns. At this stage the insolvency section of the firm was transferred to Pannell Kerr Forster, Worcester. Rabjohns has always had premises in College Yard and has had a strong connection with the cathedral, its accommodation having originally been provided by the Dean and Chapter as part of an agreement to prepare the cathedral accounts. In 1979 it purchased the long leasehold of Nos. 2 and 3 College Yard and in 1984 acquired a short leasehold interest in No. 4.

Records: Rabjohns, 1, 2, 3 & 4 College Yard, Worcester WR1 2LB

Partnership agreements: 1949–78, dissolution 1953, notes 1959; partners' meeting minutes 1945–53, 1962–date; nominal ledgers 1945–80s; cash books 1935–80s.

RANSOM HARRISON & LEWIS (Barber, Harrison & Platt)
267 Glossop Road, Sheffield

History: Founded by Edwin Ransom Harrison, an incorporated accountant, who commenced practising at 54 Bank Street, Sheffield, South Yorkshire, in 1912. By 1925 the firm was known as Ransom Harrison & Lewis. It moved to 9/11 Fosters Buildings, 22 High Street, in 1929; to National Provincial Chambers, York Street, in 1934; and to 269 Glossop Road in 1958. In 1970 the firm merged with Jarvis Barber & Sons (*qv*) and Sissons, Platt & Co, to form Barber, Harrison & Platt (*qv*).

Records: Barber, Harrison & Platt, 2 Rutland Park, Sheffield S10 2PD

Partnership agreements 1912, 1918, 1947; accounts 1955–69; bill book 1959–68; ledgers: nominal incl. some balance sheets and profit and loss accounts 1928–70, general office 1923–30s; cash book 1955 on; wages books 1941–48, 1958–67; lease of 11 York Street 1933; photograph, E Ransom Harrison n.d.

RAWLINSON & HUNTER
1 Hanover Square, London W1A 4SR

Also at Douglas, Ewell, Guernsey and Jersey

History: Founded by Alfred William Rawlinson, John Hannaford and Robert Hunter who left the firm of Chas W Rooke, Lane & Co, Norfolk Street, London, in 1933 and set up in practice in Aldwych House, Aldwych, under the style Rawlinson, Hannaford & Hunter. The firm was renamed Rawlinson & Hunter in 1938. At an early date the firm began to specialise in taxation work and international asset protection. Many overseas clients were acquired through Hunter's travels abroad, including Ciba-Geigy and other Swiss multinational pharmaceutical companies. The firm has also acted for a number of clients in the entertainment business, the Nestlé group of companies, the Campbell Connelly Group, music publishers, Alfred Blossom, architect, and the proprietors of various football pools. The firm has five offices outside the UK. Its London office moved to 51 Green Street in 1959; 105 Park Street in 1969; and the present address in 1978.

Records: Rawlinson & Hunter, 1 Hanover Square, London W1A 4SR

Partnership accounts 1933–date; working papers 1933–date; fees ledger 1953–76; ledgers: 1943–55, Paris 1937–40, private 1937–77 (w), nominal 1943–60; index to clients' files 1954–68; monthly salaries book 1935–43; photographs: Bush House n.d., Aldwych House *c.* 1923.

R Spooner, *Rawlinson & Hunter, Chartered Accountants: Its Formation, Development and Growth, 1933–84* (The firm, 1990)

READS & CO
71 Mark Lane, London EC3R 7RD

History: Founded in 1869 by George Norton Read who set up in practice at 3 Milk Street, London, as G N Read & Co. By 1871 he had taken a partner, William Dangerfield, and the name was changed to Read & Dangerfield. The firm was subsequently restyled: Read, Dangerfield & Smith (1872); G N Read, Smith & Co (1876); G N Read Son & Co (1878); G N Read, Son, Cocke & Watson (1921); and Reads, Cocke & Watson (1927). The firm moved to 51 Queen Street in 1872, and then successively to 49 Queen Victoria Street in 1882, 44 Gresham Street in 1898 and 47

Gresham Street in 1927. In December 1940 the offices were damaged in a bombing raid and moved temporarily to Friars House, New Broad Street, with such records as could be salvaged. Offices were opened in Guernsey, Channel Islands, in 1900; Bristol, Avon, in 1904; Newfoundland, Canada, in 1905; and Jersey, Channel Islands, in 1928. The Bristol and Newfoundland offices were closed in 1909 and 1933 respectively. During the German occupation of the Channel Islands the Guernsey practice was administered by another local firm and was reopened after the Second World War. In 1964 the firm merged with Drury, Thurgood & Co (*qv*), London. The name Reads, Cocke & Watson was retained until 1969 when the present style was adopted. There was a further merger in 1971 with the London firm of Thomas L Theobald & Son (est. 1867). The combined firms of Reads & Co and Drury, Thurgood & Co moved to the present address in 1987 and in the same year the Guernsey and Jersey offices became independent of the London firm. The firm continues to practise under the names of both Reads & Co and Drury, Thurgood & Co.

Records: Reads & Co, 71 Mark Lane, London EC3R 7RD

Partnership agreements 1925–date; partners' meeting minutes 1940–46, 1962–81, 1987–date; report on the Jersey branch during the German occupation 1944; private office files 1965–81; papers, merger with Drury, Thurgood & Co 1964–65; time summary 1936; accounts 1934–44, 1960–date; fees: journals 1933–63, analyses 1961–72, rendered 1964–68; private and expense ledgers 1925–69; private journals 1951–53; cash books 1933–71; trust cash book 1932–49; clients' disbursements 1964–68; book debts 1920–33; insurance register, ledger and journal 1930–49; correspondence 1965–75; salaries books: weekly 1936–45, 1963–68, monthly 1918–45; office manual 1971; leases, 44 & 47 Gresham Street and related correspondence 1899, 1927–82; photographs, 47 Gresham Street 1980s.

REVELL & REVELL (Revell Ward)

7 St George's Square, Huddersfield, West Yorkshire

History: Founded by Alfred Revell who started practising in Huddersfield, West Yorkshire, in 1886. Revell was admitted as an associate member of the ICAEW in 1896 and practised under his own name at 55 New Street, Huddersfield, until 1899 when he was joined by his son, Frank Ethelbert Revell, the practice being restyled Revell & Revell. Alfred Revell's grandson, Eric, became senior partner of the firm in 1948. The firm moved to 69 & 71 New Street in 1901 and to St George's Square in 1935. In 1967 Revell & Revell merged with Steel Ward & Co, also of St George's Square, to form Revell Ward.

Records: Revell Ward, Norwich Union House, High Street, Huddersfield HD1 2LN

Alfred Revell's diary 1886; cash book 1886–87; profit and loss accounts and balance sheets 1886–87; photograph, Alfred Revell c. 1900.

ROBT A PAGE & CO

16 Pelham Road, Nottingham NG5 1AR

History: Started in 1897 by Alfred Charles Woodroffe Rogers and Robert Alexander Page. In 1902 they merged with the practice of Charles Rogers, Temple Buildings, Albert Square, Nottingham, Nottinghamshire, and the firm became Rogers, Son & Page. The firm moved to Milton Chambers, Milton Street, in 1904. Charles Rogers died in 1906 and A C W Rogers and Page continued until 1923 when Rogers moved his share of the practice by mutual consent to Cheapside, Nottingham. Page carried on the firm under the style of Robt A Page & Co and admitted his son, who qualified in 1925, into the partnership. The firm moved to Alexandra House, 43 Alexandra Street, in 1975 and to the present address in 1981. The firm of A C W Rogers is now known as Rogers, Spencer & Co and also practises in Pelham Road.
Records: Robt A Page & Co, 16 Pelham Road, Nottingham NG5 1AR

Partnership agreements 1902, 1954; fees: ledgers 1950–81, journal 1968–69; clients' disbursements book 1899–1965; accounts and working papers 1939–date; private ledgers 1902–date; cash book 1965–70; register of deeds 1902–47; salaries books 1959–81; articles of clerkship 1889–1975; leases, 19 Milton Street 1904, 1969; photographs, partners c.1900–40.

ROBERT MILLER TATE

3 Portland Terrace, Newcastle upon Tyne NE2 1QQ

History: Founded by Robert Miller who started practising under his own name at 46 Sunderland Street, Houghton-le-Spring, Tyne and Wear, in 1926 having served his articles with A W Price & Rose, Newcastle upon Tyne, Tyne and Wear. The practice became Robert Miller & Co in 1930 and was sold in 1944 when Robert Miller died. In 1944 an office was opened at 13 Mosley Street, Newcastle upon Tyne, which became, in 1954, Robert Miller Tate. The firm moved to 31 Oxford Street in 1948; Milburn House, Dean Street, in 1970; 15/17 Sandhill in 1971; and 3 Portland Terrace in 1987.

Records: Robert Miller Tate, 3 Portland Terrace, Newcastle upon Tyne NE2 1QQ (enquiries to W S Tate, FCA)

Partnership agreement 1954; partners' meeting minutes 1970s–date; accounts 1954–date; fees journals 1954–date; nominal ledgers 1954–date; cash books 1954–date; monthly salaries book 1957–66; photograph, Robert Miller n.d.; technical material 1950 on.

S E COTTAM & SON

77 King Street, Manchester, Greater Manchester

Also at London

History: Founded by Samuel Ellsworth Cottam in Manchester, Greater Manchester, as a firm of accountants and general agents. The firm was carried on by his son, Samuel, and by the First World War was practising at 77 King Street. An office was opened in London in *c.* 1945. The firm appears to have ceased practising in 1951. Clients of the firm in the 1800s included William Harrison Ainsworth; Sir Henry R Bishop; Manchester Guardian Society for the Protection of Trade; the Society for the Preservation of Footpaths; Royal Exchange Library; the Gentlemen's Glee Club; Churchwardens of St John's Church, Manchester; the Photographic Society; the Clerical Medical & General Life Insurance Co; the Lancashire Commercial Clerks' Society; and the Botanical and Horticultural Society.

Records: Manchester Central Library, Archives Department, St Peter's Square, Manchester M2 5PD

Estate ledgers 1841–1902; letter books, Association for the Preservation of Ancient Public Footpaths 1858–67; general correspondence 1837–97; Samuel Cottam's: private ledger 1841–84, out-letter books 1877–82; papers, Manchester Grammar School 1850–64; minute book, Daltonian Professorship and Monument Committee 1844.

Clients: Association for the Preservation of Ancient Public Footpaths: details of annual meetings, correspondence 1856–73; **Lancashire Commercial Clerks' Society**: minutes 1813–23, 1835–51, 1859–64, letters 1818–21, annual reports 1802–82, register of members 1802–22, accounts 1841–82, summaries of accounts 1802–22, ledgers 1824–72, cash books 1802–07, 1836–69, claimants' pay book 1860–76, letter books, correspondence 1848–64 (w), list of members 1802–49; **Manchester Royal Eye Hospital**: list of committee members 1858, subscribers' accounts 1868–76; **Mayes' Charity**: accounts of chief rents 1846–92; **Platt Bros**, Oldham, Greater Manchester: annual reports and balance sheets 1867–80, accounts 1853–81, list of shareholders 1853–72; **St Thomas's Chapel**, Pendleton, Greater Manchester: accounts, details of building and opening 1767–1810.

S E SHORT & CO

6 Fairfield Road, Chesterfield S40 4TP

History: Founded by Samuel Edward Short, an incorporated accountant, who set up in practice under his full name in 1890 at 31 Gluman Gate, Chesterfield, Derbyshire. The firm carried on the business of accountants, auditors, estate agents and managers, and insurance brokers. From 1914 the firm operated from one address under the styles Saml Edwd Short & Co, accountants and auditors, and Saml Edwd Short & Co, estate and insurance agents. This continued until 1956 when the estate agency side demerged. The firm moved to 17 Gluman Gate in 1904 and to the present address in 1974. It amalgamated with Middleton & Stewart (est. 1929), Chesterfield, in 1974.

Records: S E Short & Co, 6 Fairfield Road, Chesterfield S40 4TP

Partnership agreements 1914–date; accounts 1952–date; tax computations 1916; bill books 1899–1912; ledgers: nominal 1958–68, private 1927–58; cash book 1905–80; copy letters to clients 1912–14; monthly salaries books 1926–74; weekly wages books 1899–1919; papers, correspondence: Short's estate incl. executors' accounts, copy will, list of investments, 1913–23, Liberal Association and elections 1908–14; historical notes 1914, 1974.

SHARP, PARSONS & CO (KPMG Peat Marwick)
115 Colmore Row, Birmingham, West Midlands

History: In 1880 J Luke & E M Sharp were practising at 47 Ann Street, Birmingham, West Midlands. In 1882 the practice moved to 120 Colmore Row. By 1888 the firm's name had changed to Sharp, Parsons & Co. An office was opened at 28 & 29 St Swithin's Lane, London, in 1890. In 1908 the Birmingham office moved to 115 Colmore Row. In 1961 the Birmingham practice amalgamated with Peat, Marwick, Mitchell & Co (*qv*), now part of KPMG Peat Marwick.

Records: Archives Division, Birmingham Central Library, Chamberlain Square, Birmingham B3 3HQ

Private ledger 1888–1900; record of charges to clients 1888–95.

SIDNEY H HOSSELL & CO (Wenham Major)
Prudential Buildings, 48 Corporation Street, Birmingham, West Midlands

History: Founded by Sidney H Hossell who qualified as a chartered accountant in 1886. He practised under his own name, at Hatherton Chambers, Old Square, Birmingham, West Midlands, until 1900 when the practice became Sidney H Hossell, Cox & Co. The name Sidney Hossell & Co was adopted in 1903. During the First World War the firm moved to Lansdowne House, 16 Union Street, and later, in 1928, to Prudential Buildings, 48 Corporation Street. In 1935 it merged with Wenham Brothers & Co (*qv*), now part of Wenham Major (*qv*).

Records: Wenham Major, 89 Cornwall Street, Birmingham B3 3BY

Private ledgers 1924–47; articles of clerkship, Sidney H Hossell 1876.

SIMPSON WOOD

Bank Chambers, Market Street, Huddersfield HD1 2EW

Also at Penistone

History: Founded by Fred Lockwood who started practising at Church Lane, Moldgreen, Huddersfield, West Yorkshire, in 1880, moving to Albert Chambers, Victoria Lane, in 1881. From 1892 to 1896 he was clerk to Armitage & Norton (*qv*). Thereafter he set up in practice under his own name at Market Place Chambers, New Street, where the firm remained until 1913 when it moved to the present address, previously known as District Bank Chambers. The firm was restyled Lockwood, Turner & Wood in 1909; H V Wood & Co in 1918; Simpson, Wood & Co in 1954; and Simpson Wood in 1981. An office was acquired in Penistone, South Yorkshire, in 1987. The firm has acted for many clients in the textile and engineering trades.

Records: Simpson Wood, Bank Chambers, Market Street, Huddersfield HD1 2EW

Partnership agreements 1909–date; accounts 1918, 1950s–date; analysis of profit and loss account 1908; income tax assessment 1913; clients' ledgers 1970–date; particulars of audits 1895; ledgers: nominal 1924–83, private 1908–70, balances 1918–35; cash journal 1943–58; bank passbooks 1909–30s; list of clients 1921; salary records 1918–24, 1950–60s; employment applications 1920–24; tenancy agreements 1919, 1938; valuation, office furniture 1925; photograph, office premises *c*.1910.

SMART & SNELL

22 Queen Street, London

History: Founded by Frederick Bertram Smart who was practising at 72 Basinghall Street, London, in 1859 and subsequently moved to 38 Gresham Street in 1864; 85 & 86 Cheapside in 1868; 53 Cannon Street in 1878; and 22 Queen Street in 1888. In 1865 Smart took into partnership James Thomas Snell and the firm was restyled Smart & Snell, and then Smart, Snell & Co in 1868; Fdk Bertram Smart & Co in 1879; Fdk B Smart & Co in 1880; Fredk B Smart, Jeffreys & Co in 1897; and Fredk B Smart & Co in 1913. The firm appears to have ceased practising in 1965.

Records: Guildhall Library, Aldermanbury, London EC2P 2EJ

Partnership agreement 1865.

SMEDLEY, SARGANT & CO (KPMG Peat Marwick)

25 Waterloo Street, Birmingham, West Midlands

Also at London

History: Practised as Smedley & Corder from *c*.1879 to 1888 at 57 Colmore Row, Birmingham, West Midlands. In 1888 it was restyled Smedley & Sargant, moved to 25 Waterloo Street and acquired an office at Lonsdale Chambers, 27 Chancery Lane, London. In *c*.1900 the practice became W S Aston & Co. This eventually became Aston Wilde & Co, the Birmingham office of which merged in 1963 with Thomson McLintock & Co (*qv*), now part of KPMG Peat Marwick.

Records: Archives Division, Birmingham Central Library, Chamberlain Square, Birmingham B3 3HQ

Profit and loss accounts 1888, 1889; ledger balances 1889.

Clients: Bretts Stamping Co Ltd: disbursements, *c*.1890; **John R Ellerman**: private diary 1879–82; **Tube Investments Ltd**: letters from Arthur Chamberlain re chairmanship 1898–1909.

SMITH, SON & WILKIE

22 Darlington Street, Wolverhampton WV1 4HX

History: Founded by Benjamin Smith who set up in business as an insurance agent at 56 Darlington Street, Wolverhampton, West Midlands, in 1861, moving to 59 Darlington Street in *c*. 1868 and 22 Darlington Street in *c*. 1873. By 1880 the firm was carried on by Lawley Tavener Smith, Benjamin's son, under the style Benjamin Smith & Son. The firm was restyled Benjamin Smith, Sons & Wilkie, when Mein Wilkie was admitted as a partner, in 1888; Benjamin Smith, Son & Wilkie in 1892; and Smith, Son & Wilkie in 1964.

Records: Wolverhampton Borough Archives, Central Library, Snow Hill, Wolverhampton WV1 3AX

Partnership agreements 1888–1961; time: ledger 1968–75, journal 1958–60, sheets 1954–69 (w), summary 1953–60; income account and balance sheet 1954; accounts working papers 1954–55; fees ledger 1888–1936; clients' disbursements books 1916–90; bill books 1872–99, 1910–83 (w); bills rendered books incl. analyses of office expenses and receipts 1943–68; ledger 1888–1952; cash books: 1874–77, 1932–61, clients' account 1937–66; receipts and payments book 1952–57; out-letter books 1880–1926; correspondence: staff 1929–45, partnership agreement 1910–15, London & County Land & Building Co Ltd 1924–35, dispute between L T Smith and George Aitkin 1890s; copy reports on accounts audited 1895–1937; index to clients' records *c*. 1924; weekly wages books 1952–63, 1979–80; employment: application 1921, agreements 1888–1915; office: leases 1961, 1968, 1974, inventory 1936; appointment, agent for the Norwich Union Life Assurance Society 1877; articles of clerkship 1908–15, 1965, 1969; photographs: office exterior 1901, Darlington Street and Queen Square 1907,

Mein Wilkie *c.* 1915; circular letter, partnership change 1877; agents' register, Norwich Union Fire Insurance Society 1863–77.

Clients: Adam Boulton & Co: register of members and share ledgers 1939–65, transfers register 1962, register of dividends paid 1963–72, share certificates 1939–62, directors' and general meeting minutes 1939–65, annual accounts *c.* 1922–36, Adam Boulton dec'd estate ledger and accounts 1916–51, annual accounts 1936–61; **E D Crane**, dec'd: private ledger 1953–64; **William Hodson**, dec'd: ledgers 1890–98, 1930–63, cash books 1890–1952, balance sheet books 1912–61; **Industrial Pressings (Wolverhampton) Ltd**: private ledger 1947–66; **George Bernard Jenks**, dec'd: ledger 1956–70, cash book 1956–70; **John Barrington & Co Ltd:** ledgers 1938–72; **Raymond Clark**, dec'd: trust fund ledger 1943–61, cash book 1917–56; **London & County Land & Building Co Ltd**: directors' meeting minutes 1944–49, annual reports and accounts 1911–28, share ledger 1912–48, ledger 1916–49; **Samuel Loveridge**, dec'd: estate accounts 1906–84, trust ledgers 1906–65, investments ledger 1906–62, cash books 1906–58; **Priestfield Iron & Brick Co Ltd**: register of members 1952; **Queen Square Syndicate Ltd**: directors' meeting minutes 1907–62, shareholders' meeting minutes 1907–53, register of members 1907–58, share register n.d., shareholders' attendance book 1907–55, share certificate book 1962, annual returns register 1950–61, private ledgers 1908–61; **R M Shelton**, dec'd: private ledger 1939–62, cash book 1939–62; **Side Welders Association**: private ledger 1944–46; **South Staffordshire Golf Club Ltd**: annual reports and accounts 1907, 1926, 1932, house committee accounts and statistics 1926–35, research board reports 1931; **South Staffordshire Iron & Steel Association**: cash book 1937–79; **Weaver & Mason Ltd**, Wednesbury, West Midlands: nominal ledgers 1945–59, private ledgers 1922–58; **Mrs C A Wellesley**: marriage settlement fund ledger 1899–1930; **White & Poole (Engineers) Ltd**: ledgers 1941–71; **George Golightly Wilkie**, dec'd: annual accounts 1942, ledgers 1929–58, investment ledger 1938–60, cash book 1929–59, correspondence 1948–60; **Mein Wilkie,** dec'd: estate papers, executorship accounts 1936; **Wolverhampton & District Butchers Hide, Skin, Fat & Wool Co**: memoranda and articles of association 1886, register of members and share ledger 1886–1967, register of directors 1948–64, annual reports and accounts 1964–73, register of mortgages and bonds 1886–99, share allotment book 1886, share certificates 1887–73, dividends book 1925–73, ledger 1962–73, private ledgers 1932–59, cash books 1961–73, wages books 1966–73, correspondence re shares 1967, liquidator's cash book 1973–75; **Wolverhampton Freeholders Permanent Benefit Building Society**: annual accounts 1870, accountants' report 1869, Benjamin Smith's report to shareholders re deficiencies of Society 1869; **Wolverhampton New Waterworks Co Ltd**: ledger 1856–69; **Wolverhampton Society for the Blind**: annual reports and accounts 1883–1904.

SOLOMON HARE
Oakfield House, Oakfield Grove, Clifton, Bristol BS8 2BN

Also at Chippenham, Chipping Sodbury and Cirencester

History: Founded by Solomon Hare who started practising in Bristol, Avon, in the 1870s. By 1885 the practice was at 44 High Street and moved to University Chambers, 48 Wine Street, in 1891; 3 Mary le Port Street, High Street End, in 1895; Brighton Chambers, 6 St Stephen's Avenue, in 1901; 39 Broad Street in 1935; 10 Union Street *c.*1955; and Oakfield House, Oakfield Grove, in 1987. The style Solomon Hare & Co was first used in 1903. This was shortened to Solomon Hare in 1988. The firm opened offices in Chipping Sodbury, Avon, in 1981; Cirencester, Gloucestershire, in 1984; and Chippenham, Wiltshire, in 1985.

Records: Solomon Hare, Oakfield House, Oakfield Grove, Clifton, Bristol BS8 2BN

Private ledgers 1874–91, 1916–40; leases, office premises 1935, 1949; photographs: Edward Hare n.d., Solomon Hare n.d.

Clients: Bristol Tramways Co Ltd: accounts 1876.

SOMERSET, COWPER & CO (Saffery Champness)
199 Piccadilly, London

History: Originated in 1914 as John James, Denton-Clarke, at 4 Walbrook, London, and renamed James & Cowper in 1919; C S S Cowper in 1931; and Somerset, Cowper & Co in 1933. The firm moved to 199 Piccadilly in *c.*1945. An office opened at Newbury, Berkshire, in 1922, reformed as a separate practice in the 1930s, and continues to practise under the name James & Cowper (*qv*). Somerset, Cowper & Co merged with J H Champness, Corderoy, Beesly & Co (*qv*) in 1973 to form Champness, Cowper & Co (*qv*), now part of Saffery Champness.

Records: Saffery Champness, Fairfax House, Fulwood House, Fulwood Place, Gray's Inn, London WC1V 6UB

Partnership agreements 1956–71.

SPAIN BROTHERS & CO
Westgate House, 87 St Dunstan's Street, Canterbury CT2 8AE

Also at Ashford, Dover, Folkestone, Sittingbourne, Tonbridge, Tunbridge Wells

History: Founded by Henry Spain, who was employed by Harding, Whinney, Gibbons & Co (now part of Ernst & Young) in 1869 and set up in practice at Gresham Buildings, Basinghall Street, London, in 1871. Shortly after he took Charles Andrews into partnership and the firm was restyled Spain & Andrews. William Augustine Spain joined the partnership in 1875 after which it was restyled Spain, Andrews & Spain; Spain Brothers, Andrew & Co; and, in 1881, Spain Brothers & Co. The firm moved to 76 Coleman Street in 1881 and to 45 London Wall in 1908. A second London office, at 1 Old Burlington Street, was opened in 1948. By 1960 the firm had offices in Brighton and Hastings, East Sussex (opened 1934 and 1949 respectively); and Tunbridge Wells, Sutton, Tonbridge and Ashford, Kent (opened 1949, 1951, 1957 and 1958 respectively). Through a merger with Andrews & Co in 1965 the firm acquired offices in Canterbury and Dover, Kent. All of the firm's offices traded under separate names. In 1961 these offices divided into Sutton, Hastings, Brighton and Worthing, which continued to practise under their individual names, and London, Tonbridge and Tunbridge Wells which retained the style Spain Brothers & Co. In 1982 the London office of Spain Brothers & Co amalgamated with Wilkins Kennedy, London. In 1987 Spain Brothers & Co amalgamated with Kingsford, Garlant & Co, Maidstone and Sittingbourne, Kent.

Records (1): Spain Brothers & Co, 16 Lonsdale Gardens, Tunbridge Wells TN1 1NU

Partnership agreement 1911; letter, terms of partnership 1934; lists: clients 1927, staff 1945; office notices 1935, 1941, 1952; appointment, Henry Spain as receiver of Henry Brooks Ltd 1891; historical notes n.d.

Records (2): Folkestone Library, 2 Grace Hill, Folkestone CT20 1HD

Clients: Burlington Mansions Ltd: ledgers 1898–1946; **Folkestone Chamber of Trade**: papers *c.*1899–1978; **Folkestone Hotel Syndicate Ltd**: minutes, title deeds 1815–1945; **Folkestone Pier & Lift Co**: ledger, journals, statements of accounts, deeds, insurance policies *c.*1885–1968; **Leas Pavilion (Folkestone) Ltd**: minutes, registers, share certificates 1902–80; **Mansions Syndicate Ltd**: ledgers 1904–48; **William Muddle**, grocers: minutes, ledgers, cash books, registers 1914–73; **Philip Sassoon Model Housing Society Ltd**: minutes accounts 1919–69.

SPOFFORTHS

Tudor Court, 52 Richmond Road, Worthing BN11 1PR

Also at Bognor Regis, Chichester, Horsham, Littlehampton and Storrington

History: Founded by Arthur Stubbs who started practising as a bookkeeper and accountant at 5 Bath Place, Worthing, West Sussex, in 1898, moving to 26 Grafton Road in *c.* 1908. Stubbs was joined by his son, Arthur, *c.* 1921 and the firm was restyled Arthur Stubbs & Son. In 1932 Stubbs, senior, was introduced to Stanley A Spofforth, an expert in taxation matters, who was acting for a mutual client in Worthing whilst still articled to Armitage & Norton (*qv*) in Leeds, West Yorkshire. Spofforth left Leeds and joined Stubbs in partnership in 1934, when the firm became Arthur Stubbs &

Spofforth. The firm moved to 10 Shelley Road *c.* 1930 and to 52 Richmond Road in 1952. In the 1940s a London partnership was formed under the style Spofforth & Prince. This practice was subsequently restyled Stanley A Spofforth & Co and, following a merger with Morgan, Brown & Haynes in 1990, Morgan Brown & Spofforth. In 1973 the Worthing firm amalgamated with West, Barrett & Co, Littlehampton, West Sussex, becoming, for a short time, Spofforth Hews & Burn, West Barrett & Co and then Spofforth, West & Hews, in 1973, and Spofforths in 1988. In 1991 the firm amalgamated with Harrison & Taylor, Horsham, West Sussex.

Records: Spofforths, 41 Beach Road, Littlehampton BN17 5JD

Partnership agreements 1947–date; partners' diaries 1930s–*c.* 45.

SPRAGUE, NICHOLSON, MORGAN & CO (MacIntyre Hudson)
Chancery House, Chancery Lane, London

Also at London, Richmond and High Wycombe

History: P E Metzner set up a practice at 3 Serle Street, Lincoln's Inn, London, in 1882. By 1887 he was listed as in practice both at 63/64 Chancery Lane and at Leyton but in 1893 moved his residence to Richmond, Surrey, where he became prominent in church and council affairs. He opened an office in High Wycombe (31 High Street), Buckinghamshire, in 1900 and another in Richmond (40 George Street) in 1901. He was joined in partnership by Henry Douglas Sprague, a member of the Edinburgh Society of Chartered Accountants, in 1902 and two years later the name of the firm was changed to Metzner & Sprague. There was a further change in 1925 when the name became Sprague, Nicholson, Morgan & Co, a title which was retained until the merger with MacIntyre Hudson (*qv*) in 1971.

Records: MacIntyre Hudson, Equipoise House, Grove Place, Bedford MK40 3LE

Fees ledgers 1932–54; clients' disbursements book 1949–73.

Stanford Letts, *MacIntyre Hudson; May 1880 – May 1980* (MacIntyre Hudson, 1980)

SQUANCE & CO (KPMG Peat Marwick)
Douro House, Douro Terrace, Sunderland, Tyne and Wear

Also at Darlington

History: Founded by Thomas Coke Squance who set up in practice in 1855 at 35 Frederick Street, Sunderland, Tyne and Wear. He moved in 1873 to 31 Fawcett Street and in 1875 to 32 Fawcett Street. The practice became T C Squance & Son, when he was joined by his son in 1877, and T C Squance

& Sons, when he took into partnership a second son, in 1888. The firm then moved to 26 John Street. The firm merged in 1948 with John Parker & Sons, 110 High Street West, Sunderland, and in 1962 with Rawlings & Wilkinson, 55 John Street, Sunderland. The firm was then restyled Squance & Co. In 1956 an office was opened in Conniscliffe Road, Darlington, Durham, and in 1957 the Sunderland office moved to Douro House in Douro Terrace. The firm merged in 1966 with Thomson McLintock & Co (*qv*), now part of KPMG Peat Marwick.

Records: KPMG Peat Marwick, Maybrook House, 27 Grainger Street, Newcastle upon Tyne NE1 5JT

Partnership agreements 1928–66; tax files 1962–66; fees: ledgers 1897–1966, journals 1880–1966, rendered book 1874–92; ledgers: 1877–97, private 1907–66; journals 1877–1956 incl. balance sheets from 1880; cash books 1877–1972; registers of securities 1890–1969; out-letter books 1876–1922; correspondence: staff and partnership matters 1960–63, office premises 1966–71; circulars, partnership changes 1911–72; register of clerks 1876–1942; staff record books 1876–1901, 1911–58, 1959–71.

Clients: Miscellaneous wills and trust documents 1879–1947; **Easington Coal Co Ltd**: directors' meetings minutes 1898–1902; **Hindustan Steam Shipping Co Ltd**, Sunderland: debenture trustees' minutes 1903–11; **River Wear Commission**, Sunderland: annual accounts 1859–87; **Sunderland Joint Stock Banking Co**: directors' meetings minutes 1857; **Wearmouth Coal Co Ltd**: directors' meetings minutes n.d.

STOY HAYWARD & CO (Stoy Hayward)
95 Wigmore Street, London

History: Founded by Albert Frederick Stoy who set up in practice at 224 Dashwood House, New Broad Street, London, in 1903. The style of the firm was changed to Stoy, Threlford & Co in 1910; A F Stoy & Co in 1915; and Stoy, Hayward & Co in 1932. The firm moved to 114/115 High Holborn in 1903; 119/120 London Wall in 1910; 103 Cannon Street in *c.*1918; 5 Giltspur Street in *c.*1945; 97 & 99 Park Street in 1956; and 95 Wigmore Street in 1968. In the 1920s an additional office was opened in Hanover Square which expanded and later moved to Upper Grosvenor Street. After the Second World War the firm handled a number of important flotations and developed an expertise in the area of property work. The firm took over a number of London practices including: Lavy, Ascher & Co, in 1965; Lawrence Fenton, in 1969; and Herbert Hill, in 1971. In 1975 Stoy Hayward & Co amalgamated with the London firm Hesketh, Hardy, Hirshfield & Co, a member of Horwarth & Horwarth International, which brought to the firm a hotel consultancy division. The firm's name was shortened to Stoy Hayward in 1985.

Records: Stoy Hayward, 8 Baker Street, London W1M 1DA

Schedules incl. work-in-progress, analysis of fees journal, notes, trial balance, analysis of clients' ledgers, time written off 1959–60.

THOMSON MCLINTOCK & CO (KPMG Peat Marwick)
70 Finsbury Pavement, London

Also at Aberdeen, Belfast, Birmingham, Bristol, Darlington, Dundee, Edinburgh, Glasgow, Leeds, Leicester, Liverpool, Manchester, Newcastle upon Tyne, Norwich and Sheffield

History: Founded by Thomson McLintock who set up in practice at 87 St Vincent Street, Glasgow, Strathclyde, in 1877 after training with Norrie & Anderson and then James L Selkirk. He was admitted as an associate member of the newly formed ICAEW in 1880. There was a strong family connection throughout the early history of the firm and it was Thomson McLintock's sons, William and Charles, who in 1914 opened an office in London. This was as a result of the appointment of Thomson McLintock as liquidator of the Northern Equitable Insurance Co which required the presence of a small staff in Equitable House, London, to collect debts and settle claims. A permanent office was established shortly after which later transferred to 158 Fenchurch Street. In 1918 a further move was made to larger offices in Bond Court House, Walbrook, where it remained until 1923 when new offices at 71 Queen Street were acquired. Also in 1918 the Glasgow office was moved from 149 to 216 West George Street. During the 1920s offices were opened in Manchester (57 King Street), Greater Manchester, and Birmingham (39 Bennetts Hill), West Midlands, the latter when Sir William McLintock, the founder's son, acquired the local practice of Charles Baker & Co (*qv*). After the death of Thomson McLintock in 1920 difficulties arose between the Glasgow and London offices which led to a split in 1934 (they were reunited in 1959). However, the firm continued to expand rapidly and developed a specialisation in the area of taxation work. During the 1920s and 1930s Sir William McLintock undertook advisory work for the government and public bodies and was appointed to report on the Royal Mail Group in the case against Lord Kylsant and H J Morland in 1931. The 1950s and 1960s saw growth in the firm's business at home and abroad. Mergers with several UK practices established or extended the firm's presence in many British cities. In England: a Newcastle upon Tyne, Tyne and Wear, office was opened in 1965 after a merger with Squance & Co (*qv*); the Manchester office merged with the Leeds, West Yorkshire, firm of Sir Charles H Wilson & Co in 1966; the Birmingham office merged in 1963 with the local firm Aston Wilde; in London, Martin, Farlow & Co (*qv*) was acquired in 1968 and there was a further merger, in 1974, with the Leicester, Leicestershire, practice of Baker Bros, Halford &

Co (est. *c*.1868). In Scotland there were mergers with G & J McBain in Aberdeen, Grampian (1971); Moody Stuart & Robertson in Dundee, Tayside (1975), and Robertson Maxtone Graham, in Edinburgh, Lothian (1975). The firm, part of the MML (McLintock Main Lafrentz) group, became KMG (Klynveld Main Goerdeler), a broader based international grouping of accountancy firms with a strong European emphasis, and in the UK it changed its name in 1985 to KMG Thomson McLintock. In April 1987 KMG Thomson McLintock merged with Peat, Marwick, Mitchell & Co (*qv*) and became Peat, Marwick, McLintock, now KPMG Peat Marwick.

Records (1): KPMG Peat Marwick, Finsbury Chambers, 74/78 Finsbury Pavement, London EC2A 1JD

Partnership agreements: 1930–38, drafts and related correspondence 1927, London partners 1967–84, UK unification agreements 1967–87; meeting minutes and agendas: UK council and committee 1967–87, London partners 1966–87, office managing partners 1985–87, London management committee 1973–85; papers: merger with Charles Baker & Co 1922, UK mergers 1969–84, MML 1971–79, KMG International 1980–86; cash book (London office) 1914–21; conference reports and papers (UK) 1967–86; correspondence between London and Glasgow offices 1933–34; presscuttings, UK firm 1984–87; publications, training and technical matters 1976–87.

Records (2): Archives Division, Birmingham Central Library, Chamberlain Square, Birmingham B3 3HQ

List of salaries and proposed bonuses 1941–42.

M F Bywater, 'Sir William McLintock', in David J Jeremy (ed.), *Dictionary of Business Biography*, Vol. 4 (London, Butterworth, 1985)

Jack House, *A Tale of Two Houses* (Edinburgh, the firm, 1980)

John Owen, *KMG Thomson McLintock (formerly Thomson McLintock & Co), a Record of Achievement, Ten Years to Merger 1977–1987* (Unpub., 1989)

Rex Winsbury, *Thomson McLintock & Co: The First Hundred Years* (London, the firm, 1977)

THORNTON & THORNTON (Grant Thornton)

Nuffield House, 41/46 Piccadilly, London

Also at Banbury, Bicester, Birmingham, Evesham, High Wycombe, Horsham, Oxford, Princes Risborough, Thame and Witney

History: Founded by Reginald Walker Thornton who commenced practising in 1904 at Lloyds Bank Chambers, Oxford, Oxfordshire, with H J Webb, under the style Thornton, Webb & Co. The firm was renamed R W

Thornton in 1906, when Webb left to become president of various companies in Canada; Thornton & Thornton in 1910; Thornton, Murray & Thornton in 1911; and Thornton & Thornton in 1924. The first office in Lloyds Bank Chambers moved to 38 Queen Street in 1907; 140 High Street in 1917; 3 & 4 King Edward Street in 1925; and 8 King Edward Street in 1937. During his early days in practice, Thornton met William Morris, later Lord Nuffield, founder of Morris Motors, and the firm obtained the Morris audit. In 1936 the firm advised on the flotation of the company and acquired the audit of various companies acquired by Morris in Europe. A year after the opening of the Oxford office, an office was opened in London by Thornton's cousin, Francis Thornton, at 17 Philpot Lane. This office was subsequently moved to 9 Walbrook in 1910; Moorgate Station Chambers in 1915; Southampton Street, Strand, in *c.*1945; and Nuffield House in 1949. Other offices were opened in Reading, Berkshire, in 1912; Banbury, Oxfordshire, in 1919; Leamington, Warwickshire, in 1923; Birmingham, West Midlands, in 1929; Bournemouth, Dorset, in 1930; Thame, Oxfordshire, in 1943; Princes Risborough, Buckinghamshire, in 1945; Witney, Oxfordshire, in *c.*1945; Bicester, Oxfordshire, in 1947; Evesham, Hereford and Worcester, in 1948; Horsham, West Sussex, in 1950; and High Wycombe, Buckinghamshire, in 1954. In 1959 the firm merged with Baker & Co (est. 1868), Leicester, Leicestershire, and Northampton, Northamptonshire, to become Thornton Baker & Co, now Grant Thornton (*qv*).

Records: Grant Thornton, 1 Westminster Way, Oxford OX2 0PZ

Partnership agreements: 1938–59, dissolution 1924; statements of profits, Oxford, London, Reading, Banbury 1912–30; time summary, Banbury 1923–24; cash accounts 1924–26; correspondence 1924; partners' meeting minutes: general 1946–59, Oxford office 1956–59; report on investigation into organisation of the Oxford office 1955; schedules of fees and profits 1905–59; accounts 1942–59; private ledgers: 1904–09, 1947–66, and cash books 1910–48; cash books: 1904–12, 1924–27, private 1946–67; costs journal 1904–24; office costings 1952–61; letter, negotiations for an amalgamation with Cooper Brothers and Cooper's merger with Carter & Co of Birmingham 1959; wages book 1914–39; pension fund deeds, 5 & 5a King Street, Oxford 1876–1970; leases and tenancy agreements, 9 King Edward Street 1955–75; photographs, partners and staff 1930s–1950s; historical notes 1950s–1970s.

Peter Hubbard, *Grant Thornton – A Brief History* (Unpub., 1991)

VALE & WEST

Victoria House, 26 Queen Victoria Street, Reading RG1 1TG

History: Founded by Henry Busby Vale who opened an office in Bridge Street, Caversham, Berkshire, in 1894. After the First World War he moved offices to Market Place, Reading, Berkshire, and in 1923 to King Edward Buildings, Station Road. In 1926 he was joined by Harry Maurice West and the style Vale & West was adopted. The firm moved to 154/155 Friar Street in 1932 and to its present address in 1980. Clients of the firm have included Smedleys Ltd; Angel, Sons & Gray Ltd, builders; Joynes Ltd, builders; Louis Rogers Ltd, butchers; Drews Ltd, wholesalers; and the National Canning Co Ltd.

Records: Vale & West, 26 Queen Victoria Street, Reading RG1 1TG

Private ledger 1926–50; balance sheets 1950–77.

VINEY MERRETTS (BDO Binder Hamlyn)

Empire House, St Martin's-le-Grand, London

History: Formed in May 1969 when Viney, Price & Goodyear (*qv*) amalgamated with Merrett, Son & Street (*qv*). In 1970 the firm was joined by Greenwood & Loryman (est. 1916), Empire House, St Martin's-le-Grand, London. In 1980 Viney Merretts merged with the international firm Binder Hamlyn, now part of BDO Binder Hamlyn.

Records: BDO Binder Hamlyn, 20 Old Bailey, London EC4M 7BH

Partnership agreements 1969–79; minutes 1969–79; staff rules 1969.

Anon., *Viney Merretts, Chartered Accountants for 150 Years in the City of London* (London, the firm, 1978)

Anon., *At Your Service – Viney Merretts* (London, the firm, 1978)

VINEY, PRICE & GOODYEAR (BDO Binder Hamlyn)

Empire House, St Martin's-le-Grand, London

History: Founded by Joseph Parrinton who in 1828 was practising at 22 Milk Street, London, under the name Parrinton & Sons. The firm was restyled Joseph Parrinton & Son in 1838; Parrinton & Ladbury in 1842; Parrinton, Ladbury & Co in 1857; Ladbury, Collison & Viney in 1861; Collison & Viney in 1885; and Viney, Price & Goodyear in 1894. By 1838 the firm was practising at 16 King Street, Cheapside, and moved to 99 Cheapside in 1866, and Empire House, St Martin's-le-Grand, in 1926. Up to the First World War the firm was heavily involved in insolvency matters and throughout its life specialised in work for the textile, drapery and food trades. In 1969, Viney, Price & Goodyear amalgamated with Merrett, Son & Street (*qv*) to form Viney Merretts (*qv*), now part of BDO Binder Hamlyn.

Records: BDO Binder Hamlyn, 20 Old Bailey, London EC4M 7BH

Partnership agreements: 1891–1969, dissolution with William Barclay Peat 1885; accounts 1893–1928; annual balance sheet record book 1862–67;

private ledgers 1857–63, 1916–31; work-in-progress listing 1917; audit manual *c.*1915; register of articled pupils 1903–68; staff engagement lists 1914, 1939; list of staff killed in war 1944; speech 1919.

W G HAWSON & CO (Hawsons)
Hartshead Chambers, Sheffield, South Yorkshire

History: Originated from the practice of Alfred Allott who was practising under the style Hewett & Allott at Central Chambers, High Street, Sheffield, South Yorkshire, in 1856. This practice was later renamed Allott & Sully in 1868 and Allott, Hadfield, Kidner & Hawson in *c.*1876. William George Hawson was a founder member of the Sheffield Institute of Accountants (est. 1877); Alfred Allott was its first president, and a member of the first council of the ICAEW in 1880. By 1880 the firm was practising under the style Kidner & Hawson at Hartshead Chambers. It was renamed W G Hawson & Co in 1895. In 1946 the firm merged with A Leslie Wing & Co (*qv*) to form W G Hawson, Wing & Co (*qv*), now part of Hawsons (*qv*).

Records: Hawsons, Pegasus House, 463a Glossop Road, Sheffield S10 2QD

Partnership tax files 1942–46; private ledgers 1881–1924, 1931–46; private cash book 1930–46.

W G HAWSON, WING & CO (Hawsons)
Hartshead Chambers, Sheffield, South Yorkshire

History: Formed in 1946 following the merger of W G Hawson & Co (*qv*) and A Leslie Wing & Co (*qv*). In 1963 W G Hawson, Wing & Co merged with Hubert Smith & Co (*qv*) to form Hawson, Wing & Hubert Smith, now Hawsons (*qv*).

Records: Hawsons, Pegasus House, 463a Glossop Road, Sheffield S10 2QD

Papers, merger with Hubert Smith & Co incl. lists of clients, notes re salaries, division of work, choice of name, general administration, share of profits and goodwill 1961–63; accounts 1948–63; tax files 1947–63; private ledger 1947–62; private cash book 1947–62; monthly wages books 1949–63.

WAISSEN WILSON (Blakemores)
137 Victoria Street, London

History: Founded by H Waissen Wilson who was admitted to the ICAEW in 1887 and by 1888 was practising at 12 Trinity Square, Seething Lane, London. In 1911 he moved to 40 Trinity Square. In 1915 he died and his practice was carried on by Henry and James Holmes. By 1918 they were practising at 2 Fenchurch Avenue. In 1939 this office moved to 13 Fenchurch Avenue and in *c*.1940 to 20 Copthall Avenue. It moved to 137 Victoria Street in 1964. The firm had offices in Brighton, East Sussex (1940–56); Henfield, West Sussex (1951–52); and Spalding, Lincolnshire (1951–83). In 1971 the firm changed its name from H Waissen Wilson & Co to Waissen Wilson. In 1972 it merged with Westcott, Maskall & Co (*qv*) to form Westcott Wilson, now part of Blakemores.

Records: Blakemores, Pemberton House, 4–6 East Harding Street, London EC4A 3BD

Partnership agreements *c*.1950 on; accounts 1951 on; profit and loss account 1912; out-letter book 1911–12.

Clients: M N Joseph: tax notebook 1935–44; **Levant Mineral Co Ltd**: minutes 1867–95, accounts 1869, 1874; **J H Randall & Co**: audit notebook 1910–11.

WALTER HUNTER & CO

24 Bridge Street, Newport, Gwent NP9 4SF

History: The firm was started by Walter Hunter who commenced practising at 21 Dock Street, Newport, Gwent, in 1891. By 1894 he was practising under the name Walter Hunter & Co at 57 Dock Street. In 1902 he was admitted to membership of the Society of Incorporated Accountants and in 1908 moved his practice to Central Chambers. The firm acquired offices in Abertillery (Commercial Chambers), Gwent, in 1908 and Cardiff (57 Mount Square), South Glamorgan, and London (1 Great Winchester Street) in 1919. The Abertillery office was maintained until 1913 and the London and Cardiff offices until 1949 and 1957 respectively. The firm was known as Walter Hunter, Bartlett & Co from 1923 to 1931 and as Walter Hunter, Bartlett, Thomas & Co from 1931 to 1972 after which the name Walter Hunter & Co was readopted. Richard Wilson Bartlett, who joined the firm in 1912 and was admitted to partnership in 1931, was president of the Society of Incorporated Accountants 1935–37. In 1967 the firm opened offices at 2 Market Square, Caerphilly, Mid Glamorgan, and 27 High Street, Chepstow, Gwent. The Newport office has been at 24 Bridge Street since 1923.

Records: Walter Hunter & Co, 24 Bridge Street, Newport, Gwent NP9 4SF

Private ledgers: 1919–39, and cash book 1895–1906; journal 1912–40; registers of clients' files 1917–67; correspondence with clients 1950s; staff record book 1918–50; photographs: Walter Hunter *c*.1920, Richard Wilson Bartlett *c*.1935.

Clients: Bailey Trust: ledger 1945–60, journal 1945–60; **C H Bailey Ltd**, dry dock owners and ship repairers: ledgers (Barry) 1915–32, ledgers (Newport) 1917–32, private ledgers 1901–53, nominal ledger 1902–07, nominal ledgers (Barry) 1932–41, nominal ledgers (Newport) 1932–42, private journal 1912–28, journal (Newport) 1916–32, journal (Barry) 1916–32, cash book 1953–57; **Cardiff Junction Dry Dock & Engineering Co Ltd**: ledgers 1929–32, private ledger 1908–23, nominal ledgers 1932–43; **Tyne Engine Works**: private ledger 1896–1910, nominal ledger 1907–15.

WATSON, SOWTER & CO (Cooper-Parry, Prior & Palmer)
25 Iron Gate, Derby, Derbyshire

History: Founded by William Chamberlain Watson who had offices on The Wardwick, Derby, Derbyshire, in the 1850s. In 1876 he moved to 17 Corn Market and in the late 1870s was joined by Frederick Luke Sowter when the practice became Watson, Sowter & Co. The firm moved to 25 Iron Gate in 1897. Early clients of the firm included Derbyshire Royal Infirmary, Derby Corporation, Derby School, Derby Crown Porcelain Co, the Meynell Hunt and a number of local gasworks, collieries and breweries. In 1965 Watson, Sowter & Co merged with Cooper-Parry, Hall, Doughty & Co (*qv*) to become Cooper-Parry, Watson, Sowter & Co, now Cooper-Parry, Prior & Palmer.

Records: Cooper-Parry, Prior & Palmer, 102 Friar Gate, Derby DE1 1FH

Partners' diaries 1856, 1861–1906 (w); papers, merger with Cooper-Parry, Hall, Doughty & Co incl. accounts, statements of capital and goodwill, correspondence 1960–65; journals 1878–90, 1907–19; cash books 1870–91 (w); list of audits and fees 1952; correspondence, tax 1939–55; summaries of salaries 1952–53; lease, 25 Iron Gate 1962.

Clients: Derby Club: minutes 1902–13; **English Stoneware Manufacturers Association:** minutes 1923–35; **Sir Francis Ley**, dec'd: trustees' accounts 1924–52, investments accounts 1915–54, cash account 1916–41; **National Federation of General Stoneware Manufacturers**: minutes 1943–54; **Stoneware Potteries Association**: minutes 1956–63.

WATSONS (Pannell Kerr Forster)
Greenfield Lane, Balby, Doncaster, South Yorkshire

History: Started in the 1920s by W R Bell and G E Watson as a section of their auctioneers', valuers' and estate agents' business trading under the name Bell & Watson at 2 St Sepulchre Gate, Doncaster, South Yorkshire. In 1943 the audit practice was divorced from Bell & Watson and was carried on as Watson, Waddington & Sharp, incorporated accountants, at 24 High Street, Doncaster. The practice moved to Georgian House, Princes Street, in 1951; 35 Thorne Road in 1959; and Greenfield Lane, Balby, in 1987. In 1987 the firm amalgamated with J Thurgood & Co, 15 Netherhall Road, Doncaster, and the style Watsons was adopted. In 1992 Watsons merged with the national firm Pannell Kerr Forster.

Records: Pannell Kerr Forster, Greenfield Lane, Balby, Doncaster DN4 0PF

Partnership agreement 1956; firm's index of limited companies 1925–50; correspondence, lease of office premises 1956–58; lease, 43 Princes Street, Doncaster 1952; scrapbook incl. miscellaneous annual reports and accounts, correspondence, notes re companies in liquidation and technical matters 1914–60.

WENHAM BROTHERS & CO (Wenham Major)
21 Bennetts Hill, Birmingham, West Midlands

Also at London

History: Alfred Ebenezer Wenham founded the firm when he set up in practice *c.*1867 at 11 Cherry Street, Birmingham, West Midlands, moving to 50 Ann Street *c.*1872. At some time before 1881 he went into partnership with his brother, Arthur, and Thomas James Agar, practising briefly under the name Wenham Brothers & Agar. When Agar left in 1882 the practice continued as Wenham Brothers & Co. At around the same time the firm's address changed from 50 Ann Street to 114 Colmore Row, when the street was renamed. In 1904 Wenham opened an office in London at 27 Martin's Lane, Cannon Street, which moved, successively, to 36 New Broad Street (1908); 52–54 High Holborn (1930); 49–51 Bedford Row (*c.*1945); and 15 Tooks Court, Cursitor Street (1950). In 1933 Alfred Wenham died and the practice was carried on by his three sons, William, Basil and Douglas, still under the name Wenham Brothers & Co. Their main interest was trade association work and when their senior clerk, who handled the audit side, left in 1935 they merged with Sidney H Hossell & Co (*qv*), an old local firm which dated from 1886. The new firm moved in 1935 to 21 Bennetts Hill, Wenham Brothers moving from 25 Temple Row, which it had occupied since 1925. In 1962 the firm merged with Major & Co (*qv*), Birmingham, to become Wenham, Major & Clarke, now Wenham Major (*qv*), and moved to 89 Cornwall Street, the present offices of Wenham Major. The London office continued to be connected with the Birmingham office of Wenham Major until 1972.

Records: Wenham Major, 89 Cornwall Street, Birmingham B3 3BY

Partnership accounts 1920–62; fees ledger 1925–35; private ledgers 1890–1962; cash book 1910–62; photograph, Alfred Wenham n.d.

WENHAM MAJOR

89 Cornwall Street, Birmingham B3 3BY

History: Formed by the merger, in 1962, of Wenham Brothers & Co (*qv*) and Major & Co (*qv*), both of Birmingham, West Midlands. Through the merger the firm, styled Wenham, Major & Clarke, acquired a small office at 44 Bradford Street, Walsall, West Midlands, which it retained until 1967. The firm merged with other local Birmingham practices: Morrison, Pearson & Hawker, 55 Temple Row, in 1967 and Howle, Sewell & Neep, Waterloo Street, in 1968. The former brought to the firm an office at 18 Lichfield Street, Walsall, which was retained until 1988. In 1973 the Birmingham partnership severed its connection with the London office and was renamed Wenham, Major & Co. This was shortened to Wenham Major in 1983.

Records: Wenham Major, 89 Cornwall Street, Birmingham B3 3BY

Partners' meeting minutes *c.*1963–date; accounts 1963–date; private ledgers 1963–date; general correspondence 1963.

WENN TOWNSEND

30 St Giles, Oxford OX1 3LE

Also at Abingdon and Cirencester

History: Started by Arthur Edwin Preston who set up in practice in High Street, Abingdon, Oxfordshire, in 1876. By 1885 he had opened an office at 55 Cornmarket Street, Oxford, Oxfordshire, being the first chartered accountant in the city. Following the retirement of Preston in 1908 J H Hume Wenn and John Elsom were taken into partnership and the firm was restyled Wenn & Elsom. This style was changed to Wenn & Co in 1920, and Wenn Townsend & Co in 1947, following the admission to partnership of James Townsend who had had connections with the firm since 1909. The Abingdon office was closed in 1925 but another office in the town was acquired during the Second World War through the takeover of Cowley & Allen, Stert Street. An office in Cirencester, Gloucestershire, was also opened during the Second World War. The Oxford office moved from St Michael Street to 30 St Giles in 1957. The firm's name was shortened to Wenn Townsend in 1982.

Records: Wenn Townsend, 30 St Giles, Oxford OX1 3LE

Out-letter book 1909–15; historical notes n.d.

Clients: King & Barnes Ltd, brewers: annual accounts 1895, 1908.

WESTCOTT, MASKALL & CO (Blakemores)

33 Catherine Place, London

History: Established by William Westcott who commenced practising *c*.1853. By 1880 his practice was styled William Westcott & Co. This was changed to Westcott, Maskall & Co when Thomas Henry Maskall was admitted as a partner in 1899. The firm moved to 99 Gresham Street in 1888, to 29 & 30 Broad Street Avenue in 1905, and to 33 Catherine Place in 1951. The firm amalgamated with Waissen Wilson (*qv*) in 1972 to form Westcott Wilson, now part of Blakemores. For many years the firm acted for Bridewell Royal Hospital and the National Liberal Club, both still clients of Blakemores.

Records: Blakemores, Pemberton House, 4–6 East Harding Street, London EC4A 3BD

Fees journal 1919–34; private ledgers 1902–29; out-letter books: 1890–91, 1898–1901, liquidation of South West London Tradesmen's Provident Society Ltd 1912 on; staff: register 1906–52, manual 1965.

Clients: British Luxfer Prism Syndicate Ltd: directors' report and balance sheet 1924; **Hall, Beddall & Co**, builders: profit and loss accounts 1882, 1885, 1886, balance sheets 1882, 1885, questions and answers re status of company 1883; **Holyford House School**: ledger 1914; **James Marriott Ltd,** coal merchants: accounts 1922; **John Oakey & Sons**: audit certificate 1893; **Sherborne Estates**: income account 1876, 1879, 1882, profit and loss accounts 1888–90, expenditure on churches and schools restored or built under improvement loans 1883.

WHITEHEAD & ALDRICH

5 Ribblesdale Place, Preston PR1 8BZ

History: Founded by Arthur Guy Paget Rigby who left the accountancy firm of Davies & Crane in 1906 to start practising on his own at 5 Chapel Street, Preston, Lancashire. He was shortly joined by two other members of Davies & Crane, James Goodier Bradshaw and Sam Whitehead, and in 1907 the practice became Rigby, Bradshaw & Whitehead. Offices were acquired in St Anne's-on-Sea (34 St Anne's Road West), Lancashire, in 1910 and Blackpool (18 Clifton Street), Lancashire, in 1912. Between 1923 and 1925 Bradshaw ceased practising in Preston, the St Anne's and Blackpool offices split up, becoming respectively Whitehead & Howarth and Bradshaw & Booth, and the Preston office was restyled Whitehead & Aldrich after Stephen Aldrich was admitted as a partner. In 1953 Whitehead & Aldrich moved to 4 Chapel Street and in 1970 to 5 Ribblesdale Place.

Records: Whitehead & Aldrich, 5 Ribblesdale Place, Preston PR1 8EZ

Partnership agreements 1960–date; accounts 1912–15; fees journals 1906–67; private ledgers 1912–22, 1953–date; cash books 1908–23, 1959–61; correspondence: James Bradshaw's tax 1924, staff and articled clerks 1953–60s; weekly wages book 1956–62; staff record book 1965–74.

WINTER, ROBINSON & CO (Coopers & Lybrand)
16 Market Street, Newcastle upon Tyne, Tyne and Wear

History: Founded by John Martin Winter who set up in practice at 76 Grey Street, Newcastle upon Tyne, Tyne and Wear, in 1870 having previously been employed as a cost clerk to a local builder. In 1878 he moved to Tynemouth, Tyne and Wear, where he became actively involved in local politics. The practice became John M Winter & Sons in 1896. Offices were opened at 1 Howard Street, North Shields, Tyne and Wear, in 1906 and 24 Coleman Street, London, in 1907. In 1928 the Newcastle and North Shields offices adopted the style Winter, Robinson & Co, the London office retaining the name of John M Winter & Sons (now Winters). In 1933 Winter, Robinson & Co merged with Sisson & Allden (est. 1880), 13 Grey Street, Newcastle upon Tyne, to form Winter, Robinson & Sisson (*qv*), which merged with J G Benson & Sons (est. 1870), Newcastle upon Tyne, in 1951 to form Winter, Robinson, Sisson & Benson (*qv*), now part of Coopers & Lybrand.

Records: Tyne and Wear Archives Service, Blandford House, Blandford Square, Newcastle upon Tyne NE1 4JA

Private ledgers 1926–33; document register and file A–F 1924–33.

WINTER, ROBINSON & SISSON (Coopers & Lybrand)
16 Market Street, Newcastle upon Tyne, Tyne and Wear

History: Formed in 1933 as a result of the merger between Winter, Robinson & Co (*qv*) and Sisson & Allden (est. 1880), 13 Grey Street, Newcastle upon Tyne, Tyne and Wear. Winter, Robinson & Sisson amalgamated with J G Benson & Sons (est. 1870), Newcastle upon Tyne, in 1951 to form Winter, Robinson, Sisson & Benson (*qv*), now part of Coopers & Lybrand.

Records: Tyne and Wear Archives Service, Blandford House, Blandford Square, Newcastle upon Tyne NE1 4JA

Private ledger 1933–51; private cash books 1933–51; document register and file 1933–51.

WINTER, ROBINSON, SISSON & BENSON (Coopers & Lybrand)
16 Market Street, Newcastle upon Tyne, Tyne and Wear

History: Formed in 1951 as a result of the merger between Winter, Robinson & Sisson (*qv*) and J G Benson & Sons (est. 1870), 27 Grey Street, Newcastle upon Tyne, Tyne and Wear. In 1969 the firm amalgamated with Deloitte, Plender, Griffiths & Co, which in 1978 became Deloitte Haskins & Sells (*qv*), now part of Coopers & Lybrand. Robert Pearson Winter was president of the ICAEW 1963–64.

Records: Tyne and Wear Archives Service, Blandford House, Blandford Square, Newcastle upon Tyne NE1 4JA

Private cash books 1951–69; register and document file 1951–60.

WM F SMART, SON & BLOOR (Chantrey Vellacott)
Africa House, 64–78 Kingsway, London

History: Established in 1861, the firm was practising at 16 Basinghall Street, London, under the name Wm F Smart & Son by 1880. Restyled Wm F Smart, Son & Bloor in 1915, the firm occupied 16 Basinghall Street until 1902 and 255 Finsbury Pavement House, 120 Moorgate, from 1903 to 1970. It had offices in Brentwood (London Road), Essex, 1902–33; Whetstone (Burleigh House, High Road), London, *c.*1940–50; and Streatley-on-Thames (Churn Lodge), Berkshire, 1957–65. The London office moved to Africa House, 64–78 Kingsway, in 1970 and merged with Chantrey, Button & Co (*qv*), now part of Chantrey Vellacott, in 1972.

Records: Chantrey Vellacott, Russell Square House, 10-12 Russell Square, London WC1B 5LF

Nominal ledger 1890–99.

WOOD & CO (Chantrey Vellacott)
1 Old Burlington Street, London

Also at Reading

History: Founded *c.*1870 by Richard Wood who by 1897 was practising at 155 Leadenhall Street, London, with C A Radermacher under the name Wood & Radermacher. The firm had offices at 1 Jeffreys Square, St Mary Axe (1897–1900), 36 Camomile Street (1900–36) and South Street, Moorgate (1936–48). In 1948 it changed its name to Wood & Co and moved to 1 Old Burlington Street. It opened an office in Reading, Berkshire, in 1977. In 1978 it merged with Wright, King & Co (est. 1939), London and Surbiton, Surrey, and became Wood, King & Co. This firm amalgamated with Chantrey, Button & Co (*qv*) in 1984, to form Chantrey Wood King, which merged with Hill Vellacott (*qv*) in 1988 and became Chantrey Vellacott.

Records: Chantrey Vellacott, Russell Square House, 10–12 Russell Square, London WC1B 5LF

Fees day book 1896–1902.

The Institute of Chartered Accountants in England and Wales and its constituent bodies: lists of records

LIVERPOOL SOCIETY OF CHARTERED ACCOUNTANTS

1 Old Hall Street, Liverpool L3 9HG

History: Founded in January 1870 as the Incorporated Society of Liverpool Accountants, a company limited by guarantee. The oldest of the ICAEW's founding bodies, the Society started as an informal meeting of prominent Liverpool accountants, held at the offices of Harmood Banner & Son at 24 North John Street, Liverpool, Merseyside. Harmood Banner, senior partner of Harmood Banner & Son (est. 1805, now Coopers & Lybrand), became the Society's first president in 1870; Anthony Wigham Chalmers, of Chalmers & Wade (est. 1796, now Kidsons Impey), was its first secretary, its second president (1878–84) and a petitioner for the royal charter of the ICAEW. The Society's objects were the protection of the character, status and interests of Liverpool accountants; the promotion of honourable practice; the settlement of disputed points of practice; and the consideration of general questions affecting the interests of the profession, or the alteration or administration of the law. The conditions for admission to the Society were strict and in 1880, it had only thirty-one members, fewer than any of the four other English accountancy bodies. The Society assisted in the formation of the ICAEW (*qv*) in 1880. Its members were absorbed into the new Institute although it continued to retain its own identity. A students' association was formed in 1883. In 1887 the Society changed its name to Liverpool Society of Chartered Accountants. Meetings were initially held at 24 North John Street and subsequently in the offices of A W Chalmers at 5 Fenwick Street. Between 1907 and 1936 the Society occupied 13 Union Court, Cook Street, returning to 5 Fenwick Street in 1936, where it remained until 1989, when it moved to the present address. In 1992 the Society had 3,128 members and covered the counties of Merseyside, Clwyd, Gwynedd, Cheshire (except for Congleton and Macclesfield), the districts of Wigan and West Lancashire, and the Isle of Man. Its two branches, Chester and North Wales and the Isle of Man, were formed in 1948 and 1958 respectively.

Records: Liverpool Society of Chartered Accountants, 1 Old Hall Street, Liverpool L3 9HG

Meeting minutes: committee and general 1870–date, membership sub-committee 1951–58; memoranda and articles of association 1870–1947, 1964; annual reports and accounts 1917–38, 1945–date; ledgers 1916–69; cash books 1905–59; correspondence: amendments to rules 1958–65, annual dinner 1946–56; members' signature book 1870–1940; subscription registers 1914–49, 1963; roll of honour 1918; photographs: presidents, members, officers 1870s–1970s, annual dinners 1930s, centenary celebrations 1970; meeting notices and press cuttings 1894–1904, 1934; leases, tenancy agreements, 13 Union Court and 5 Fenwick Street 1907–62; library: committee meeting minutes 1920–71, ledger 1910–21, cash books 1910–64, rules and bye-laws 1910, 1922; students' association: committee meeting minutes and papers 1907–date, general meeting minutes and papers 1900–75, annual reports and accounts 1899–1914 (w), 1928–date, ledger 1962–75, cash books 1933–48, 1955–81, rules 1910, 1914, 1928–57, membership and subscriptions registers 1912–25, proceedings books, lecturers, examination questions 1887–91.

Ian Hargraves, *Centenary 1870–1970* (Liverpool, The Liverpool Society of Chartered Accountants, 1970)

INSTITUTE OF ACCOUNTANTS (Institute of Chartered Accountants in England and Wales)
3 Copthall Buildings, London

History: Formed in November 1870 as the Institute of Accountants in London. The first meeting, called by William Quilter, senior partner of Quilter, Ball & Co (est. 1833, now Coopers & Lybrand), was attended by nine leading accountants who sought to set up an association of accountants incorporated by royal charter. Since 1867, however, the Privy Council had declined to recommend further grants of royal charters and the accountants, instead, formed themselves into an association which met at the offices of Quilter, Ball & Co, 3 Moorgate Street, London. Later meetings were held at 30 Moorgate Street and from July 1877 at 3 Copthall Buildings. At the first council meeting of the Institute, William Quilter was appointed president and William Turquand, of Turquand Youngs & Co (est. *c.*1840, now Ernst & Young) was elected vice-president. The object of the Institute was 'to elevate the attainments and status of professional accountants in London, to promote their efficiency and usefulness, and to give expression to their opinions upon all questions incident to their profession'. Under the rules, membership was confined to professional accountants in London. Anyone who had been in practice as an accountant for five years would be considered by the council for admission as a Fellow. Associates were required to pass an oral examination. Accountants who were not in the profession, such as those employed in dock or railway companies, were barred from membership, as were those who carried on other business as well as accountancy. Strict entry requirements and high entrance fees kept membership figures low in the 1870s. Those who did not qualify formed the Society of Accountants in England in 1872. In the same year, the Institute, in response to complaints received from accountants practising in the provinces, opened up membership to suitable applicants from all parts of the United Kingdom, changing its name to the Institute of Accountants. Few provincial accountants in fact applied for membership, although the Society of Accountants was growing rapidly at this time. With the appointment of William Turquand as president of the Institute in 1877, the question of incorporation by royal charter was raised once more. The Society of Accountants and the accountancy bodies in Liverpool, Manchester and Sheffield were equally in favour of forming a national body but objected to the Institute's rigid entry requirements. When the Institute prepared to present a bill to Parliament proposing its incorporation in 1878, both the Society and the Sheffield Institute drew up formal petitions opposing the passage of the measure. The Institute eventually relaxed its admission requirements and the draft bill was amended to meet the objections. The bill was dropped, however, in favour of a petition to the Queen in Council for a charter of incorporation. A royal charter was granted in May 1880 by which the five existing accountancy bodies merged their separate identities in the Institute of Chartered Accountants in England and Wales (*qv*). After 1880, the Institute of Accountants did not continue as a local society, unlike the other founding bodies which became district societies of the ICAEW.

Records: Guildhall Library, Aldermanbury, London EC2P 2EJ

Meeting minutes: council 1870–80, committee 1870–80, general 1870–80; journal 1871–80; rules and regulations n.d.; letter books 1870–80.

Sir Harold Howitt (ed.), *The History of the Institute of Chartered Accountants in England and Wales, 1880–1965, and of its Founder Accountancy Bodies, 1870–1880* (London, Heinemann, 1966)

Tom Margerison, *The Making of a Profession* (London, The Institute of Chartered Accountants in England and Wales, 1980)

MANCHESTER SOCIETY OF CHARTERED ACCOUNTANTS

Brook House, 70 Spring Gardens, Manchester M2 2BQ

History: Formed in February 1871 as Manchester Institute of Accountants for the purpose of promoting and protecting the interests of the profession in the Manchester area. A preliminary meeting, held at the Clarence Hotel, Manchester, Greater Manchester, was attended by the city's leading accountants and presided over by John Thomas. The first elected president was David Chadwick. The Institute advocated the formation of a national body of accountants in the 1870s. One of its leading members, Henry Grosvenor Nicholson, of H G Nicholson & Co, was a petitioner for the royal charter of the ICAEW (*qv*) in 1880. In April 1881, following the formation of the ICAEW, the affairs of the Manchester Institute were wound up and Manchester Society of Chartered Accountants came into being. In 1883 a students' society was formed. The first meetings of the Manchester Institute were held in the offices of Chadwick, Adamson, Collier & Co, 64 Cross Street, Manchester. These were later transferred to 23 Cross Street in 1874; 18 Booth Street in 1878; and 69 Princess Street in 1895. In 1903 the Society moved to 60 Spring Gardens, where it remained until 1950. It then moved to 46 Fountain Street and in 1976 to offices in Ship Canal House, King Street. This was followed by a move to Derby House, Booth Street, in 1983 and to the present address in 1990. In 1992 the Society had 4,052 members and covered Greater Manchester (except for Wigan), the High Peak district of Derbyshire and the Macclesfield district of Cheshire. It has one branch, the Bolton Society of Chartered Accountants, formed in 1951. A North Lancashire branch, formed in 1948, became the North West Society of the ICAEW, in 1965.

Records: Manchester Society of Chartered Accountants, Suite 1c, Brook House, 70 Spring Gardens, Manchester M2 2BQ

Meeting minutes: council 1871–82, 1894–1927, committee and sub-committee 1905–date, general 1927–date; annual reports and accounts 1871–73, 1894–date; nominal ledger 1911–37; cash book incl. abstract of cash account and statement of accounts 1881–89; accounts, papers, correspondence re prizes 1938–77; rules 1896; historical notes n.d.; students' society: committee and general meeting minutes 1938–86; Bolton branch, annual reports and accounts 1957–67; North Lancashire branch, annual reports and accounts 1966–67.

SHEFFIELD & DISTRICT SOCIETY OF CHARTERED ACCOUNTANTS

2A Rutland Park, Sheffield S10 2PD

History: Established in 1877 as Sheffield Institute of Accountants to enhance the position and protect the status of accountants in the area. Early meetings were held in the offices of Tasker & Shuttleworth at Wharncliffe Chambers, Bank Street, Sheffield, South Yorkshire. Alfred Allott of Allott, Hadfield, Kidner & Hawson, of Hartshead, Sheffield, was the Institute's first president and Thomas George Shuttleworth, of Tasker & Shuttleworth, its honorary secretary. Membership in the first year was twenty-one, seventeen of whom were already members of the Society of Accountants in England, established in 1872. The objects of the Institute were 'to increase the efficiency and usefulness of professional accountants;

to protect the interests of its members; to express opinions upon all questions relating to the profession; and to do all such things as may be necessary for the attainment of these ends'. The Institute supported the idea of a national body of accountants, but petitioned against the London Institute's bill for the formation of such a body on the grounds that many members of the Sheffield Institute who were also stockbrokers or auctioneers would be ineligible for admission. The bill was eventually withdrawn. The ICAEW (*qv*) was formed in 1880, incorporating the Sheffield Institute and the other provincial bodies. The new local society of the ICAEW was registered as a company limited by guarantee, Sheffield Incorporated Society of Chartered Accountants, in 1882. In the following year a students' society was established. The Society's name was changed in 1907 to Sheffield Society of Chartered Accountants and in 1937 to the present style. The Society moved to the new offices of Tasker & Shuttleworth in Queen Insurance Buildings, Church Street, in 1885 and to the offices of Knox, Burbidge & Co in Bank Street in 1899. It subsequently moved to Campo Lane in 1948, 22 Norfolk Row in 1962, 146 West Street in 1976, and to the present address in 1978. In 1882 the Society had twenty-eight members drawn from within twenty miles of Sheffield Town Hall. In 1992 it had 1,406 members and covered the county of South Yorkshire, the districts of Bolsover, Chesterfield, north-east Derbyshire and west Derbyshire and the Bassetlaw district of Nottinghamshire.

Records: Sheffield & District Society of Chartered Accountants, 2A Rutland Park, Sheffield S10 2PD

Meeting minutes: committee and general 1882–date, sub-committee 1948–68, 1986–90; memoranda and articles of association 1882–1958; special resolutions 1937, 1962–63; annual reports and accounts 1913–date; balance sheets 1937–39, 1946–61; ledgers 1877–1970; cash books: general 1918–72, subscription 1953–63; correspondence 1960–77; rules 1877; monthly wages books 1967–77; members lists 1882–1958; subscription registers: 1958–63, articled clerks 1959–77; roll of honour 1918; photographs, presidents, officers, etc., *c.*1900, 1950, 1977; scrapbook 1977; press cuttings, dinner notices, etc., 1896–1923, 1951–date; students' society: committee meeting minutes 1956–61, 1970–75, library sub-committee minutes 1948–56, sports sub-committee minutes 1971–72, rules n.d., roll of honour *c.*1922, photographs, roll of honour n.d., group 1911, lecture programmes 1962–73.

Alan M Hoe, *The First Hundred Years: Centenary 1877–1977* (Sheffield, the Society, 1977)

INSTITUTE OF CHARTERED ACCOUNTANTS IN ENGLAND AND WALES

Chartered Accountants' Hall, Moorgate Place, London EC2P 2BJ

Also at Milton Keynes

History: Established by royal charter on 11 May 1880. The charter incorporated the five English accountancy bodies established between 1870 and 1877: the Incorporated Society of Liverpool Accountants, now Liverpool Society of Chartered Accountants (*qv*); the Institute of Accountants (*qv*); Manchester Institute of Accountants, now Manchester Society of Chartered Accountants (*qv*); Sheffield Institute of Accountants, now Sheffield and District Society of Chartered Accountants (*qv*); and the Society of Accountants in England. Under the terms of the original charter, the new body was entitled the Institute of Chartered Accountants in England and Wales. Its objects, as redefined in the supplemental charter of 1948, were, and remain:

> to advance the theory and practice of accountancy in all its aspects, including, in particular, auditing, financial management and taxation; to recruit, educate and train a body of members skilled in these arts; to preserve at all times the professional independence of accountants in whatever capacities they may be serving; to maintain high standards of practice and professional conduct by all its members; and to do all such things as may advance the profession of accountancy in relation to public practice, industry, commerce and the public service.

The royal charter listed the forty-five members of the first council (amongst them, the petitioners for the charter, namely the presidents of the founder bodies and two Manchester accountants, Edwin Guthrie and Charles Wade) and named William Turquand, former president of the Institute of Accountants, as president and Robert Harding as vice-president. Membership at the time of incorporation was 599. The charter defined two classes of membership, Fellows and Associates, and provided for examination of those applying to be associate members. From the outset the Institute aimed to raise the standards of new entrants to the profession. Its refusal to relax its strict admission requirements led, in 1885, to the formation of the Society of Accountants and Auditors (Incorporated), later renamed the Society of Incorporated Accountants, (*qv*), by 300 accountants who did not qualify for membership of the Institute. The Society eventually amalgamated with the ICAEW and the Scottish and Irish Institutes in 1957. The first application for membership by a woman was received in 1888 but female members were not in fact admitted until after the First World War when the passing of the Sex Disqualification (Removal) Act in 1919 made it illegal to bar women from membership. In 1992 the Institute had a total of over 100,000 members. It sets its own entry requirements, code of ethics and disciplinary and practising standards and monitors the activities of members and firms to ensure that the standards are maintained. It undertakes technical work and research and offers a range of advisory services to its members and to the public. It is a member of the Consultative Committee of Accountancy Bodies which includes the five major accountancy bodies in the British Isles and is represented in the major international accountancy organisations. The Institute is governed by a council of sixty elected representatives who elect a president, deputy-president and vice-president to hold office for one year. It is represented around the country by twenty-two district societies and twenty-seven branch societies. The Institute's headquarters building is Chartered Accountants' Hall, Moorgate Place, London. Built in the early 1890s, to the design of the leading Victorian architect, John Belcher, RA, the building has since been extended and developed to reflect the changing needs of the Institute. Additional administrative premises were opened in Milton Keynes in 1984.

Records (1): The Institute of Chartered Accountants in England and Wales, Gloucester House, 399 Silbury Boulevard, Central Milton Keynes MK9 2HL

Council meetings: minutes 1949–date, agendas 1967, attendance books 1954–72; standing and joint committee meeting minutes: various 1949–76, accountants' joint parliamentary 1964–69, applications 1947–66, auditing practices 1973–87, coordination 1946–55, chartered accountants' joint standing 1901–05, 1957–72, courses 1967–85, development 1961–64, disciplinary 1949–82 and agenda books 1949–72, district societies 1938–86, education and training 1959–60, 1972–83, education 1962–73, education and training directorate 1978–83, examination 1951–72, finance 1950–69, financial and management accounting 1973–76, future plans joint steering 1964–70, general purposes 1950–66, general purposes and finance 1950–88, grants 1972–78, internal services 1966–86, investigation 1947–71 and agenda books 1963–68, joint ethics 1969–76, joint product development 1983–84, joint standing 1948–72, P D Leake 1950–73, library 1957–66, members' education and training 1978–81, moderators 1956–64, overseas relations 1954–87, parliamentary and law 1951–88, post-qualifying education 1972–76, post-qualifying instruction 1967–69, public relations 1960–68 and agendas 1968–77, public relations and communications advisory 1978, research 1964–74, small practitioners 1976–80, steering 1963–66, students education and training 1978–82, summer course 1955–67, taxation and financial relations 1942–59, taxation and research 1950–65 and sub-committee 1953–73, technical advisory 1966–81, technical and research 1965–82, technical services 1979–84, others 1949–76; sub-committee meeting minutes: accounting courses 1978–82, accounts 1969–70, articled clerks 1954–73, auditing courses 1978–82, finance and administration 1988–89, financial investments 1956–64, financial policy 1957–63, industry courses 1982, internal economy 1946–57, journals 1958–75, 1981–88, management development courses 1978–82, organisation 1957–71, practice courses 1982–85, publications 1967–69, taxation courses 1978–85, training 1973–85, trust 1971–72; boards, *ad hoc* committees meeting minutes: accounting education consultative board 1977–81, accounting standards review group 1978, advisory board of accountancy education 1970–76, royal charter special meeting 1963, board of accreditation of authorised principles 1973–82, board of accreditation of colleges and courses 1973–83, consultative committee of members in commerce and industry 1958–66, certificate in management information board of examiners 1967–72, editorial board 1974–84, FCA Ltd 1961–77, inflation accounting steering group 1976–79, joint accountancy bodies 1949–63, special committee on development policy 1970, work of the institute *ad hoc* committee 1969; general meeting minutes 1958–74; committee reports 1951–70; International Congress minutes 1952; autumnal meetings: minutes 1953–59, press cuttings 1951–59; ledgers 1946–63; journals 1941–63; investments: accounts book 1925–61, changes 1968–74, market values 1956–74; staff pensions fund: minutes 1959–72, trustees' minutes 1947, journal 1934–53, cash book 1966–75; benevolent fund ledger 1926–61; seal books 1954–79; lists of members 1881–date; registers: articled clerks 1950–82, former articled clerks of the Society of Incorporated Accountants 1958–61; statistics on articled clerks' registration 1962–date; preliminary examination reports 1950–63; roll of honour 1945; notes for honorary secretaries of district societies and branches 1954; Chartered Accountants' Charities Ltd: minutes 1957–82, ledger 1960–73, cash books 1957–66, seal book 1955–72; Merrett Estate: transactions 1961 on, joint account 1971–74, settlement account 1964–73, cash book 1961–71; Chartered Accountants' Trustees journal 1957–76; P D Leake Custodian Trustees Ltd: minutes 1953–72, reports and accounts 1953–66, trust fund cash book 1952–64, seal book 1953–72.

Records (2): Guildhall Library, Aldermanbury, London EC2P 2EJ

Council meeting minutes 1880–1949; committee meeting minutes: various 1880–1949, applications 1883–1947, co-ordination 1942–46 and agendas 1942–47, examination 1882–1951, finance 1880–1950, general purposes 1883–1950, investigation 1881–1947, and decisions discontinued *c.*1927, library and publications 1897–1956, moderators 1936–56, parliamentary and law 1886–1951, planning 1945–51, students, societies grants 1904–36, taxation and financial relations 1942–50 and sub-committee 1942–54, war bye-laws 1939–53; general meeting minutes 1881–1957; draft bye-laws 1881; committee reports 1880–1950; accountants advisory selection panel minutes 1939–40; joint accountancy bodies minutes 1938–49; international congress minutes (fourth) 1933; autumnal meetings: proceedings 1923–37, papers functions 1893–1913, 1921–47; provincial meetings proceedings 1898–1913; ledgers 1880–1945; private ledger 1946; journals 1880–1941; balance book 1904–36; letter book 1880; correspondence and papers 1930s; circulars 1881–1948; legal advice books 1880–1943; precedents of complaints 1881–1939; staff record book *c.*1900–30; roll of membership 1880–1946; registers: articles 1882–1950, applications not acceded to 1880–1902, successful candidates at examinations 1882–1912, certificates of exemptions 1882–1948; examinations:

results 1882–1925, reports 1882–1949; prize fund vouchers 1914–49; roll of honour 1939–45.

A C Harper, *The Institute of Chartered Accountants in England and Wales: A Short Sketch of its Inception, 11th May, 1880* (London, The Institute of Chartered Accountants in England and Wales, 1930)

Leon Hopkins, *The Hundredth Year* (Plymouth, Macdonald & Evans, 1980)

Sir Harold Howitt (ed.), *The History of the Institute of Chartered Accountants in England and Wales, 1880–1965, and of its Founder Accountancy Bodies, 1870–1880* (London, Heinemann, 1966)

Philip Magnus, *The History of the Institute of Chartered Accountants in England and Wales 1880–1959* (Unpub., 1959)

Tom Margerison, *The Making of a Profession* (London, The Institute of Chartered Accountants in England and Wales, 1980)

SOCIETY OF INCORPORATED ACCOUNTANTS (Institute of Chartered Accountants in England and Wales; Institute of Chartered Accountants in Ireland; Institute of Chartered Accountants of Scotland)

Incorporated Accountants' Hall, Temple Place, Victoria Embankment, London

History: Formed in 1885 as the Society of Accountants and Auditors (Incorporated) under the Companies Act, 1867 and subsequently renamed the Society of Incorporated Accountants and Auditors in 1908, and the Society of Incorporated Accountants in 1954. The impetus to form the Society came from the growing number of practitioners who sought professional status but were unable to comply with the rigid conditions for admission to the ICAEW (*qv*), incorporated by royal charter five years earlier. Amongst these were clerks to practising accountants who had insufficient length of service and accountants who were in business, or in the service of corporations and public bodies. At the Society's first annual general meeting in May 1886 Joseph Shaw Green, of Warrington, Cheshire, was elected president and James Martin, of Martin & Farlow, London (est. 1882, now KPMG Peat Marwick), was made vice-president. Examinations were first held in 1887; however, in the early years the number of candidates was small and admission to the Society was mainly upon election by Council. The admission of women was first mooted in 1899, but it was not until 1918 that the constitution was amended to provide for their membership, and the first woman passed the final examination and was elected as an associate member in 1920. Early meetings of the Society were held at 57 Moorgate Street and from 1886 in the offices of James Martin, secretary of the Society (1886–1919), at 3 Newgate Street, London. In 1888 the Society moved to 4 King Street, Cheapside and in 1909 to 50 Gresham Street. It acquired its own building, which became Incorporated Accountants' Hall, Victoria Embankment, in 1929. The Hall, built in 1895 to the design of John Loughborough Pearson, RA, for the first Lord Astor, was occupied by the Society until its integration in 1957 with the Institute of Chartered Accountants in England and Wales (est. 1880), the Institute of Chartered Accountants in Ireland (est. 1888) and the Institute of Chartered Accountants of Scotland (formed, in 1951, through the merger of the three accountancy bodies in Edinburgh, Glasgow and Aberdeen). By 1957 the Society had over 11,000 members, with nine branches in Scotland, Ireland and the Commonwealth (Australia, Canada, South Africa and Southern Rhodesia), established between 1886 and 1954. The Scottish branch originated as the Scottish Institute of Accountants (founded in 1880), which amalgamated with the Society in 1899. The Society also had twenty-three district societies, including two in India, which were founded between 1886 and 1950, and seven students' societies, the oldest of these being London, established in 1890.

Records (1): Guildhall Library, Aldermanbury, London EC2P 2EJ

Meeting minutes: council 1886–1958, general 1925–57; committee meeting minutes: executive and finance 1886–1930, articles and bye-laws 1946–55, branches and district societies 1936–56, disciplinary 1902–57, examination and membership 1930–62, finance and general purposes 1930–31, 1936–57, parliamentary 1936–56, research 1936–54, management 1950, special 1890–1930, young incorporated accountants 1949–50, miscellaneous committee 1936–57, mechanical accounting sub-committee 1949–50, *Accountancy* editorial conference minutes 1950–57; cash book 1958–62; joint liquidators' report and receipts and payment account 1957–1959; seal register 1958; visitors' book 1929–38; staff superannuation scheme: minutes 1937–57, ledger 1938–58; membership applications book 1948–57; registers of members and subscriptions 1885–1947; registers of articled clerks 1886–1957; examination results 1924–52, 1957–62; benevolent fund: trustees' minutes 1936–61, particulars of cases 1945; illuminated address presented to James Martin 1907; London students' society minutes 1894–1910, 1930–36; South African branch committee minutes 1896–1960; London district society minutes 1936–58.

Records (2): The Institute of Chartered Accountants in England and Wales, Gloucester House, 399 Silbury Boulevard, Central Milton Keynes MK9 2HL

Lists of members 1885–1957.

A A Garrett, *The History of the Society of Incorporated Accountants, 1885–1957* (Oxford, Oxford University Press, 1961)

Name index

Includes names of firms, companies, record repositories and individuals. References to record locations – firms, libraries, record offices, etc. – are included in this index and do not appear in the place index in any form.

The page references for the principal entries are set in bold and those for record locations in *italics*.

Names of firms are indexed as they appear, e.g. 'A W H Peach', not 'Peach, A W H'

In the case of items differentiated by a comma, the item without the comma appears first.

Place index